MALWA IN TRANSITION
THE FIRST PHASE
1698-1765

MALWA IN TRANSITION

OR

A CENTURY OF ANARCHY

THE FIRST PHASE
1698—1765

BY

RAGHUBIR SINH, M.A., LL.B., D.Litt.

WITH
A FOREWORD BY

SIR JADUNATH SARKAR, Kt., C.I.E., D.Litt.,

Honorary Member, R.oyal Asiatic Society of Great Britain and Ireland,
Corresponding Member, Royal Historical Society (London).

KALPAZ

ISBN: 978-93-5128-915-9(HB)

First Published in 1936
Indian Reprint in 2017

Published by

Kalpaz Publications
C-30, Satyawati Nagar,
Delhi – 110052
E-mail: kalpaz@hotmail.com
Website: kalpazpublications.com
Ph.: +91-9212142040

DEDICATED

TO

THOSE THREE *GURUS*

WHO

BY TURNS TAUGHT ME

HISTORY

AND

MADE ME CAPABLE OF

WRITING

THIS THESIS

FOREWORD

Malwa was one of the most notable provinces of India during the Hindu and early Muslim periods of our history, and its influence on Hindu culture was of an abiding character. In the expansion of the Delhi Empire to the South, this province played a most important part by reason of its position in the map of India. And yet it has up to now lacked a history worthy of its past. Sir John Malcolm's *Memoir of Central India* (1820), written in the infancy of modern historical studies relating to our country and based on imperfect materials handled without sufficient criticism, has remained our only authority on the subject, though it has long been recognized as quite obsolete.

In the course of the 116 years that have elapsed since Malcolm wrote, all the original State papers of the Marathas, forming an immense mass, have seen the light, and quite a large number of contemporary Persian sources, unknown to Malcolm, have been discovered and utilised by scholars. The result amounts to a complete revolution in our knowledge of the history of Malwa in the 17th and 18th centuries. The present work forms the first portion of an attempt to replace Malcolm's primitive *Memoir of Central India* by gathering together the fruits of the accumulated discovery and research of the past century.

It is fortunate that Malwa is at last going to have a history worthy of her past glories, through the pious endeavour of one of her sons, Maharaj-Kumar Raghubir Sinh, M.A., D.LITT., LL.B., the cultured heir of the Rathor Maharajah of Sitamau. He has utilised all the available materials, printed and manuscript, in the Persian, Marathi, Hindi, English and French languages that can throw any light on the province's past during the period chosen. In addition to borrowing all my MSS. bearing on the subject, he has procured photostatic copies of the other necessary MSS. in the British Museum and India Office, which were wanting in my collection. With immense labour he has critically sifted and then pieced together a large number of minute details from the *Persian ākhbārāt* and official letter-books (all unprinted) and reconstructed the history of many an unknown episode and period of the provincial history. To this he has added his intimate knowledge of the topography and genealogy of Malwa, which no outsider can equal. The result is a study at once intensive, accurate and exhaustive.

Besides throwing true light on many names of places and princes, this book makes two very important corrections in the known history of the province : he has conclusively proved that Girdhar Bahadur and Daya Bahadur were both killed on the same day and in the same battle, and that the Hindi Mandloi letters are a pure fabrication. His sections on the economic condition, social changes and culture of the province supply a very important and interesting element which is usually ignored by our research students. This book is as readable as it is packed with learning, and I feel sure that it will stand forth as a model and exemplar for other provincial histories of India in future.

JADUNATH SARKAR.

CONTENTS

PAGE

FOREWORD by Sir Jadunath Sarkar vii
ABBREVIATIONS EXPLAINED xii
CHAPTER I—MALWA AT THE CLOSE OF THE 17TH CENTURY ... ... 1—23
Geographical 2
Economic 4
Strategical 10
Political 11
Administrative 16
Social life 18

CHAPTER II—MALWA DURING THE LAST DECADE OF AURANGZIB'S REIGN (1698-1707) ... 24—87
1. The Epoch beginning in 1698 : The new period and its keynote 24
2. Mālwa and its governors, (1698-1707) ... 31
3. Chhatra Sāl Bundela and Mālwa 42
4. Rebellion of Gopāl Singh Chandrāwat (1698-1706) 47
5. Mālwa and the Marathas : Their early invasion and first touch with Mālwa (1698-1707) ... 52
6. Other minor disturbances (1698-1707) ... 67
7. Modern Mālwa in the making : Condition of the people (1698-1707) 70
APPENDIX A.—The Maratha raids on Mālwa during the years 1690-98 A.D. 85

CHAPTER III.—THE INCREASING IMPORTANCE OF MALWA (1707-1719) ... ... 88—126
1. The Main currents of the period 88
2. Mālwa and its governors (1707-1719) ... 91
3. The Marathas reach Mālwa : The legalization of their title in the Deccan (1707-1719) ... 107

PAGE

4. Mālwa and the princes of Rājputānā, (1707-19) 112
5. The Development of modern Mālwa, (1707-19) 120

CHAPTER IV—THE MUGHAL-MARATHA STRUGGLE—FIRST STAGE (1719-1730) ... ... 127—207

1. The struggle for a footing in Mālwa ... 127
2. The Nizām's first governorship (February 20, 1719—August 29, 1722) 131
3. First governorship of Girdhar Bahādur (Aug 30, 1722—May 15, 1723) 144
4. Azimullāh's deputy-governorship (May 15, 1723—June 2, 1725) 149
5. Girdhar Bahādur's second governorship—His defeat and death (June 2, 1725—Nov. 29, 1728) 153
6. Governorship of Bhawāni Rām (November 29, 1728—November, 1729) 165
7. Second governorship of Jai Singh (Nov., 1729—Sept. 19, 1730) 177
8. Other internal affairs of Mālwa during the period : 1719-1730 181
9. The real cause of the Maratha invasions on Mālwa 186

APPENDIX 1.—The letters of the Mandloi *Daftar* ... 196

APPENDIX 2.—The Question of the dates of the defeat and death of Girdhar Bahādur and Dayā Bahādur 199

CHAPTER V—THE MUGHAL-MARATHA STRUGGLE : SECOND STAGE (1730-41) ... ... 208—287

1. The loss of Mālwa to the Empire 208
2. Muhammad Bangash in Mālwa : His failure; (September 19, 1730—October 12, 1732) ... 211
3. Sawāi Jai Singh's last governorship (Sept. 28, 1732—Aug. 3, 1737) 222

CONTENTS

PAGE

4. The last struggle for Mālwa and its failure: The loss of Mālwa; (Aug. 3, 1737—July 4, 1741) 253
5. The Development of modern Mālwa (1730-1741) 274

CHAPTER VI—THE CONSOLIDATION OF THE MARATHA HOLD ON MALWA AND THE END OF THE EPOCH (1741-1765) ... ... 288—321
1. The main currents of the period (1741-65) ... 288
2. The consolidation of the Maratha Power (1741-1759) 291
3. The Durrāni clash, the battle of Pānipat and after (1759-1765) 306
4. The end of the epoch 316

CHAPTER VII—CONDITION OF MALWA DURING THE PERIOD (1698-1765) ... ... 322—339
Political situation summed up 322
Administrative 323
Justice and Public Peace 326
New routes in Mālwa 328
Economic condition of the province 329
Agricultural and industrial products of Mālwa ... 332
Social changes in Mālwa 333
Linguistic and Literary movements 336
The Fine Arts and Architecture 337
The period is transitional and hence devoid of any great creative effort 338

BIBLIOGRAPHY 341
INDEX 357
ADDENDA ET CORRIGENDA

MAPS

1. Mālwa, 1695-1765 ... ... facing p. 1
2. Chimāji's Invasion of Mālwa and the Battle of Amjherā, Nov.-Dec., 1728 facing p. 204

ABBREVIATIONS EXPLAINED

[For full titles and other particulars of the works cited consult the bibliography at the end of the work].

Ahwal—*Ahwal-ul-Khawaqin* by Muhammad Qāsim (Ref. in Irvine).

Aiti Patre or *Aiti*: *Aitihasik Patravyavahar* etc., Vols. I-II, Ed. by Sardesāi and others. (Letter Nos. are quoted).

Ajaib—*Ajaib-ul-Afaq.*

Akhbarat—*Akhbarat-i-Durbar-i-Mualla.*

A.M.D.—Mandloi *Daftar*, collected by Mr. S. V. Athalye of Shiposhi. (Letter Nos. are quoted).

Ashob—*Tarikh-i-Shahadat-i-Farukhsiyar wa Julus-i-Muhammad Shah.*

Athalye's Dhār—Dhār *Daftar* collected by Mr. S. V. Athalye of Shiposhi. (Letter Nos. quoted).

Aurangzib (Vol. III & V.)—Sarkar's *History of Aurangzib.*

Azam—*Azam-ul-Harb.*

Bahādur—*Bahadur Shah Nama* by Dānishmand Khān Ali (Ref. in Irvine).

Bayan—*Bayan-i-Waqqi* by Abdul Karim Kāshmiri (Ref. in Irvine).

Bernier—Bernier's *Travels*. Ed. by V. A. Smith.

Bhāgwat—*Holkarshahi Itihasanchi Sadhanen* Ed. by A. N. Bhāgwat. (Letter Nos. are quoted).

Bhimsen—*Nuskha-i-Dilkasha* by Bhimsen.

B.I.S.M.Q.—*Bharat-Itihas Sanshodhak Mandal Quarterly.*

Bramh. or *Bramhendra*—*Brahmendra Swami Charitra* by Pārasnis. (Letter Nos. are quoted).

Burhan—*Burhan-ul-fatuhat* (Ref. in Irvine).

Chahar—*Chahar Gulshan* by Chatarman Saksenā.

Chahar Gulzar—*Chahar Gulzar* by Harcharan Das. (Ref. in Irvine).

Dharcha etc.—*Dharchya Pawaranche Mahatva wa Darja* by Oak and Lele.

Duff—Grant Duff's *History of the Marathas.*

Elliot—*History of India as told by her own historians* by Elliot and Dowson.

Gaz.—The Gazetteer.

Ghulām Ali—*Muqaddam-i-Shah Alam Nama* (Ref. in Irvine).

Holkaranchi—*Holkaranchi Kaifiyat*—(2nd Ed.) Ed. by A. N. Bhāgwat.

Ibrat.—Muhammad Qāsim Lahori's *Ibratnama* (Ref. in Irvine).

Ināyetullah—Ināyetullah's *Ahkam-i-Alamgiri.*

India of Aurangzib—by J. N. Sarkar.

Iradat Khan—*Scott*—Irādat Khan's *Tarikh.* Translated by J. Scott in *History of the Deccan,* Vol. II. Part IV, pp. 1—130.

Irvine—W. Irvine's *The Later Mughals.* Vols. I-II, Ed. and augmented by J. N. Sarkar.

Jarrett's *A'in*—*A'in-i-Akbari.* Vol. II. Translated by Jarrett. (Bib. Ind.).

J.A.S.B.—Irvine's *History of the Bangash Nawabs of Farukhabad* published in the *Journal of the Asiatic Society of Bengal.* 1878, Part IV.

J.P.H.S.—Translations of the Journal of Ketelaar's Travels, published in the *Journal of the Punjab Historical Society,* Vol. X, Part I.

Kalimāt-i-T—*Kalimat-i-Tayyibat.*

Kāmrāj—Kamraj's *Ibrat-Nama.* (Ref. in Irvine).

Kāmwar—*Tarikh-i-Chagtai*

Khāfi Khān or K.K.—*Muntakhab-ul-Lubab,* Vol. II. (Bib. Ind.)

Khajista—Sāhib Rai's *Khajista-i-Kalam.*

Khande—Jadunāth Kavi's *Khande Rai Raso.*

Khare—*Aitihasik Lekh Sangrah.* Vol. I. (Letter Nos. quoted).

ABBREVIATIONS EXPLAINED

Khulasat or Sujan Rāi—Sujān Rai's *Khulasat-ut-Tawarikh.*
Khush-hāl—Khush-hal's *Nadir-uz-Zamani* (Ref. in Irvine).
Lāl—Lal Kavi's *Chhatra-Prakash.*
M.A.—*Maasir-i-Alamgiri.* (Bib. Ind.).
Madhya—Sardesai *Marathi Riyasat—Madhya Vibhag. Vols.* I—IV.
Main Currents—Sardesai's *Main Currents of Maratha History.* (2nd Ed.).
Malcolm—Malcolm's *A Memoir of Central India.* Vols. I—II (1823).
Malcolm—Report—Malcolm's "Report on the Province of Mālwa and adjoining Districts (1927 reprint).
Manucci—Manucci's *Storia Do Mogor.* Ed. by W. Irvine.
Mirat—*Mirat-i-Ahmadi.* (G.O. Series).
Mirzā—*Roznamcha.*
Mughal Administration—by J. N. Sarkar (2nd Ed.).
M.U.—*Maasir-ul-Umra.* 3 Vols., (Bib. Ind.).
Nawāzish—Nawāzish Khan's *Letter-book.*
Ojhā : *Rajputana*—G. H. Ojhā's *Rajputane Ka Itihas.*
Ojhā : *Udaipur*—G. H. Ojha's *Udaipur Rajya ka Itihas.*
Pārasnis—*Peshwe Daftarantil Mahiti*—(*Itihas-Sangrah*).
Phālke—*Shindeshahi Itihasanchi Sadhanen.* Vols. I, II. Ed. by Sardār A. B. Phālke (Letter Nos. quoted).
Purandare—Purandare *Daftar.*
Qānungo : *Jats*—*History of the Jats,* by K. R. Qanungo.
Rājwāde or Raj.—Rājwāde's *Marathanche Itihasanchi Sadhanen.* Vols. I, II, VI, VIII, etc.
Rustam Ali—Rustam Ali's *Tarikh-i-Hindi.*
Sarkar—J. N. Sarkar's *The Fall of the Mughal Empire.* Vols. I—II.
Shiv—Shiv Dās' *Munawar-i-Kalam.* (Br. Mus. MS.).
Shrivāstava—A. L. Shrivāstava : *The First two Nawabs of Oudh.*
Siyar—*Siyar-ul-Mutakherin.*

S.P.D.—*Selections from the Peshwa's Daftar.* Ed. by G. S. Sardesai. (Letter Nos. quoted except where pages are specially referred to).

Sujan—Sudan's *Sujan Charit.*

Tavernier—Tavernier's *Travels.* Vols. I-II Ed. by Ball (Macmillan).

Tieffenthaler—*Description de L'Inde,* par le père Joseph Tieffenthaler, S. J. Tome I, (Berlin, 1786).

Tod—Tod's *Annals and Antiquities of Rajasthan.* Vols. I—III (Oxford).

Vād—*Selections from the Peshwa's Diaries.* Ed. by Vād and Pārasnis. (Letter Nos. are quoted except where the pages are specially mentioned).

Vamsh—Surya Mal's *Vamsha Bhaskar.* Vol. IV.

Vir Vinod or *Vir*—*Vir Vinod* by Shyāmaldās.

Wārid—*Mirat-i-Waridat.*

N.B.—The references are to pages except where letter numbers are specially given.

MĀLWA IN TRANSITION

A CENTURY OF ANARCHY

CHAPTER I

MĀLWA AT THE CLOSE OF THE 17TH CENTURY.

The 18th century is rightly known in Indian history as a dark age, a century of anarchy. The anarchy was rampant not merely in affairs political, but also in matters cultural and social. The old structure was definitely crumbling away. Even a disinterested onlooker like Manucci felt : "It looks as if everything was being made ready for some remarkable revolution."[1] There were no signs of remaking. In reality the century may be called a century of revolution. The social and cultural map of India was completely changed. Many an old political entity was wiped off from the map of India. The effacement of Mālwa as a geographical, political and, above all, administrative unit was complete, and a historian, writing at the beginning of the 19th century, talked of "Central India" and

[1] Manucci, III, p.249.

not of Mālwa.[1] Yet to the student of Indian history of the 18th century Mālwa was a factor not to be ignored. The province of Mālwa, as one of the component parts of the Mughal Empire, had a definite geographical boundary and its administrative machinery, though medieval in form, was quite in line with that of all the other provinces of the Empire. More than all this, it had a history behind it. The beginning of the change can be marked from the year 1698, which heralds the commencement of a new epoch not only in the history of Mālwa but also in the geography of the province.

Geographical. In 1695 the *subāh* of Mālwa comprised within its limits 12 *sarkārs* and 309 *mahals*, but by 1697, a slight change was effected, the *sarkār* of Bijāgarh having been transferred to the *subāh* of Burhānpur. The province now comprised 11 *sarkārs* and 250 *parganāhs* only.[2] These 11 *sarkārs* were, Ujjain,

---

[1] Malcolm, I, pp.vi-vii.

[2] Khulāsāt (p.34a) mentions Bijāgarh as one of the *sarkārs* of Mālwa. The territory is now comprised in the Nemād district of Indore State. (*Indore Gaz.*, I, pp.413-4; *India of Aurangzib*, p.xxvi; Manucci, II, pp.413-4.)

The change seems to have continued even afterwards. Chahār does not mention it also (1720), pp.80a, 80b; *India of Aurangzib*, pp.lix, 141-2.

Raisin, Chanderi, Sārangpur, Māndu, Handia, Gāgron, Kotri Parayā, Garh, Mandesor and Nandurbār.[1] The Narmadā in the south, the Betwā in the east and the Chambal in the north-west roughly marked its boundaries. The provinces of Kānthal and Bāgad separated Mālwa from Rājputānā and Gujrāt,[2] while the tract known as Hādoti formed the extremest limit on the north-west. Bundelkhand and Gondwānā surrounded Mālwa on the eastern and south-eastern side. The country within the province was mainly a plateau, with alluvial tracts scattered all over the land. The jungle was also dense in many places, big game was abundant all over the country and even elephants could be encountered in Mālwa. The climate was temperate, the nights of

---

[1] In Chahār there are slight differences: Nandurbār appears as Shāhbād, which, according to Sarkar, may be a copyist's mistake; Garh is the same as Kanauj mentioned in *A'in* containing 57 *mahals,* one of them being named Garh. Khulāsāt gives Kobhri for Kotri Parayā. Jarrett's *A'in,* II, p.197; Chahār, p. 80b; Sujān Rai, p. 34*a*; *India of Aurangzib,* pp.lix *n.,* lx, 57 *n.,* 142 *n.*

[2] Bāgad comprised the Guhil States of Bānswādā and Dungarpur, Kānthal of Partābgarh. Both these terms mean a hedge. Over all these States Mewād claimed right of suzerainty, though not accepted by the Mughal Emperors. Partābgarh extends even into Mālwa.

the summer in Mālwa being simply delightful ; it was not an unenviable spot in the Empire.

The province could claim many big cities also, not merely big trade centres, but also some like Ujjain with a history behind them. The chief cities were Ujjain, Chanderi, Dhār, Māndu, Garh (Māndal), Sironj, Narwar, Kotāh and Mandesor. The whole country was traversed by trade routes, with arrangements made for the travellers on the main roads.[1]

Economic. The province had been a centre of culture and civilization for centuries. For a century and a quarter it enjoyed the protection and patronage of the Mughals, and Mālwa received its due share of the prosperity which enriched the Mughal Empire. The roads that passed through Mālwa were military roads as well as trade routes. The industrial activities of the province received an added impetus from these routes. The European traders, who had settled on the western coast, generally travelled by Mālwa routes. During the rains it was closed, due to the many rivers that had to be crossed, but the

---

[1] Manucci, I., p.68; Chahār, pp.120-121b.

In the various routes traced by Sarkar on the basis of the road book of Chahār, there are mentioned many serais forming stopping places, where no town nor village existed near-about. *India of Aurangzib*, pp. xcii-cxv, 168-171.

other route through Ahmedabad, though more direct and always open, was only resorted to in the rainy season in case of great necessity as "the rājās through whose territories the traveller had to pass, (while on that route), generally interfered with trade and claimed that the goods ought to pass their territory and that the customs should be paid."[1] Tavernier mentions an exchange house at Sironj (in Mālwa) which would give letters of exchange for Surat at the rate of 3%.[2]

Industrially Mālwa occupied the first rank among the Mughal *subāhs* after Gujrāt.[3] "Cloth of the finest texture was woven here."[4] "There is made at Sironj", says Tavernier, "a description of *muslin*, which is so fine that when it is on the person you see all the skin as though it were uncovered. The merchants are allowed to export it and the governor sends all of it for the great Mughal's seraglio and for the principal courtiers. This it is of which the Sultānās and the wives of the great nobles make for themselves shifts and garments for the hot weather

[1] Manucci, I., Introduc. lvii-lviii, Chap. XVIII.
[2] Tavernier, I., p.36.
[3] *Aurangzib*, V., p.380.
[4] Jarrett: *A'in.*, II., p.195; *India of Aurangzib*, p.lxi.

and the king and nobles enjoy seeing them wearing those fine shifts and cause them to dance in them."[1]

Mālwa was famous for its coloured cloth too, which it produced in abundance.[2] It was known as *chintz* and was exported to foreign countries also. These calicoes were made in many places, but those made and printed at Sironj were the most famous. It was said that the calicoes dyed in Sironj did not merely look lively, but their colour would appear all the more beautiful the more they were washed. This speciality was attributed to the water of the river, which passes by Sironj, and specially when they were washed in its disturbed waters.[3] The *chintz* made in Mālwa was exported to Persia in large quantities, where it was used by the common people for their dresses, bed-covers and table-cloths. It was all the more popular among the females there, and the manufacturers in Sironj made it to order to suit the taste and customs of the place. It was

---

[1] Tavernier, I., pp.36-7.

It is not clear whether the State maintained any State factory at Sironj, the nearest being at Burhānpur. The officials were ordered to watch the local industries and to send its best products to the Court. Other nobles too patronized these industries. Manucci, II., p.431; *Mughal Adminis.*, p.187-90.

[2] Manucci, II., p.425.

[3] Tavernier, I., p.56; II., pp.29-30.

exported to Turkey also.[1] The trade in this cloth was in the hands of the Armenian traders, who dwelt there, but many times European traders also came there to do business in cloth.[2] These *chintz* were sold at from 20 to 60 rupees the corge or there-about.[3]

"Mālwa was rich in agricultural wealth (too)—producing large quantities of the higher crops, such as opium, sugar-cane, grapes, musk, melons and betel-leaf."[4] While crossing the province Tavernier met with fields of wheat and rice, which strongly reminded him of the French fields at Beausse.[5] "Both crops of the year", says Sujān Rai, "grow excellently, wheat, poppy, sugar-cane, mango, melon and grape grow well. In some places, especially Hāsilpur (in *sarkār* Māndu), the vine bears fruit thrice in the year. Nandurbār was also famous for grapes. Betel grows wonderfully well."[6] Melons of Mālwa used to be served on the table of the Emperors as also on those of great nobles at the

[1] Tavernier, I., p.56; II., p.5.
[2] Manucci, I., p.68.
[3] Tavernier, II., p.5.
[4] *Aurangzib*, V., p.380.
[5] Tavernier, I., p.57.
[6] Khulāsāt, p.34a; *India of Aurangzib*, p.56.

court, where large supplies were sent.[1] Fine tamarinds were a speciality of the Bijāgarh *sarkār*.[2] Salt was also manufactured in Mālwa.[3]

Beautiful forests rich in natural products covered large tracts of the province. Manucci writes of having come across inaccessible mountains, with numerous beautiful trees and traversed by crystal streams.[4] The jungles of Bijāgarh, Hindiā and Garh were noted for sheltering wild elephants.[5] In the jungles of Dhār there were big long bamboos. Lac was made in Dhār and lac-makers were often required there for the purpose.[6]

During the first century of Mughal rule in Mālwa the province reached the height of its prosperity in the middle of the 17th century, the provincial revenues collected in 1654 amounted to Rs. 1,39,32,933,[7] which was the highest ever realized and recorded. It was practically double the figure given in the *A'in-i-Akbari*, which was

---

1 Nawāzish, pp.2b, 3a.
2 *India of Aurangzib*, p.lxi.
3 Manucci, II., p.430.
4 Khulāsāt, p.34a.
5 *India of Aurangzib*, pp.lxi, 56.
6 Nawāzish, p.29b.
7 *Dastur-ul-Amal* in *India of Aurangzib*, pp.ix, xxix.

Rs. 60,17,136.[1] The war of succession of 1658 had its own effect, but in 1697 the income stood at Rs. 99,06,250.[2] The province was once again enjoying a period of comparative peace, and in 1700 it reached another high watermark of Rs. 1,02,08,667.[3] The prosperity was, however, soon to end.[4] The ease with which the sudden drops in the revenue disappeared shows the prosperous

---

[1] Jarrett : *A'in.*, II., p.197; *India of Aurangzib,* pp.xxxlii, lx.

[2] Manucci, II., p.413.

[3] *Dastur-ul-Amal,* MS. C. in *India of Aurangzib,* pp.xxxii, ix.

[4] A comparative statement of changes in revenue is given below :—

1665—Rs. 91,62,500. (Bernier, p.457) 9 *Sar.* 190 *Parga.*

1695—Rs. 92,25,425. (Khulāsāt, p.34a) 12 *Sar.* 309 *Mahals.*

1697—Rs. 99,06,250. (Manucci, II., p.413) 11 *Sar.* 250 *Parga.*

1700—Rs. 1,02,08,667. (*Dastur-ul-Amal*) 12 *Sar.* 117 *Mahals.*

1707—Rs. 1,00,97,541. (Ramucio in Harris, *Voyages*).

1707—Rs. 1,00,99,516. (Jagjivan Dās Gujrāti).

Manucci, II., p.413. He takes the figure from Jagjivan Dās Gujrāti's 'Muntukhub-ut-Tawarikh' (Br. Mus. Add. MS. No. 26,253, fol. 51 *et seq.*) which gives it on the basis of estimates prepared for Bahādur Shāh in 1707.

1720—Rs. 90,04,593. (Chahār, p.79) 11 *Sar.* 259 *Mahals.* *India of Aurangzib,* pp.lix, ix, pp.56, 141.

condition of Mālwa during the closing years of the 17th century.

Strategical. The strategical importance of Mālwa was very great. It was the link which joined North India with South India. All the military routes to the Deccan passed through it, so also the routes to Gujrāt and to the sea-ports on the western coast. For striking at Rājputānā, Gondwānā or Berār, Mālwa afforded an excellent military base.[1] The importance of Mālwa increased with Aurangzib's wars in the Deccan. Aurangzib had, therefore, made it a point to appoint to its governorship either some prince of the Royal blood or some most trusted officer.[2] This importance was to grow in the period that followed. When Aurangzib was fighting in the Deccan and the Marathas began their aggressive policy, they began to attack Mālwa, in order to cut off the communication between the Royal camp and Northern India. After Aurangzib's death the Mughal capital again shifted back to the North. Soon, however, the fall of the Empire was presaged by two movements, *viz.*, to carve out new kingdoms out of the declining Empire and to establish the

---

[1] *Aurangzib,* V., p.381.

[2] Manucci, II., p.430.

Maratha supremacy. Each party tried to control Mālwa to achieve its own aim. The effects were very disastrous and far-reaching. The strategical importance of Mālwa increased in the 18th century because of anarchy.

Mālwa was never fully dominated by the Muslims, even though it was once ruled over by the independent Muslim kings of Mālwa. Specially in the later days of that local Sultanate the Hindu domination was rather a rule than an exception; Basant Rāi was long a minister, while the Rajputs too held dominant position for long. The population was predominantly Hindu. It was composed of more than one element. There was the original cultivating class with other similar Hindu elements. The original aboriginal tribes also lived there, Bhils, and Minās in the western and north-western regions, Gonds in the southern tracts; while there were many tribes similar to the gypsies, which had no settled home. The Jāts were settled in the north and north-western areas. The Rajput society of this period was cut into two distinct divisions. First, there were those Rajputs who had established themselves in Mālwa, when the Rajputs dominated the whole of India (in the 7th and 8th centuries), or those who had retired to these tracts when the Political.

first rush of the Muslims in India swept many of the Rajputs chiefs from the north. These Rajputs had lost their touch with those of Rājputānā; they had made Mālwa their home, its problems were their problems, and above all, its kingdom was their own kingdom; they practically identified themselves with Mālwa. Many of these races maintained touch with the fighting races of the locality, and thus became intermixed with them. They were the landholders when the Mughals established their control over Mālwa. Many of them continued to hold land even later. There, however, grew up many intermixed races, such as the Bhilālās and Sondhiās,[1] who were found practically over the whole of Mālwa, specially in the central and southern regions. Many of these early Rajput races continued to guard the purity of their blood and were acknowledged as such by a certain section. In 1698, there was, however, another set of Rajputs in Mālwa, who classed themselves as true Rajputs of the purest blood and as such purer than those of the first set. This set consisted of those Rajputs who came from the Royal families of Rājputānā, who had served the Mughals very faithfully, had

[1] Malcolm, I., pp.511-516.

proved their mettle and were rewarded with grants of land in Mālwa. These Rajput grandees brought their relatives, friends and dependents with them in Mālwa and founded States, many of which exist to this day. Connected as these Rajputs were with the ruling families of Rājputānā, to whom history has given importance and who enjoyed power due to the Imperial favour, these Rajput Princes and their circle of society became dictators in the social matters of the Rajput race in Mālwa. They had only recently been introduced into the political and social life of Mālwa and, though politically not very firmly rooted there, they enjoyed great influence in the province.

In addition to all these, there was the Muslim element in the population. The Afghāns had scattered throughout Mālwa, but they had mainly settled in different centres, while the Mughal element was limited to big towns only, or to places where there were outposts of the government.[1] In number they all formed a very small minority.

Constituted as the population was of such diverse elements, the firm rule of the Mughals gave a peaceful and uneventful administration to the

[1] *Mughal Adminis.*, pp.55-6.

province till the near end of the 17th century; exceptions there were but very rare.[1] With the beginning of the new century this long period of peace ended. The disturbing factors in the province itself were not wanting. "The undeveloped primitive races," says Sir Jadunath Sarkar, "which had taken refuge in out-of-the-way corners and among the hills and jungles, were too uncivilized and too much divided to count for anything, though in mere number they formed the largest substratum of the population."[2] In times of anarchy, however, they were capable of taking advantage of the situation and making life and property quite unsafe. The Jāts and the Gonds were tribes which could be kept subdued only by means of a strong hand; fermentation in both these tribes was going on in 1698, which was sure to affect Mālwa. "Any disturbance in Berār or Gondwana, Bundelkhand or the eastern Rajput States would immediately spread by contagion to Mālwa."[3] In Mālwa itself the old set of Rajputs and Afghāns supplied enough material to increase the disturbances. These Rajputs felt their own humiliation, their loss of lands and independence.

---

[1] *Aurangzib,* V., p.382.

[2] *Aurangzib,* V., p.380.

[3] *Aurangzib,* V., p.381.

The Afghans too felt the same thing, and they joined in all disturbances in Mālwa, not caring in the least to think whether they were helping the Rajputs or the Marathas; to them even that puritan Emperor appeared to be an enemy. Their opposition and resentment was all centred against the Imperial authorities.

The new set of Rajputs and their newly-granted landed-estates supplied the necessary factor of stability and support to the Empire. They were the creations of the Mughal Empire, and as such very rarely stood up in opposition to the Imperial authority. It can well be asserted that the establishment of these States and the creation of these new landed interests in Mālwa was the outcome of a definite policy of the Mughal to create buffers between the South and the North,—buffers, which would always be true to the Empire. They even served as checks on other turbulent States of Rājputānā, which did not always stand in obedience to the Empire. The creation of Kotāh as a full-fledged State marks the beginning of this policy.

But these States had their weak points too. In many cases the descendants of those brave founders turned out to be weak men. In other States which had been founded in the last years of Aurangzib's reign—and the number of such States was the greatest in Mālwa—the founders as well as their early descendants did not get enough time to organize their States nor to secure their hold over the lands and the people within the State, as they were kept busy in the distant South with the Imperial army. And the States, yet unorganized and unstrengthened, could least help the Empire in times of disorder, for they had first to grapple with the question of their own existence. Thus alone can the secret of the utter failure of the Imperial authorities in Mālwa be explained. The States helped the Empire as long as they hoped that the Empire would win in the end, but when the utter break-up of the Empire became evident, they began to think of making their own position safe, and the Imperial forces were thus left to fight single-handed against the Marathas invading from the Deccan and their helpmates in the province itself.

Administrative.

Hence the province was full of all those discordant factors and weaknesses which could make it the most turbulent in the Empire. During the first century of Mughal rule the province was the midway station for the armies moving towards the South and back, but for the last twenty-five years the armies of the Empire had mainly been concentrated in the

South. To add to that, the forces of disorder which had been disturbing the fringes of the province could not yet be put down successfully, which greatly reduced the prestige of the Imperial forces. The policy of religious fanaticism enforced by Aurangzib caused much heart-burning among the common Hindu population.[1] The administration had, on the other hand, been getting weaker. The decline was apparent in Mālwa too. "The new classes of *subedārs* and *faujdārs* were too low in rank and armed strength to repress them."[2] It was a vicious circle from which there was no way out. The income of all the officers including the governors also, was dwindling even on paper, and it was not possible to gain anything even from the landholders. This diminished income forced the governors to keep fewer men in their pay. "Except some, who had ancestral estates, *viz.*, Rāo Dalpat, Rāmsingh Hādā and Jai Singh Kachhāwāh," says Sir Jadunath, "I have not come across a single noble, who kept even a thousand troopers in his contingent."[3] Mālwa was

---

[1] Fight in Ujjain, April 1670, *Akhbarat*, 13th year, Sheet 17. Amin-i-Jaziyā killed in Ratlām, *Akhbarat*—June, 8, 9, 1695. *Aurangzib*, III, pp.321-2.

[2] *Aurangzib*, V, pp.10-11, 451-2; Bhimsen, II, pp.139a, 140a.

[3] *Aurangzib*, V, 453-4.

no exception; and with additional troubles in the years to come the whole system of provincial administration was to prove a failure.[1] Mughal rule had failed to create any nationality in Mālwa; on the other hand, it had destroyed what little of it was there. The province had evidently soon to face a sweeping flood, for which it was the least prepared.

Social life. "No person," says Sujān Rai, "whether a peasant, *baniyā*, artisan, skilled mechanic or any other, is without a weapon of war."[2] Hindu society was divided into four divisions with many more sub-divisions and sub-castes which not merely made it more complex, but rigid too. The Brahmans had ceased to possess their former domination over the Hindu society in general, and even more signally over the Rajputs, who generally dominated the whole social life of the province. Their economic condition was also not good, nor were they very learned, many were not proficient in religious rites too.[3] Ujjain, however, was still a great religious centre,

---

[1] *Aurangzib,* V, p.452.

[2] Khulāssāt, p.34a; *India of Aurangzib,* pp.lxl, 56.

[3] This section is mainly based on Malcolm's *Memoirs* (Vol. II) with due omission of the facts that were introduced by the Maratha domination. Malcolm, II, p.124.

and, even though in ruins, it continued to attract pilgrims.[1]

The chief points of difference between the two sets of Rajput society have already been mentiond. It may be added that the recently immigrated Rajputs did not intermarry nor did they take to agriculture, as was the case with the other set of local Rajputs. Even as late as the beginning of the 18th century, Sir John Malcolm felt that the features of the Rajputs of the former class could distinctly be marked as quite foreign to Mālwa. Their chief occupation was fighting. Their head-dress and other dresses greatly resembled the court-dress of the Mughal Emperors. The Rajputs ladies strictly observed the *purdāh*. The use of opium was not limited to children only, but was prevalent among all other classes too.[2] Their favourite pastime in times of peace was hunting. They brought with them from Rājputānā many of the festivities (*i.e., Akshaya Tritiyā*) and introduced them into Mālwa. The attachment of these new set of Rajputs to Rājputānā was so great that wherever they settled they practically colonized the place. The influence of the

---

[1] Manucci, II, p.430; *India of Aurangzib,* p.ix.

[2] Malcolm, II, pp.127-8, 140, 144, 146, 147, 150-151; Khulāsāt, p.34a; *India of Aurangzib,* pp.lxi, 56.

bards who form more than one clan, *viz.*, Bhāts, Chārans, Rāos, etc., was great on the Rajputs. They were not merely historians, but also the custodians of the military traits and valour of the Rajputs; they accorded praise to all good deeds and censure to wrong acts.

Even the Bhilālās and the Sondhiās, though bound to the soil, kept up their military traditions. "They were cultivators or plunderers, according to the strength or weakness of the government over them, but they had always a tendency to predatory war, and cherished its habit even when obliged to subsist by agriculture."[1] The other local Rajputs, though they continued to be landholders and were quite powerful, were not treated on terms of equality by the new immigrants. The main difficulty lay in their relation being one of rulers and the ruled. But the period to follow was to begin the slow process of amalgamation, when the local Rajputs began to supply the fighting forces to save the existence of the new immigrants.

The trading classes were of two types; there were those who like Banjārās moved from place to place and formed the chief source of communication

---

[1] Malcolm, II, pp.127-8, 150, 131-9, 153.

and the main means of transport. There were *baniyās* too, who had their own banking system and carried on the trade of the province. They mostly belonged to the Jain religion, while many were Hindus, adhering to the Vaishnava sect.[1] There was one more important class of society which was of a very recent growth only, *viz.*, the *Kayasthas.* They supplied the Persian-knowing clerks of the States and by their keen intellect became the keepers of the land-revenue and other records in the province.[2] Many times this class supplied a series of ministers and administrators to the newly formed States.

The province was undergoing a definite change at this time and hence there are no traces of any great literary or artistic effort at this time. Supporters of the fine arts and the higher instincts were wanting at this period. Education was carried on by private enterprise.[3] The fanatical religious policy of the Emperor did not greatly disturb the local society, and the records do not give account of any tension between the Hindus and the Muslims over religious affairs. There were many religious and superstitious beliefs and usages which were equally shared by the

---

[1] Malcolm, II, pp.152, 160-2.
[2] Malcolm, II, pp.165-7.
[3] Malcolm, II, pp. 190-1.

followers of both religions. The *Holi* festival was practically celebrated by Muslims also.[1] Slavery was found in Mālwa, but was generally restricted to females and was a speciality of the Rajputs and the Muslims, who generally needed it.[2] The *suttee* was common among the higher Hindu castes; so also was female infanticide which was generally limited to the Rajputs. The practice of self-immolation on special festivities was to be found among the lower classes. Belief in witch-craft prevailed in Mālwa to an extraordinary degree.[3] Dancing girls were to be found in the large centres of the province. Rope-dancers and like people supplied amusement to the villages.[4]

The Muslim population was mainly constituted of those whose conversion was forced upon them or had been bought about in the early days of Muslim rule. These converts not merely retained the Hindu practices but also Hindu names and old tribal differences. Many of these were cultivators by profession.[5] Those who had taken to the military

---

[1] Malcolm, II, pp.194-5.
[2] Malcolm, II, pp.199-201.
[3] Malcolm, II, pp.207, 208-10, 212-218.
[4] Malcolm, II, pp.195-7.
[5] Malcolm, II, pp.108-110.

profession were only recent immigrants like the Multānis, or Afghans, who maintained their military character. They generally lived in the towns or sought service. Many took to trade also, and many Muslim traders came from distant places for its sake.[1]

Soon, however, a few factors appeared on the political horizon of Mālwa, which were also to revolutionize the constitution of society. The Maratha inroads and, later, their conquest greatly influenced the economic life of Mālwa as well as its administrative system.

[1] Malcolm, II, pp. 113-114.

CHAPTER II

MĀLWA DURING THE LAST DECADE OF AURANGZIB'S REIGN (1698—1707)

SECTION I.—THE EPOCH BEGINNING IN 1698: THE NEW PERIOD AND ITS KEYNOTE.

The Emperor.

For forty years Aurangzib had been ruling the Empire. "To an extraordinary degree hard-working, active, moral, and inspired by a sense of duty, the Emperor had denied himself pleasure and repose, steeled his heart against the seduction of the senses and the appeals of pity and human weakness and governed his people according to the best of ideals of his age and creed." By 1681 Aurangzib seemed to have attained the summit of human happiness and glory. Every enemy was removed from his path, the whole Empire obeyed his command, the absorption of Bijāpur and Golkondā appeared inevitable,—and the wealth and culture of the Empire were increasing from the peace and order that his firm and vigilant rule had ensured to the country.

The Emperor goes to the Deccan: June, 1681.

But soon after the Emperor found that the situation in the Deccan was complicated by the revolt of Prince Akbar, who now joined the Marathas, already rising in their opposition to the Empire. He crossed the Narmadā for the last time in 1681 and the next twenty-six years of his life, which were also the last twenty-six years of his reign, he spent in tents in the South.

Aurangzib and the Marathas, 1698.

There in the Deccan the Emperor wore out the revenues of the Empire, its army, its organized administration and his days too in an unending and fruitless struggle. The two Muslim kingdoms had fallen; but the Marathas still remained unsubdued. Rājārām, the second son of Shivāji, was crowned as the Maratha king after his elder brother, Shambhāji's execution; Shāhu, son of Shambhāji, was then in Mughal captivity. Rājārām had fled away from Mahārāstra and was upto 1697 sheltering behind the walls of Jinji, which was being besieged by the Mughal forces. At this time there was no organized opposition in Mahārāstra; this lack of organization only multiplied the difficulties of Aurangzib. It now became a people's war and every Maratha captain gathered together his own retainers and other adherents and raided different quarters of the Empire on his own account. In January, 1698, the Mughals captured the fort of Jinji. Rājārām, however, escaped to Mahārāstra, the Maratha forces once again gathered together under one man's leadship, and the Mughal forces became active in Konkan.

Mālwa in 1698.

As Aurangzib became more and more entangled in the Deccan with Maratha affairs, his local agents in northern and central India grew weaker and more helpless. Chhatra Sāl Bundelā was achieving brilliant triumphs over the Mughal forces by capturing Kālinjar, Dhāmuni and plundering Bhilsā. The range of his raids was gradually extending. Bakht Buland had raised the standard of revolt in Deogarh and was trying his luck. His territories lay adjoining to Mālwa on its south-western border. Mālwa had become the happy hunting ground of these foreign invaders from these neighbouring countries. They provided the nucleus round which the lawless men of Mālwa assembled. Though the internal regions of the province were more or less peaceful and had so far enjoyed uneventful administration, the troubles on the outskirts had begun to react on the central regions too.

The new epoch : Its keynote.

The year 1698 marks an epoch not only in the history of India but also in that of Mālwa. "After Rājārām's return home from Jinji (in 1698)," observes Sir Jadunath Sarkar, "began a movement which was destined in less than fifty years to completely change the political history of the province [of

Mālwa]."[1] In 1699 Aurangzib, an old man of eighty-two, decided to conduct the war in person and capture the Maratha forts one after another and thus to uproot the Maratha power completely. The Marathas on the other hand, were reviving feudalism in their polity, first for defence and later for the expansion of their kingdom. The struggle between the weakened Mughal Empire, now on its decline, and the Maratha power, bubbling with enthusiasm aroused by the newly revived feudalism, is the keynote of the first phase of this century of anarchy. In the struggle the Mughal power is thoroughly beaten, ousted, and the Marathas come to dominate Mālwa. There they plant their own feudal institutions and give the feudal remains of the Mughal empire in Mālwa their permanency. This establishment of divided power, clashing interests and retention and strengthening of the opposing elements marks the new epoch. Its bitter result,—the internal struggles and the disorders in the province,—followed this early stage in the second phase of the transition.

End of peace, prosperity and unity of Mālwa.

The year 1698 brings to an end the long period of peace and prosperity in Mālwa. It also closes the century of united Mālwa under Mughal rule.

---

[1] *Aurangzib*, V, p.382.

The Mughal Empire was weakening and the forces of anarchy and disruption were gaining strength. In the province itself there was no possibility of the rise of any central force which could take the place of the falling Mughal Empire. The Mughals had crushed down all those people who could possibly have proved to be their saviour at this time. Thus, there was no united power, State or group of people in Mālwa which could form a nucleus in the unification of Mālwa or give Mālwa unity when the Empire was finally collapsing. The Rajput policy of the Mughals led to the plantation of a new group of Rajputs in Mālwa, but they were not yet strongly enough planted there to become the bulwark of the Mughal Empire in its falling days. The Rajputs brought with them their disintegrating tendencies too. Their hold over their own lands was not strong enough, nor were they extensive enough to give them power and position in the affairs of the province. The introduction of the Rajput element in Mālwa brought about a new complication in the provincial affairs, as these newly planted princes looked to the Princes of Rājputānā for help and guidance. This dependence increased due to the lack of any great personality in Mālwa during this period. Jai Singh alone filled this gap and for

Lack of central force: Lack of great personality.

twenty years or more, openly or secretly, guided the internal movements and intrigues of the province.

Financial difficulties: Its influence on politics.

The situation of the province, of its landholders and of the Empire, too, was weakened and became worse on account of the financial stringency that prevailed in the province throughout this new period. The influence of this stringency on the politics of the province was great. The central government could not help and the provincial government could not keep the requisite military equipment and forces. Whenever any provincial governor thought of being very exacting as regards the Imperial dues, the landholders thought and hoped that it was cheaper to keep the raiders (the Marathas) satisfied than to support the provincial machinery. They naturally supported the cause of the Marathas. This very financial stringency was to lead to the adhesion at first and opposition after 1743 of the Rajput and other landholders in Mālwa to the Marathas.

The failure of the Marathas to give Mālwa peace, prosperity, unity and the required central force.

But the Marathas too could not supply the required central force to the affairs of Mālwa, nor could they give the province peace, prosperity and unity. The feudalism of the Marathas disrupted their own forces and so long as they were busy with affairs outside the province, the defects of their system and the failure of their policy did not become apparent. Thus, the rise of a number of powers among these conquerors, each practically semi-independent and all tied together by that very weak thread called the overlordship of the Peshwā, completely destroyed what little remnants of the unity of the Mughal times were left. The new conquerors found that the various fiefs and *zamindaris* of the Mughal times had become more or less full-fledged States during this period of transition, and they accepted the state of affairs as it existed, save where later events and transactions modified the situation.

Thus the chief characteristic of the whole period of transition was the breakdown of the unifying factors and the rise of anarchical tendencies. The failure of the Marathas to put down these tendencies led to their own fall as the supreme power in Mālwa. The first phase of the period of transition, which this volume proposes to deal with, saw the breakdown of all the unifying factors. The defeat of the Marathas at the battle of Pānipat saw the breakdown of unity among the Marathas themselves; the bond that kept their own disintegrating forces under control visibly weakened. The second phase saw the undoing of the Marathas consequent upon their failure in the first phase.

SECTION 2.—MALWA AND ITS GOVERNORS (1698—1707).

The Unity of the period. The sowing of the seed.

The last nine years of Aurangzib's rule form a period by themselves. With the beginning of the year 1698, a new movement began in the Deccan, but it did not change the situation all at once. These nine years saw the beginning of various new tendencies which, though insignificant and temporary in outward appearance at the time, gradually proved to be the forerunners of considerable movements. The Great Mughal still dominated the affairs of the Indian Empire. The revolt of Chhatra Sāl was not new to the period; it had been going on for twenty years and more. There were some Maratha invasions of the province, which did not result in any conquest at that time. The Maratha power had received a set-back by the untimely death of Rājārām in 1700. Shāhu was still in Mughal captivity. The efforts of Tārā Bāi, though opening a new vision before the Maratha generals, could not create a strong nation out of them. This weakness of the Maratha power at this time becomes all the more apparent from the lull that followed the release of Shāhu in 1707. Thus, though the Marathas could not achieve any great results during this period, they showed the weak point in the Mughal power, where it could be hit with advantage. Again the other important and notable fact of this period is the beginning of the internal disturbances and troubles which greatly weakned the Mughal power in the province and were to pave the way for the Maratha conquest in the years to come. The spirit of anarchy becomes rampant and though it does not become evident in the period that immediately followed, being once aroused, it held on, and as soon as the Maratha invasions were revived after 1719, Mālwa became aflame and the Imperial government found it impossible to oppose the Maratha forces which had numerous supporters and friends in the province itself. Thus, the touch with Mālwa of the Maratha invaders and the beginning of the spirit of anarchy mark the whole period. The administrative weakness in the province made matters worse. This spirit of anarchy was to weaken the position of those people too, who had their landed interests in the province and were ardent supporters of the Empire. The seed of all these troubles of the future was sown during the last nine years of Aurangzib's reign. After his death there followed a period of another nine years during which there was a comparative lull in the affairs of the province; the seed lay germinating, unseen, below the soil.

In 1698 Mukhtiyār Khān, the father-in-law of Prince Bidār Bakht, was the governor of Mālwa. He was appointed to this post in the 41st year of the reign (sometime between March 24, 1697 and March 12, 1698). He continued to hold this office till 1701, when Abu Nasar Khān succeeded him.[1] It was during Mukhtiyār Khān's governorship that Ratan Singh, son of Gopāl Singh Chandrāwat, was converted to Islam and the series of troubles between the father and the son began, which continued even after the death of Aurangzib. The revolt of Chhatra Sāl continued unabated and Bakht Buland disturbed the province when he passed through it with his horde of rebels. The Marathas invaded Mālwa for the first time under the leadership of Krishnāji Sāwant and were allowed to return unmolested.

Mukhtiyār Khān 1697-1701.

Abu Nasar Khān was one of the sons of Shaiyastā Khān, who had figured prominently in the early years of the reign. He was known as Shaiyastā Khān II. He had already served for seven years (1690-97) as governor of Kashmir, where he was noted for his attempts to enrich himself by levying illegal cesses, in addition to his legitimate

Abu-Nasar Khān, Shaiyastā Khān II. 1701—August, 1704.

[1] Manucci, III, pp.194n.3, 194-5; M.A., p.442; M.U., I, pp.246-7; III, p.656.

dues.[1] He enjoyed the honour of being a 2½ *hazari* and commanded 1,000 horsemen. He was appointed in the middle of the year 1701, when he was given a promotion of ½ *hazari* and command of 1,500 horsemen.[2] The troubles with Chhatra Sāl had subsided for the time being, but the revolt of Gopāl Singh was still going on. The invasion of the Marathas was repeated more than once, and it was the Maratha raid of 1703-4, which finally led to his dismissal. Weak, dissolute and greedy, he dared not face the raiders, remained sheltering within the fort of Ujjain, and thus could be of no help to the Imperial armies pursuing the invaders under Firuz Jang. The Emperor peremptorilly dismissed him from the governorship.[3]

Bidār Bakht: Aug. 3, 1704 —April, 1706.

Aurangzib first thought of giving the governorship to his own grandson Bidār Bakht, who at first hesitated. For some time the Emperor was in a fix; he even had a mind to appoint Nawāzish Khān, the degraded *faujdar* of Māndu, who was now restored to favour. But, finally the Emperor appointed

---

[1] *Aurangzib,* V, pp.419-20.

[2] M.A., p.442.

[3] *Akhbarat,* Feb. 3, 1704; Kālimāt T. fol.44a, 55a; M.A., p.483.

the prince to the governorship on August 3.[1] The Prince had proved himself a brave and skilful general. He was already the governor of Aurangabad and continued to hold the appointment even now.[2] His governorship of nineteen months in Mālwa was full of activity for the Prince. He had to move from Mālwa to Khāndesh or *vice versa* as the situation demanded. Every time the treasures from the northern provinces reached Agra on transit, the Prince was called upon to make special arrangements for their escort through Mālwa and Khāndesh and to save them from the Maratha depredations.[3] The Prince had to put down the local troubles of Bhils and Kolis of Nemād and other districts in Mālwa and those adjoining it in the south. These risings were the outcome of the Maratha invasion of the previous year.[4] The *zamindar* of Awāsgarh (now

[1] Ināyetullah, fol.19a, 132b, 134b, 75b, 131a; *Akhbarat*, Aug. 3, 1704; M.A., p.483; *Aurangzib*, v. p.388.

[2] *Aurangzib*, V, pp.189, 388; M.A., 471, 470, 483. Khāndesh was to be governed by a deputy of Bidār Bakht. In 1704 Mir Ahmad Khān the *diwān sarkār* of the Prince, was appointed *Naib-Subedar* of Khāndesh. (M.A., p.480.)

[3] Many of the letters in Ināyetullāh's *Ahkam* contain the instructions to the Prince to this effect. They are too numerous to be given in detail. Many of them are not dated and as the letters are not arranged chronologically, it is very difficult to correctly arrange the events in a chronological order.

[4] Ināyetullah, fol.31a, 57b, 101b, 138a, 148b, 40a.

the principality of Barwāni) also raised his head and continued to cause trouble even after the Marathas had withdrawn.[1] The Bhils caused disturbances on the north-western frontiers also and built the fort of Gāgron.[2] After the fear of another invasion by Nimā had disappeared, the Prince had to go to Mālwa to escort the treasure, when he fell ill (Dec. 1703-Jan. 1705).[3] At this time he appointed Jai Singh of Amber, his trusted assistant, to escort the treasures and also to act as his deputy in Mālwa. The Emperor objected to this appointment, ordered the Prince to recall Jai Singh, appointed Khān Alam instead and, for future guidance, ordered that no Rajput was to be appointed *subāhdār* or *faujdār*.[4] Bidār Bakht was ordered at this time to go down to Sansani (a fort near Bharatpur), which had recently been taken by the Jāts, and to recapture it. The Prince did intend to comply, but due to his illness and other engagements in Mālwa, he could not proceed to Sansani.[5] In the rains of the year

---

[1] Ināyetullah, fol.31a, 101b, 106a.

[2] Ināyetullah, fol.64a.

[3] Ināyetullah, fol.76a, 91a, 104b, 133b, 93a.

[4] Ināyetullah, fol.94a, 105a, 133b, 134b, 138a, 68a, 72b, 74b.

[5] Ināyetullah, fol.24a, 25a, 70a, 75b, 77a, 78a, 78b; Qānungo : *Jats,* I, 47.

1705, the Prince had to stay in Mālwa.[1] During the closing months of 1705, Bidār Bakht's task was lightened. The provinces of Aurangābād and Khāndesh were taken away from his charge and were entrusted to Prince Azam who was now on his way back from Gujrāt.[2] Bidār Bakht continued to be on active service against the Marathas even in Khāndesh. He had gone to Mālwa in November, 1705 to investigate and set right the complaints in Mālwa against some of the assistants of Jai Singh. In the meanwhile, as Prince Azam, father of Bidār Bakht, left Gujrāt on the November 25, 1705, and was proceeding to the Emperor through Mālwa, Bidār Bakht went to Dhār to meet his father. The Emperor was angry with Bidār Bakht for not having returned to Burhānpur to hunt after the Marathas. Bidār Bakht had to move down to Nolāi (Badnagar) to meet the Maratha forces sent by Parsu Maratha to help Gopāl Singh Chandrāwat once again in his revolt. The province of Gujrāt was invaded by the Marathas and the Emperor summarily ordered

---

[1] Ināyetullah, fol.87b.

[2] Ināyetullah, 73a; M.A., p.496. On Nov. 16, 1705, Mālwa continued to be with Bidār Bakht. M.A., p.498.

Bidār Bakht to start for Gujrāt immediately.[1] The Prince left Mālwa in April 1706 for Gujrāt.

During his governorship, though Khān Alam was made the Deputy Governor, time and again various persons were appointed to that office, as Khān Alam had often to go on various expeditions either alone or with the Prince.[2] The condition of the forces of the Prince, too, was not very good and the Emperor often sent instructions to reinforce them and also helped him with money. Time and again leading generals were appointed to act under the directions of Bidār Bakht.[3] On the whole it can be asserted that the province was not seriously disturbed by any foreign invasion of great magnitude. In 1706, on the recommendation of Firuz Jang, peace was made with Chhatra Sāl, who visited the

---

[1] Ināyetullah, fol.81a, 83a, 83b, 84, 85a, 21; *Aurangzib*, V, pp.388, 43.

[2] Ināyetullah mentions the appointment of the following persons as *Naib-Subedār* of Mālwa; Khān Alam, 68a, 91a, 37a; Qāsim Hussain Khān, 78a; Ali Mardan Khān, 76a, 86a; Abdullā Khān, son of Amānullā Khān, was appointed *Naib-Subedar* in place of Khān Alam (90a) probably at the time of the appointment of Bidār Bakht to the governorship of Gujrāt. He continued to hold this place till 1707.

[3] Ināyetullāh, fol.34a, 38a, 46a-b, 49a, 74b, 75b, 78a, 86b, 88b, 90b, 108a.

Emperor in the Deccan. There he was honoured and lived in peace till the death of the Emperor.[1]

On the transfer of Bidār Bakht to Gujrāt, once again there was difficulty in filling this governorship. Even when Prince Azam was governor of Gujrāt, he had requested the Emperor to appoint him to the governorship of Mālwa (1705); this the Emperor refused to do and gave him the governorship of Khāndesh instead. Azam was not willing to take Khāndesh and the Emperor at last decided to transfer Mālwa to Azam (Jan., 1706); Bidār Bakht was ordered to go down to Burhānpur. Azam had obtained permission to visit the Emperor with great difficulty, and as he was on his way to Ahmednagar, he did not care to stop in Mālwa.[2] When Bidār Bakht was leaving for Gujrāt, the Emperor felt that Khān Alam was not the proper person for Mālwa, most probably because he was ill at that time. Khān Alam proposed that Munawwar Khān be given this

---

[1] M.U., II, p.512; Bhimsen, II, 157b. Sarkar puts this event in 1705 A.D. I believe that it could not have occurred earlier than late in 1705 or beginning of 1706. Ināyetullāh mentions the plans of Bidār Bakht to put down Chhatra Sāl, fol.30a, 29b. These letters were probably written in April or May, 1705. *Aurangzib*, V, p.399; Bhimsen too puts it in the year 1706.

[2] Ināyetullāh, fol.73a, 74a, 80a, 84a; Khāfi Khān, II, 541.

governorship, which was not acceptable to the Emperor (July, 1706). Finally, Khān Alam was made the governor of Mālwa and Nejābat was ordered to act in place of Khān Alam so long as the latter did not recover from his illness.[1] But Khān Alam does not appear to have remained in Mālwa as its governor for long, as he was busy fighting the Marathas in Khāndesh. Later he went to Ahmadnagar. Abdullā Khān, son of Amānullāh Khān, who was appointed the deputy governor of Mālwa early in 1706, carried on the government till April 1707, when Azam appointed Nejābat Khān as the governor of Mālwa.[2]

Khān Alam 1706.

Azam starts for Mālwa : The Emperor's death and Azam's return. Feb., 1707.

In February 1707, the Emperor saw his own end very near and he decided to send his sons way. On February 13, he sent Azam to Mālwa "to set the matters of the province right." Azam knew the real facts and before he had gone no further than forty miles in a week, he heard of the death of his father (Feb. 20, 1707). Azam hurried back to the Imperial camp.[3]

---

[1] Ināyetullāh, fol.85a, 21b, 21a, 22a; M.A., p. 512.

[2] Ināyetullāh, fol.90a, Irādat Khān : Scott, p.16; M.U., I, p.816; II, p.871; Azam, pp.193-4.

[3] *Aurangzib*, V, pp.256, 258; Khāfi Khān, II, pp.548, 566; M.A., (p.520) states that the Prince took leave. It must

The Administration of Mālwa: its decline: causes.

During these nine years the administration of the province had been steadily going down. "The inflated expenditure and incessant warfare in the Deccan," says Sir Jadunath Sarkar, "adversely re-acted on the situation in Northern India."[1] The best soilders, the ablest officers and all the collected revenues were sent to the Deccan. Time and again orders were sent for the enrolment of soldiers and for sending them to the Deccan, and no regard was paid to the fact that in some cases the forces were needed in that province too.[2] There went on much looseness and bribery in the fulfilment of the Imperial orders and even the highest officers were ready to ignore the discrepancies in the execution of the orders.[3] The administration was being weakened by the poverty of the various officers. The Emperor himself knew this fact and in his letter to Zulfiqār Khān agrees that Nawāzish Khān could not rule well because of his own poor circumstances and small retinue.[4]

---

have been on the orders of the Emperor and against his own will that the Prince had been forced to take leave.

[1] *Aurangzib*, V, p.451.

[2] The orders for supplying men and money given in the *Akhbarat* of Aug. 2, 1700 is noteworthy. The invasion of Krishnāji Sāwant had occurred only a few months before.

[3] *Vir Vinod*, II, pp.741, 751-52.

[4] Ināyetullāh, fol.132b.

Cases of oppression of poor subjects by the officers were not also few; embezzlement of the State revenues and oppression of the people made the people appeal to the higher authorities for redress, which often did not come.[1] Even able officers like Prince Bidār Bakht had to complain to the Emperor of the lack of sufficient forces.[2] Again in the administration of the province, the weakness in the management of the *zamindāris* already transferred to grantees provided an added source of danger, for they could least be relied upon in the event of a raid or disturbance. And at a time when the spirit of disorder was beginning to prevail, the weakness of the administration was to have the most fatal consequences.

SECTION 3.—CHHATRA SAL BUNDELA AND MALWA

Chhatra Sāl Bundelā had been invading the north-eastern border of Mālwa for a decade and more previous to the year 1698. The Mughal forces had on the whole failed to subdue him and as the Emperor became more and more entangled in

---

[1] Ināyetullāh, fol.64a. In spite of this inquiry and representation, Hidāyatullah appears to have continued to hold the *faujdari*. Irādat Khān: Scott, p.16-7.

[2] Ināyetullāh, V, fol.86a, 108a.

the affairs of the Deccan, Chhatra Sāl became increasingly active, extending his field of activity and carving out a kingdom for himself in Eastern Mālwa. By the year 1698, he had made his position in his own principality secure and was busy broadening its limits. By 1699 he had not merely captured Kālinjar and Dhāmuni and plundered Bhilsā, but had also captured many minor places. He raided and exacted *chauth* from Matāundhā district; he further proclaimed his own domination over Ghurraurā, Thurhāt, Kotāh, Kachirāhi, Khadāutu and Jalālpur.[1]

Battle and siege of Suraj-Mau. 1699.

After capturing Jalālpur, Chhatra Sāl went to Banhauli and encamped there. Sher Afkan, the *faujdār* of Rānod, and his son Shāh Quli, both moved against Chhatra Sāl. After a severe battle Chhatra Sāl took refuge in the fort of Suraj-Mau. Sher Afkan besieged and took the fort. Chhatra

[1] The chief authority on the affairs of Chhatra Sāl is his court-poet Lāl's work, *Chhatra Prakash*. It does not give details. Again, it exaggerates the successes of Chhatra Sāl. The details from Muslim authorities have been used to correct and date the various events. Lāl, p.146; *Aurangzib*, V, pp.395-7, 397-8.

All the places referred to are small villages in that territory; Kotāh is Kotrāh in Bundelkhand and should not be confounded with Kotāh of Rajputana. Kachirāh is Kachir Kākarwai, near Jhānsi.

Sāl escaped. Sher Afkan had gained this victory single-handed and lost about 700 men and exhausted his own private means. His forces were strengthened soon after as Chhatra Mukut Bundelā came over to the Mughal side. Sher Afkan followed up his victory by conquering the *parganāh* of Gāgron which had been held for the last twenty years by Chhatra Sāl's son Gharibdās. The Emperor rewarded Sher Afkan and appointed him *faujdār* of Dhāmuni too, in place of Khairandesh Khān, who had not co-operated with Sher Afkan in this campaign. He got the *parganāh* of Gāgron and big amounts in cash in addition as reward.[1]

Battle of Purā Ghāt: Death of Sher Afkan: April, 1700.

But Chhatra Sāl had his revenge next year. On April 24, 1700, Sher Afkan attacked Chhatra Sāl near Jhunā and Bārnā on the Purā Ghāt. A severe battle was fought. Chhatra Sāl was wounded and about 700 of his men were killed and the rest were dispersed. But Sher Afkan was mortally wounded and carried away by the flying soldiers of Chhatra Sāl. Chhatra Sāl wrote to

---

[1] *Akhbarat*: April 21, 25; June 28 and July 26, 1699; Lāl, pp.146-8; *Aurangzib*, V, pp.398-9.

Gāgron is situated just 1 mile north of Jhalarāpātan Chhaoni (Long. 76°, 10′; Lat. 24°, 56′).

It is difficult to identify Suraj-Mau as there are two Mau's in Bundelkhand.

Jāfar Ali, one of the sons of Sher Afkan, "Your father has little life left. Send your men and take him away." The *palki* arrived too late only to carry back Sher Afkhan's dead body.[1]

Khairandesh Khān was once more made the *faujdār* of Dhāmuni and was ordered to punish Chhatra Sāl. According to Lāl, Shāh Quli headed an expedition with an army of 8,000 men to take his revenge on Chhtra Sāl, in which he was helped by one Nand Mahārāj. The combined forces moved down to Mau and besieged the fort. An attack was delivered in which Nand Mahārāj was severely wounded. The Mughal forces withdrew and encamped, but Chhatra Sāl attacked them at night and defeated Shāh Quli so thoroughly that he had

Later campaigns of 1700—1701.

---

[1] *Akhbarat*: May 12, 21, 1700: *Aurangzib*, V, pp.398-9. Lāl differs here from the incidents as reported in *Akhbarats* and as such his version cannot be accepted. He says that Sher Afkhan's life was saved by Said Latif Khan, the *Qiledar* of Kotrā. Latif agreed to pay *chauth* and other exactions. This news reached the Emperor. Sher Afkan now became a *faqir* and gave over his charge to his own son. It is difficult to locate many of these villages and the Ghāt. The movements of Sher Afkan in Gāgron district in 1699, suggest the possibility of these battles having been fought in the neighbourhood of Gāgron. Bārnā may be identified with Baran and Purā Ghāt with Sālpurā 25 m. S.-E. of Baron (Kotāh State).

to accept all the terms dictated by Chhatra Sāl.[1] He evacuated the fort Shāhbād, which was taken possession of by Devi Singh, son of Shāhman Dhamdherā. The *faujdār* of Gwalior recovered it in October, 1700.[2]

After these failures, the Mughal campaigns against Chhatra Sāl, were not undertaken with great vigour. In April, 1702, Khairandesh Khān was ordered to besiege the fort of Kālinjar, where the family of Chhatra Sāl was then staying, but this attack evidently failed.[3] Khairandesh Khān continued to be in charge of the campaign against Chhatra Sāl even after this failure.[4] In 1703, Chhatra Sāl invited Nimā Sindhiā to Mālwa, but the success of Firuz Jang in the battle of Sironj, frustrated all his intention. Bidār Bakht proposed to the Emperor to be allowed to undertake an expedition against Chhatrā Sāl. But nothing was done as the rainy season was near at hand.[5] In the closing months of 1705 or early in 1706, Firuz Jang induced the Emperor to make peace with the irrepressible

---

1 Läl, pp.149-150.

2 *Akhbarat* : June 11, Oct. 23, 1700; *Aurangzib*, V, p.399.

3 *Akhbarat* : April 4, 1701; *Aurangzib*, V, p.399.

4 Inäyetullāh, fol.29b.

5 Inäyetullāh, fol.30a, 32a.

Bundelā. Chhatra Sāl was created a 4 *hazari* in the Mughal peerage and induced to visit the Emperor in the Deccan where he lived in peace till the death of Aurangzib in 1707.[1]

SECTION 4. REBELLION OF GOPAL SINGH CHANDRAWAT (1698—1706).

The policy of religious fanaticism begun by Aurangzib was the chief cause of more than one trouble in the province. "A preponderantly Hindu province with a sturdy population, was not likely to take Aurangzib's policy of temple destruction and poll-tax on the Hindus with tame submissiveness."[2] There were some cases of the Hindu population fighting the agents of Islam in defence of their religion and of people fighting with the rude agents of *jaziya* collectors.[3] But these troubles were more or less local and did not give rise to any great revolt; nor was there any organized opposition to this policy in the province. There was, however, one great incident which was the outcome of this policy of Aurangzib

Policy of Fanaticism: its results—Disturbances.

[1] Bhimsen, 157b; M.U., II, p.512; *Aurangzib*, V, p. 399.

[2] *Aurangzib*, V, p.381.

[3] *Akhbarat*: April 7, 1670; *Akhbarat*: 13th year of Aurangzib's rule, sheet 17, *Akhbarat*, June 8, 9, 1695.

and it was the revolt of Gopāl Singh Chandrāwat of Rāmpurā in 1698.

The State of Rāmpurā: Gopāl Singh and Ratan Singh.

On the north-western border of Mālwa, between the States of Kotāh and Deoliā (Partābgarh), there was the small principality of Rāmpurā ruled over by the Chandrāwat clan of the Sesodiā Rajputs. It was the buffer State between Mālwa and Mewād and had formed part of Mewād before Akbar made it an independent principality. Since then, the ancestors of Gopāl Singh had served the Mughal Emperor faithfully. Gopāl Singh succeeded to his ancestral domain in 1689. In 1698 he was serving under Prince Bidār Bakht in the Deccan. He had sent his son, Ratan Singh, to Rāmpurā to manage the affairs of the State. Ratan Singh, however, managed to gain the supreme power there, displaced his father's officers and refused to send money to him.

Ratan Singh seizes Rāmpurā: He embraces Islam, 1698.

Gopāl Singh requested the Emperor to summon his son to the Court; the Emperor paid no heed to this request. After some time Ratan Singh became a convert to Islam through Mukhtiyār Khān's efforts and got the title of Islām Khān and the gift of his ancestral home, Rāmpurā, which was renamed Islāmpurā. At this, Gopāl Singh left the army of Prince Bidār Bākht and went to Rāmpurā. He tried to gain possession of Rāmpurā by collecting a force (June, 1700).[1] He was helped by Bhim Singh, son of Rām Singh Hādā of Kotāh, with money and presents of cloth.[2]

The Emperor decided to take steps to put down this revolt. On July 10, 1700, Bidār Bakht was ordered to proceed to Mālwa, but, a week later, as Azam had started for Mālwa, he did not go.[3] Azam was ordered to look after the operations to put down Gopāl Singh's rising.[4] Before Azam had gone far he was ordered to attend, first, to the rebellion of Bakht Buland as Firuz Jang was summoned to the Court; Azam reached Mālwa only after June, 1701, when he was ordered to proceed to Gujrāt as its governor.[5]

In the meanwhile, Mukhtiyār Khān, the governor of Mālwa, sent his son Iftikhār Khān against Gopāl Singh, who now fled to the territory

---

[1] Bhimsen, II, p.130a; *Akhbarat,* June 10, 1700.

[2] *Akhbarat*: June 11, 1700.

[3] *Akhbarat*: July 10, July 17, and Sept. 16, 1700.

[4] Bhimsen, II, p.133b. Khāfi Khān does not say that Azam was sent against Gopāl Singh (II, p.474). Bhimsen is quite explicit on the point.

[5] Bhimsen says that the appointment of Azam was made when he was at Burhānpur (II, p.130b). M.A. explicitly says that he was at Dhār when orders were received (M.A., p.442), which view is supported by the *Akhbarat* (Dec. 1, 1701).

of the Mahārānā of Udaipur, in spite of all the arrangements to guard the roads and to arrest him, as ordered by the Emperor.[1] The Mahārānā was well disposed towards Gopāl Singh and, at his instigation, Udaibhān Sakatāwat, the *jāgirdar* of Malakā Bajānā, gave Gopāl shelter; the Mahārānā also helped him with money (February, 1701).[2] In December, 1702, Abu Nasar Khān, then governor of Mālwa, was informed by Ratan Singh and Kirti Singh, son of Rāwat Pratāp Singh of Deoliā (Partābgarh), that the forces of the Mahārānā had marched into the territories of Rāmpurā. Abu Nasar Khān immediately summoned Bāgh Mal, the agent of the Mahārānā, and called upon him to explain. He gave out that the report was incorrect and gave a security that no such outrage on the Imperial territories would be perpetrated.[3]

Gopal Singh's submission. His second revolt: 1706-07.

As the Mahārānā had failed to do anything for Gopāl Singh, the latter made his submission to the Emperor in 1703. He was pardoned by the Emperor and restored to his *mansab*. He was appointed *faujdar* of Kaulās (in Haiderabad). His

---

[1] Bhimsen, II, p.130b; *Akhbarat*, February 26, 1701.

[2] *Vir Vinod*, II, pp.741-2.

[3] *Vir Vinod*, II, pp.747-8.

ancestral estate was not restored to him.[1] In 1705, Gopāl Singh again fell into poverty, as he was deprived of his *faujdari*, and he joined the Marathas. In January, 1706, he sought the help of Parsu Maratha and thought of entering Mālwa by way of Māndu and Dhār. As Bidār Bakht marched to Nolāi (Badnagar) to check him, this effort was given up.[2] Gopāl Singh, however, accompanied the Maratha forces that raided Gujrāt in March, 1706.[3]

For some years all was quiet in Rāmpurā. Ratan Singh continued to rule there. When Bidār Bakht was governor of Mālwa, Ratan Singh was with the Imperial army. In November, 1705 he left the army of the Prince without permission, and went to Ujjain, whence he returned to Rāmpurā.[4] He entered into correspondence with the Mahārānā to gain his favour. The Mahārānā wrote in reply that his attitude depended on that of Ratan Singh himself.[5] On February 7, 1706, Ratan Singh wrote to the Mahārānā assuring him of his faithfulness and

---

[1] *Akhbarat.* Bhimsen, II, p.145b. Tod's statement that "Rana took up arms and Mālwa joined in the tumult" (I, p.463) is not corroborated by any authority.

[2] Bhimsen, II, p.155a; Ināyetullah, p.45a.

[3] Bhimsen, II, p.156a; *Aurangzib,* V, pp.310-1.

[4] Ināyetullah, fol. 75a, 87a.

[5] *Vir Vinod,* II, pp.760-61.

obedience. Later events show that the Mahārānā could not have been favourably disposed towards Ratan Singh. Thus, though this revolt was to lead in future years to many political complications and intrigues, it did not cause much trouble save some disturbances, when Gopāl Singh tried to raise a revolt in Rāmpurā. Though an outcome of religious policy, this revolt was mainly political in its nature and character.

SECTION 5.—MALWA AND THE MARATHAS : THEIR EARLY INVASION AND FIRST TOUCH WITH MALWA

(1698—1706)

The Marathas and Mālwa.

There could not be any point of contact or affinity between the Marathas and Mālwa. Geographically, they were far apart, culturally, too, they had nothing in common, and, socially, they differed widely from each other. The fact that the Marathas represented the spirit of opposition to the policy of fanaticism and Muslim cultural domination in India could not also make the Hindu population of Mālwa feel one with the Marathas. To them and, more specially, to the Rajput element, who were admirers of Mahārānā Pratāp, the Marathas appeared to be mere upstarts. To the leading Rajput Princes and generals, fighting in the distant Deccan for the Imperial cause, the Marathas appeared more as enemies than as friends. Exceptions to this general rule were few and far between.

The true nature of the raids: Their importance.

In 1698, on his return to Mahārāshtra, Rājārām introduced feudal institution into Maratha policy and thus laid the foundation of the great Maratha confederacy. But Rājārām could not complete the rebuilding of the Maratha power, and the seed that he had sown, lay germinating below the soil. In the meanwhile, the first raid on Mālwa was organized and proved a success. Thus, when Tārā Bāi began to plan the counter-offensive against the Mughal Empire, she included Mālwa in her scheme. But these plans were not carried into effect by any organized body at the instigation of or under orders from the head of the Maratha power. The central government of the Maratha power practically broke down after Rājārām's death and the various Maratha generals, whether they were under Rājārām's successors or not, began to invade the Mughal dominions and swept down into Mālwa whenever they could conveniently do so. The main importance of these raids lay in the fact that they opened a new path for the Maratha invaders, showed them a new field for their activity, and above all, established a contact between these factors. And thus it was that, when the Peshwās and their generals began to plan their schemes of conquest and extension of the limits of their own domination, they only followed the path which had already been opened by these early invaders. Bālāji Vishwanāth prepared the way and Bāji Rāo carried into effect the policy and plans of Rājārām, and these invaders form the missing link between them.

Krishnāji Sāwant's raid : 1699-1700.

The first invasion of Mālwa by Maratha bands occurred in 1699.[1] In the month of November, when Aurangzib was on his way to besiege the fort of Satārā, Krishnāji Sāwant, a Maratha general, at the head of 15,000 cavalry, crossed the Narmadā and ravaged some places near Dhāmuni and returned. "Since the time of the early Sultāns", adds Bhimsen, "the Marathas had never crossed the Narmadā till now. He plundered and returned to his home unmolested."[2] "The path thus opened,"

[1] Malcolm in his *Memoirs* mentions the raids on Dharampuri as early as 1690 and the fall of Māndu in Maratha hands in 1698. See Appendix A to this chapter for a discussion of these facts.

[2] Bhimsen alone mentions it (p.129a). There is available only one reference about Krishnāji Sāwant, previous to the raid, that he was captured by Bakht Buland of Deogarh in

says Sir Jadunath Sarkar, "was never again closed till at last in the middle of the 18th century Mālwa passed into regular Maratha possession."[1]

Death of Rājārām 1700. Tārā Bāi and her new policy.

On March 2, 1700, Rājārām died of fever and was succeeded by his son Karna, who also died, within three weeks of his succession, of small-pox. Tārā Bāi, the wife of Rājārām, crowned her son, Shivāji, a boy of ten years, and began to rule with the help of Rāmchandra Pandit.[2] Immediately, she offered submission to the Emperor, who rejected this offer and demanded all the forts of the enemy.[3] Now she began to plan a new offensive against the Mughal Empire. Khāfi Khān thus describes her policy:

> "She took vigorous measures for ravaging the Imperial territories and sent armies to plunder the six *subahs* of the Deccan as far as Sironj, Mandisor and the *subah* of Mālwa. They penetrated into the old territories of the Imperial throne, plundering and destroying

---

April, 1699 (*Akhbarat*). He probably escaped in June from Deogarh, when it was taken by Hāmid Khān. Nothing is heard about Krishnāji after this raid.

[1] *Aurangzib*, V, p.382.

[2] *Akhbarat*, April 1 and 4, 1700; M.A., p.420; Bhimsen, II, fol.130a; *Aurangzib*, V, pp.135-6, p.199.

[3] *Akhbarat*, March 12, 1700; *Aurangzib*, V. pp.136-7.

wherever they went. The commanders of Tārā Bāi cast the anchor of permanence where-ever they penetrated and having appointed *Kamāvishdārs* (revenue collectors), they passed the years and months to their satisfaction with their wives and children, tents and elephants. Their daring went beyond all bounds. They divided all the districts (*parganahs*) among themselves and, following the practice of Imperial rule, they appointed their *subahdars* (provincial governors) *Kamāvishdārs* (revenue-collectors) and *rāhdārs* (toll-collectors)."[1]

Khāfi Khān further adds, "They attack and destroy the country as far as the borders of Ahmedābād and the district of Mālwa and spread their devastations through the provinces of the Deccan to the environs of Ujjain."[2] A study of the Marathi sources makes it clear that though Mālwa was included in the scheme, much could not be done there. Outposts were established and grants of lands were made as far as the province of Khāndesh only.[3] Evidently Tārā Bāi could plan a scheme,

[1] K.K., II, pp.516-7; Elliot, VII, pp.373-4.

[2] K.K., II, pp.517-8; Elliot, VII, pp.347-8.

[3] The document of partition of the possessions of Buāji Pawār proves this statement. His possessions were limited to

but the weakness of the Maratha power did not allow her to carry it out fully. It was left to the whims and fancies as well as to the personal interest and convenience of the various generals to carry out the schemes of Tārā Bāi, and all their efforts to get a footing in Mālwa failed at this time. Bālāji Vishwanāth had to begin anew after 1713.

The schemes of Tārā Bāi, however, gave new life to the Maratha power and, in 1703, the efforts to reach and raid Mālwa recommenced. Early in 1703, when the Emperor was involved in the seige of Kondānā (Sinhgarh), the Marathas crossed the Narmadā again and caused disturbances up to the environs of Ujjain. After a few months, another band, after plundering Burhānpur, came upon and ravaged the city of Khargon "within a part of the *Subah* of Mālwa lying south of Narmadā."[1]

Nimā Sindhiā's raid into Mālwa. 1703-1704.

These minor raids were soon followed by another of great magnitude. After the rains of 1703 were over, Nimā Sindhiā burst into Berar in October, defeated Rustam Khān, the deputy governor in Berar, raided the district of Hushāngābād and then crossed the Narmadā and invaded

Khāndesh only. Lele and Oak: *Dhar cha Pawaranche Mahatwa*, etc., pp.5-7.

[1] *Aurangzib*, V, pp.382-3; Bhimsen, II, p.144b; *Akhbarat*, February 11, 1703.

Mālwa. "As Nimā Sindhiā was not on good terms with Dhanā and other Maratha generals, he in pride crossed the Narmadā, marched into Hindustan and raided up to the neighbourhood of Sironj. At the instigation of Chhatra Sāl Bundelā he devastated the province of Mālwa."[1] According to Manucci, the bribes offered by the governors to these raiders to save their own province from plunder and devastation were sufficient temptation for the raiders.[2] The Maratha horde consisted of 50,000 horse. Before moving towards Hushāngābād, the invaders divided themselves into two groups. While one went down to the Māndu side,[3] the other, under the leadership of Nimā, entered Mālwa near Hāndia and marched down to Sironj, plundering and burning many of the villages on the way.[4]

As soon as the Emperor heard of the Maratha raid on Mālwa, he grew anxious and the more so,

---

[1] Bhimsen, II, p.148; *Aurangzib*, V, p.383.

[2] Manucci, III, p.502.

[3] Manucci (III, p.426) mentions this division of forces, and the details of the raid on Māndu are supplied by Nawāzish Khan's letter-book (fol. 17b-18b). Sir Jadunath Sarkar does not trace this inroad.

[4] *Aurangzib,* V, p.384; Bhimsen, II, fol. 147a; Ināyet-ullah, fol.30b.

because the treasures from the northern provinces were then on their way to the Deccan and waiting for an escort at Sironj. He ordered Prince Bidār Bakht on October 31, 1703, to proceed against the Maratha invaders by forced marches, to punish them and to escort the treasures.[1] Azam was then in Gujrāt, and he was ordered to go down to Mālwa to punish the Maratha raiders.[2] Bidār Bakht was too far off and his army was not in a condition to undertake the expedition, while the help of 1,000 horse ordered by the Emperor was inadequate.[3] Azam, too, did not move.[4] In the meanwhile, Firuz Jang entered Khāndesh in pursuit of another Maratha band (November, 1703), and the Emperor ordered him to undertake the pursuit and to punish the raiders. Firuz Jang left his heavy baggage and camp at Burhānpur and started for Mālwa.[5] Bidār Bakht, who also was moving towards Burhānpur, was ordered by the Emperor to

[1] Ināyetullah, fol.43a, 45, 31a-b, 58, 12a; *Aurangzib*, V, p.384.

[2] Ināyetullah, fol.12a.

[3] Ināyetullah, fol.46a-b, 12a; Manucci, III, 509; *Aurangzib*, V. p.384.

[4] Ināyetullah, fol.14b.

[5] Bhimsen, fol.148b; M.A., 483.

hundred and fifty-five bags of letters and fifty-five baskets of fruits reached the Emperor. But the treasure had still to be brought from Ujjain and to be sent to the Deccan, and the minor revolts that had broken out due to the Maratha invasion were to be put down. Again, it was not yet known definitely whether Nimā had returned to the Deccan or not. The camps of the Marathas near Sironj were swept off.[1] Bidār Bakht left Khargon and started for Mālwa; Zulfiqār Khān was also ordered to join the Prince.[2] But soon after, when Firuz Jang reported that Nimā was in Berar and there was not much danger in Mālwa, Zulfiqār Khān was ordered not to proceed to Mālwa. The Prince, too, was advised that it was not urgently necessary for him to undertake the expedition as the rains were near.[3] Bidār Bakht had already moved on to Mālwa, he had reached Sironj, and no sooner did

Bidār Bakht's expedition to Mālwa: March-May, 1704.*

---

* The details of this expedition have been collected from the letters of Ināyetullah. They are not dated, nor are they arranged chronologically. A detailed study of these letters makes me think that the expedition must have been undertaken in March-May 1704, even though Bidār Bakht was not yet made governor of Mālwa.

[1] Ināyetullah, fol.61a, 63b, 28a, 30a, 31a, 32a-b, 58a.

[2] Ināyetullah, fol.129a, 59a, 32a.

[3] Ināyetullah, fol.29b, 40b.

the Marathas hear of the approach of Bidār Bakht, then they fled towards Bundelkhand and Allahabad.[1] He returned immediately to Ujjain and after arranging for the despatch of the treasure, he came down to Khargon. Here he tried to put down the Bhils and Kolis and also to subdue Mohan Singh, the rebellious *zamindar* of Awāsgarh.[2] The Prince had planned an expedition against Chhatra Sāl Bundelā, which could not be undertaken as the rainy season was not far off.[3] It was during this expedition that the Prince saw, as he later reported to the Emperor, that the devastation caused by the Maratha raids was great. Khāndesh was wholly ruined and the half of Mālwa adjacent to Khāndesh was also desolated.[4] It was this desolate state which made Bidār Bakht hesitate to accept the governorship of Mālwa, when it was offered to him.[5] Soon, however, the prince was ordered to go down to Burhānpur as there was no possible danger from the Marathas in Mālwa.[6]

---

[1] Ināyetullah, fol.29a, 128a.
[2] Ināyetullah, fol.128a, 40a.
[3] Ināyetullah, fol.30a, 32a-b, 29b.
[4] Ināyetullah, fol.15a, 60a, 61a.
[5] Ināyetullah, fol.19a, 132b.
[6] Ināyetullah, fol.106b.

Deogarh, who had rebelled and was besieged at Deogarh by Hāmid Khān, escaped from the fort and entered Mālwa. He went down to Garh by way of Dhāmuni and on his way caused much disturbance in the province. Though he did not appear again in Mālwa, his Muslim allies caused disturbances in the province during the year 1703 and 1704.[1]

In February, 1700, another Afghan named Nisār disturbed the province with his band of 2,000 men.[2] A few months later, Jujhār Rāo broke into rebellion, attacked and burnt the villages in the *parganāh* of Khātoli and, after a fight, carried away the cattle.[3] Gopāl, the Chaudhāri of Sironj, had been in captivity and no sooner was he released than he again began to oppress the people and to show a defiant attitude. The Emperor ordered him to be brought to the presence. His mother, too, refused to pay the State dues. But when, at the time of Nimā's raid on Sironj, he defended the fort against the invaders, he was rewarded by the Emperor. But the watchful eye of the Emperor never lost sight of

---

[1] *Aurangzib*, V, pp.408-10; *Akhbarat*: July 5, 6, 1699; M.A., p.404.

[2] *Aurangzib*, V, p. 389.

[3] *Akhbarat*: May 27, 1700.

this disturber of peace and enquiries were often made about his movements.[1]

In January, 1705, when a Muslim tax-collector visited the *zamindāri* of Devi Singh, son of Brahm Deo Sisodiā, the men of the *zamindar* plucked the beard and mustaches of the former and let him go.[2] In his letter-book, Nawāzish Khān gives the details of the various minor expeditions he had to undertake to put down these revolts and disturbances; every time treasure or any other goods had to be escorted through the province, difficulties had to be faced. He mentions one Abbās Afghan who was raiding the highways and stopping the mails near Ujjain; and the Afghan had a following of 5,000 men.[3] In 1703-4, when the raids of the Marathas occurred, the whole of southern Mālwa was disturbed. Mohan Singh, the *zamindār* of Awāsgarh, joined the Maratha invaders, and, later, the Bhils and Kolis also rose in revolt. Not only did the Bhils and Kolis rise in southern Mālwa, but there was a rising in the north also, where one Mādho

[1] Ināyetullāh, fol.3b, 26b, 15a, 84a.

[2] *Akhbarat*: January 28, 1705.

[3] Nawāzish, fol.17b. There is known to exist only one copy of this letter-book of Nawāzish Khān, which belongs to Sir Jadunath Sarkar (*Aurangzib*, V, p. 389).

Bhil laid the foundation of the fort of Gāgron. In 1704, Mohan Singh raided and plundered in the neighbourhood of Nandurbār and Bijāgarh.[1] Bidār Bakht, too in his letters to the Emperor, mentions many minor expeditions. It was no wonder then, that Nawāzish Khān thought it a relief to be removed from Mālwa, and even "the eminent pearl of the Mughal Empire" (Bidār Bakht) hesitated to accept the governorship of the province.[2]

SECTION 7.—MODERN MALWA IN THE MAKING: CONDITION OF THE PEOPLE: 1698—1707.

Factors in the making of Mālwa in the 18th century.

Modern Mālwa was not the creation of any single individual, nor of any single power; more than one factor contributed to its present shape. The rapidly falling Mughal Empire, the ever increasing Maratha power and the local elements slowly, but steadily, moulded Mālwa. In the closing decades of the 18th century a new factor in the shape of the British Power entered the political arena of the province. As events occurred and as the days rolled on, the disintegrating forces became more and more

---

[1] Nawāzish, fol.18b; Ināyetullah, fol.31a, 57b, 101b, 138, 148b, 40a, 106a, 64a.

[2] Nawāzish, fol.7b; Ināyetullah, fol.19b, 132b.

active, and out of the Mughal province of Mālwa there arose a Mālwa which was no more than a group of many ill-strung States, small as well as big. History has given importance to these States, and their present position makes it necessary to trace their origin and growth.

The local element during the days of change counted for much in the history of Mālwa, but unfortunately no account of this factor has yet been taken by the historian, and as such this aspect of the history of the province offers a virgin field for study and research. The material for its study is very scanty. The political anarchy of the period is responsible for the loss of a good deal of material, while what little was left lies rotting in the archives of the various States, which would not let any historian lay his hand on them in the honest fear, born of ignorance, that its revelations might lower their present position. The main facts, however, remain correct, for they are based on the general trend of events and tendencies, which are clearly discernible in spite of the scantiness of the available records.

The local element and its importance: the scarcity of material for its study.

It is a belief, as widely held as it is mistaken, that the various States of modern Mālwa were created by the Mughals. The Mughal Emperors created only one State, *viz.*, that of Kotāh on the border of Mālwa. All the others were mere *jāgirdārs* and *zamindārs* enjoying simple *diwāni* rights, criminal powers being reserved for the Imperial authorities. The *zamindārs* were those who enjoyed permanent and hereditary grants of land, while the *jāgirs* were granted for the tenure of service only. There were many holders who were *zamindārs* as well as *jāgirdārs*, who were not merely permanent grantees but had also to render some service to the Emperor : with the increase of their *mansab* and status, they generally got additional grants and honours which were for the most part personal. Those *zamindārs* and *jāgirdārs*, who held lands in Mālwa in the last days of the Mughal domination in the province, and who became powerful enough to maintain their fiefs in the days of its decline, slowly usurped other powers too, and in the anarchy which followed the weakening of the Mughal hold, they became full-fledged States and thus exercised all sorts of powers and jurisdictions. The fall of the Mughal Empire, as well as the peculiar policy and position of the Maratha invaders, and, above all, the ever-increasing scope and area of their activities, created full-fledged States out of these *jāgirs* and *zamindāris*.

The rise of the Mālwa States.

The introduction of the new Rajput element in Mālwa, which later resulted in the rise of these States, may well be ascribed to a definite Mughal policy to colonize Mālwa with those Rajputs who had proved to be the most faithful and loyal adherents of the Mughal Empire. At the time of the Mughal conquest of Mālwa, the two races that dominated it were the Afghans and the local Rajputs. The former had ruled over the province for long, while the latter had enjoyed a position of independence and at times controlled the affairs of the Muslim kingdom itself. It was but natural that they would never be loyal to the Mughal Emperors. The Mughal Emperors, however, always desirous of the extension of their Empire in the Deccan, felt the necessity of creating a loyal Mālwa. The creation of a group of vested interests in the province, the continuance of which depended on the good-will and pleasure of the Emperor, would strengthen the position of the Empire. Hence, they went on making grants in Mālwa to the younger sons and brothers of the Rajput princes of Rājputānā, and thus colonized Mālwa with a new set of Rajputs. Akbar created the Khichi State of Bajrang-garh (now known as Rāgho-garh). Shah Jahan created Kotāh and granted Ratlām and other *parganāhs* in its neighbourhood to

The Rajput colonization of Mālwa by the Mughal Emperors.

Ratan Singh Rāthor, and Aurangzib granted Badnāwar to Rājā Bhim Singh, brother of Mahārānā Jai Singh, and recreated the Rāthor State of Sitāmau by fresh grant after confiscating that of Ratlām.

This colonization of Mālwa created a new social problem in the Rajput society of the province and the more so when the grantee was called upon to put down a local chieftain and occupy his lands. In many cases the new grantees did not get enough time to strengthen their hold on their lands sufficiently to raise them as bulwarks against the aggression of the southerners. Again, the grants were too small to create any real power in the province. But many of these grantees, though they failed to check the invaders, managed to keep their existence and to develop their own holdings and *zamindāris* into full-fledged States. The British Power, when it came completed the work by recognizing these States.

To begin from the north, there was the State of Shivpuri ruled by the Kachhāwāh dynasty which had once ruled before and was to rule once again over Narwar. Rājā Anup Singh ruled over the principality and with the help of Khānde Rai, who later became his general, subdued all the disturbers of peace near about, as also the Bais Rajputs of

Dhamdherā. At the time of the death of Aurangzib the Rājā was on Imperial service with Prince Muazzam at Kabul.[1] Politically, this State was directly under the governor at Agra. But being on the northern border, it had exercised an influence in the affairs of Mālwa in that part. It also held a strategical position on the imperial road to the South.

Further down on the east, there was the State newly-created by the rebel Chhatra Sāl Bundelā. In the east, further south, was the Ahirwādā, where, with Sironj as its capital, ruled the Khichi dynasty of the States of Bajrang-garh, which had risen to prominence during the days of Akbar and Jahangir. Rājā Dhirāj Singh was ruling over this State and was mainly busy putting down the rebellious Ahirs and restoring order. West of Ahirwādā were the States of Rājgarh and Narsinghgarh. The Umat rulers and their Umat subjects gave this tract their own name.

Just north of Umatwādā was the Kotāh State. It had been raised to the full status of a sovereign State by Shah Jahan, but was yet in its infancy. Rāo Rām Singh Hādā was the ruler of the State. He was a brave soldier and enjoyed the confidence

[1] Khānde, pp.733-80, 537-545.

of the Emperor. During the last decade, he was busy fighting against the Marathas in Deccan. After the death of Aurangzib, he espoused the cause of Prince Azam and was killed fighting on the battle-field of Jājau. The sister State of Bundi lay on the north-western side of Kotāh. It was ruled by Rāo Budh Singh, who had succeeded to the *gadi* in 1695. Budh sided with Prince Muazzam. On the recommendation of the Prince, the district of Pātan was transferred back to Bundi, even though temporarily it had been granted to the ruler of Kotāh State. The additional grant of Tonk district further strengthened the State of Bundi.[1] On the south-west of Bundi was the principality of Rāmpurā, the affairs of which have already been referred to in connection with the revolt of Gopāl Singh and the conversion of his son, Ratan Singh. Close to its border was the State of Deoliā. Though mainly situated in the hilly tract, it extended even into Mālwa on account of the few districts that were granted to its ruler by Akbar. It continued to be under the nominal suzerainty of the Mahārānā of Udaipur until 1660, when it was finally separated by Aurangzib

[1] *Akhbarat*: July 22, 1695. According to *Vamshbhaskar*, it is Dec. 23, 1695, which was probably the date of his ceremonial accession (IV, pp. 2897, 2923-24).

and made an independent State.[1] In 1698, Rāwat Pratāp Singh succeeded to the *gadi;* he laid the foundation of the town of Partābgarh, which later became its capital. Probably the State was under the control of the governor of Mālwa, due to its vicinity to that province.

The Sesodiā State of Bāgād lay on the western and southern side of Deoliā. It was a State ruled jointly by the two houses of the family, both of which were equally strong. It was yet semi-dependent on the Mahārāna of Udaipur. In 1702, Rāwal Khumān Singh died after a short rule and his son, Rām Singh, went to the Emperor and accepted service in the Imperial army. He was granted 1000 *zat* and 1000 horse *mansab.* The family feud between the two houses was ended by the Emperor and a partition of the State was made. Rām Singh was granted the *jagir* of Dungarpur, and Bānswādā was made over to Khush-hāl Singh. As the newly created State of Bānswādā was on the border of Mālwa, Khush-hāl Singh had to pay half of his tribute to the governor of Mālwa and the other half was paid in the treasury of Gujrāt.[2]

---

[1] *Vir Vinod,* II, pp.439-442.

[2] *Mirat-i-Ahamadi.* Supplement Text (G.O.S. No. 50) p.225; Ojha: *Dungarpur Rajya Ka Itihas,* p.122.

The Rāthor States of Amjherā and Jhābuā lay south of Bānswāda and separated Mālwa from Gujrāt. Since its reinstatement by Shah Jahan in 1634, the Rāthor family was ruling over the State of Jhābuā. Khush-hāl Singh, who ruled in 1698, was an incompetent ruler; he alienated much of the land to his younger sons and brother and was too weak to rule his State effectively. His weak rule and inefficient administration were to prove points of advantage to the Maratha invaders.[1] Just close to Jhābuā on its south lay the State of Amjherā. It was ruled by Jairup Rāthor, whose younger brother Jagrup Rāthor actively co-operated with Nawāzish Khan in clearing the fords of all disturbers. Jagrup's services were rewarded by the grant of a *mansab* and other dignities.[2]

South of the Narmadā lay the principality of Awāsgarh (now known as Barwāni). In 1698, one Jodh Singh was ruling over the State. He had a bitter enemy in his step-brother Mohan Singh. Mohan Singh, however, managed to get Jodh Singh assassinated (about the year 1700), and got control of the State. He, however, proved a thorn in the side of the Imperial authorities. He sided with the

[1] Ināyetullāh, I, fol.34b.

[2] Nawāzish, fol.10a, 11b-12a.

Maratha invaders, and in 1703-4 guided them in their attack on Māndu and continued to cause trouble even after the Marathas had dispersed by joining the Bhils and Kolis and plundering in the neighbourhood of Nandurbār and Bijāgarh. At this time, the Mughal authorities appear to have supported the cause of Jodh Singh's son, Parbat Singh, but the latter could not stay long and after 1708 Mohan Singh once again became the master of Barwāni State.[1]

Central Mālwa was the scene of many rapid changes. After the death of Ratan Singh Rāthor in the battle of Dharmat against Aurangzib in 1658, his descendants continued to rule over the State of Ratlām, which they held as a *zamindāri*. In 1695, however, this State was wiped out of existence due to Imperial displeasure. Keshodās, the second grand-son of Ratan Singh, who was ruling over Ratlām then, was away in the Deccan on Imperial service. At Ratlām his men put to death the *Amin-i-Jaziyā* of the place, with the result that no sooner was it reported than the *zamindāri* and *jāgir* were confiscated and transferred to the officers of Prince

---

[1] *Barwani State Gaz.* (1908) p.4; Ināyetullah, fol.31a, 101b, 106a; Nawāzish, fol.18a.

Azam; and Keshodās was degraded in his rank.[1] For six and more years the fortunes of the Rāthor family were evidently on the wane. But Keshodās stuck to Imperial service in the Deccan.[2] The Emperor was soon after pleased with him, and in 1701 he granted the *zamindāri* and *jāgir* of the district of Titrod (present territories of Sitāmau State) to him, in addition to lands which had been granted to him before this. Thus, the modern State of Sitāmau was founded by an Imperial grant dated the 31st October, 1701.[3] It was further extended in 1714, when the Emperor Farukhsiyar granted the neighbouring *parganāh* of Alot to Rājā Keshodās.[4]

During the years that followed the foundation of the State of Sitāmau, Chhatra Sāl, the fifth son

---

[1] *Akhbarat*: June 8, 9, 1695.

[2] Keshodās was mentioned in Imperial despatches for his services even during the days of his disgrace. *Akhbarat*: Sept. 3, 1699 and another of 1699. Keshodās was the *faujdār* and *quledār* of Nalgundā in the Deccan.

[3] Imperial grant of Sitāmau State. Its wording shows that the lands in the possession of Keshodās, before this grant was made, were practically double of the district of Titrod. The papers in the State archives show that at one time the district of Nahārgarh was also under Sitāmau State. Exact date and year of its grant cannot be ascertained. It can be conjectured that the district of Nahārgarh was granted to Keshodās before the grant of Titrod.

[4] State records of Sitāmau State.

of the great Rāthor Ratan Singh, founded the State of Ratlām anew. He was serving in the Imperial army and enjoyed the confidence of Prince Azam. At the time of the deposition of Keshodās of Ratlām, Chhatra Sāl, who was his uncle, also received his portion of the bad luck and was dismissed from the *qiledāri* of Penukondā; his *jāgir* was confiscated and transferred to someone else.[1] But like his nephew, he too continued to be on active service and the end of the 17th century brought better days, when he received promotion in the Imperial army.[2] In April, 1701, Chhatra Sāl's eldest son Hāthe Singh was killed by the shot of European artillery-men, when storming the Panhālā fort.[3] Lack of definite historical evidence makes it impossible for the historian to give the date when the present State of Ratlām was founded, but, roughly, it can be stated that by 1705 it had come into existence. Soon after Chhatra Sāl died leaving behind him one grandson and two sons.[4] Before his

---

[1] *Akhbarat*: June 9 and 10, July 9, 1695.

[2] *Akhbarat*: June 13, July 22, 1695: Sept. 3, 1696, Oct. 20, 1700.

[3] *Akhbarat*: April 30, 1701. The dates of the death of Hāthe Singh, as given in the family chronicles and the Gazetteers are wrong.

[4] The Gazetteers give the date of Chhatra Sāl's death as

death Chhatra Sāl divided his holdings into three equal divisions, giving one-third to each of his descendants and deciding that all of them were to enjoy equal privileges and honours. This partition was to be the source of much trouble ten years later (1718). Historically, the modern State of Ratlām has got nothing to do with that of Ratan Singh, which was founded and had ceased to exist in the 17th century, but traditions die hard and historical truth is dimmed and lost in the mist of legends and popular beliefs.

In central Mālwa, there was one more State of note, *i.e.*, Badnāwar ruled by the descendants of Rājā Bhim Singh, brother of Jai Singh, Mahārānā of Udaipur. Rājā Bhim Singh's son, Surjmal, ruled till 1700, when he was killed, fighting against the tribes of the north-western frontier. He was succeeded by his son Sultān Singh. In the onrush

---

1709. The family records, however, state the event to have taken place during 1705-6 (1762 *Vikram*). The latter date appears to be more correct. In 1703 Chhatra Sāl was promoted to be the commander of 1,500 horse and a year later, he was made the *qiledār* of Satara (M.A., 424; *Aurangzib*, V, p. 391 *n.*) It is probable that the grant of Ratlām to Chhatra Sāl was made in 1703, when he got a promotion in his *mansab*. Lack of authentic evidence on the point makes it difficult for the historian to assert anything definitely.

of the Marathas this State was wiped out of existence (*c.* 1736) and the descendants were left with their possessions in Mewād only.

In addition to these prominent States, there were hundreds of other small landlords and *zamindārs*. Many of them were serving under the Imperial authorities in the province, while others were maintaining their life by plunder and pillage. Though many of these small holdings continued to exist even during the days of disorder that followed this decade, they could not leave any mark on the history of the province and as such deserve no special attention.

A study of the history of the States makes one point evident; it is the sudden fall of the glory of the rulers or families in the various principalities. The foundation of a principality meant localization of their interests and this meant their being cut off from greater avenues. Such was the history of the rulers of Jhābuā, of Rāghogarh and other places, and was to be the future of other States too, to whom the bigger avenues were to be closed by the depredations of the Marathas and the break up of the Empire. The fact that the holdings were, more often than not, small and that many of them were still newly-founded, made the position of their rulers difficult, especially after the weakening of the central authority.

Condition of the people. The condition of the people of the province was getting from bad to worse. The internal disorders combined with the raids of foreign invaders, made the people poorer, rendering the condition of those, who tilled the land and lived on agriculture worse and worse. Financial exhaustion was producing its own result. The lack of safety on the roads made communication difficult and trade almost impossible. The misery of the peasant was great, and even the *zamindārs* found it difficult to realize their dues from their estates. The whole of southern Mālwa was reduced to one desolate tract; in the words of Bidār Bakht, it was wholly ruined. The Imperial revenue also suffered from the same causes. The people as a whole ceased to have any special attachment for the Empire. In addition to the imposition of *Jaziyā*, the continued oppression by the governors, the bribery, the unsound way of assessment of the land dues, and, above all, the lack of protection made them seek out ways to protect their own interests. Their confidence in the Empire was lost.

APPENDIX A.

THE MARATHA RAIDS ON MALWA DURING THE YEARS 1690-98 A.D.

On the authority of the revenue records of Dharampuri and the manuscript supplied by Sheo Lal, the descendants of the former *zamindārs* of Māndu, Sir John Malcolm asserts the following facts in his *Memoirs*.

1. The Maratha raids on Dharampuri began from the year 1690 and were repeated in 1694, 1696 and 1698.
2. The raids thus continued for full seven years and were abandoned on the advance of Sawāi Jai Singh of Amber.
3. In their raid of 1696-8 the Marathas took Māndu and, after a siege of three months, captured the fort of Dhār also.
4. Sawāi Jai Singh was on friendly terms with the Maratha invaders and, when he was accused of it, he went to Māndu and the Marathas retreated.
5. They, however, returned in a few years and the standard of Udāji Pawār was

planted at Māndu. He was soon after compelled to retreat (1709 A.D.) (*Memoirs*, Vol. I, pp.60-64 with footnotes.)

The various sources of the history of Mālwa in Marathi, Persian and other languages are all silent on these events. The first reported Maratha invasion on Mālwa occurred in 1699 and was led by Krishnāji Sāwant. It is not possible that so great an event as the fall of Māndu and Dhār would have gone unrecorded in *Massir-i-Alamgiri* or would not have been reported in the *Akhbārāts*, had they occurred before 1707. In the light of the latest researches, the historian of Dhār asserts that the public career of Udāji Pawār began only after 1709 or at the most a couple of years earlier. (*Dhār Sansthān chā Itihās*, I, p.9.)

Jai Singh of Amber succeeded to the *gadi* after his father's death in 1700 (*Akhbārāt*, Feb. 18, 20, 1700; *Vamsh*, IV, pp.2936-37) at the age of twenty-one years (according to *Vamsh*, twelve years) only. Even in 1704-5, after he had proved his abilities at the siege of Khelnā in 1702, the Emperor thought Jai Singh as dependent on others and very young (Ināyetullah, fol. 29a, 78b): it seems impossible that he could have taken any active part in 1795-8 when he was yet an heir.

The events as dated and given by Sir John Malcolm conflict with known history; they cannot be accepted. It seems probable that Malcolm committed a mistake in turning the Arabic, Mālwi on *Fasli* years into those of the Christian era. The fall of Māndu into Maratha hands, the advance of Sawāi Jai Singh on Mālwa and the retreat of the Marathas from Māndu occurred only in 1729-30 and not in 1698, as Malcolm asserts. Malcolm probably pre-dated the events of 1723-30 by 32 years and narrated them as he had done.

CHAPTER III.

THE INCREASING IMPORTANCE OF MALWA (1707—1719).

SECTION 1.—THE MAIN CURRENTS OF THE PERIOD

The history of Mālwa during this period does not contain anything sensational or important. Yet it is worth studying as the period of the rise of various tendencies which were to dominate the history of the province during the next decades, when it had to face the storm of the Maratha invasion, conquest and, finally, occupation.

On the death of Aurangzib, the Emperor returned once again to the North, with the result that the centre of interest reverted to northern India. But the Deccan *subāhs* still retained their importance and engaged the covetous eye of every adventurer, who thought of taking advantage of the situation. Again, the control of those *subāhs* meant the acquisition of a great power. But to control the Deccan necessitated some domination over Mālwa, which alone commanded the route between the North and the South. The prosperity of Mālwa, too, made it important. Thus, for reasons political and financial, the various nobles at the Court struggled for the control of the province. But it did not gain anything from this struggle. The governors, who were more often than not absentees, did not pay much attention to its internal administration. This official disregard for its internal affairs helped the growth of the various principalities in Mālwa.

The political situation and the evident weakness of the Empire tempted other powers also to tamper with the affairs of Mālwa. The neighbouring States of Rājaputānā were desirous of gaining their own ends. The Mahārāna of Udaipur was anxious to regain his lost province of Rāmpurā. The triumvirate, which was formed in 1708, indirectly introduced Jai Singh of Amber into the politics of Mālwa and gave him prominence in the eyes of the Rajputs of the province. It, however, increased at the time of his governorship of Mālwa. The rise of Jai Singh in Mālwa introduced a new complication in the provincial affairs. He had his own leanings towards the Marathas, and the coming in of the Marathas into Mālwa brought them together again. Jai Singh now dreamed of a kingdom from the Jamunā to the Narmadā and made every effort to make his dream a reality.

The Marathas, too, were slowly approaching the borders of Mālwa. The early years of the rule of Shāhu were occupied with the work of internal reorganization and fighting out the civil war with the younger house of Kolhāpur. The position changed with the coming in of Bālāji Vishvanāth as Peshwā. He strengthened the position of Shāhu and planned an aggressive policy. By the close of this period, the Marathas had reached the borders of Mālwa, with their position legalized by the grant of a *farmān* which acknowledged their right to levy *chauth*. Moreover, the period saw the beginning of a new policy for the Empire. First, its officers and, later, the Emperor himself began to offer terms to the Marathas, who threatened to dominate the scene in the coming decade.

With the strengthening of the Maratha power in its neighbourhood and the evident weakening of the Central power, with the neglect of internal administration and, above all, the crystallizing of the Rajput power in Mālwa, led and influenced by Jai Singh of Amber, the stage for the coming struggle for domination over the province of Mālwa was set, and everything was awaiting the right moment. It was to come only nine years after the close of this period. There is, however, no denying fact that this period saw the seed germinating below the surface.

SECTION 2.—MALWA AND ITS GOVERNORS (1707—1719).

Azam proclaims himself Emperor: March 4, 1707 A.D.

On February 13, Azam was sent away from Ahmadnagar for Mālwa, but he was not destined to rule over the province. On hearing of the death of his father on February 20, he returned to Ahmadnagar and performed all the funeral rites. Azam then proclaimed himself Emperor and disregarded the will of his father,[1] who had suggesed the partition of the Empire among the three brothers. Preparations for the struggle for undisputed ascendency over the whole Empire were hastened. Bidār Bakht, then in Gujrāt, was ordered to proceed directly to Agra and check the advance of Prince Muazzam. Abdullāh Khān, the governor of Mālwa, was ordered to join him. These orders were soon cancelled and Bidār Bakht was asked to wait in Mālwa till Azam's arrival. Disbanding all his troops in accordance with the orders of his father, Bidār Bakht started for Mālwa: he reached

[1] *Aurangzib,* V, pp.262-3; Irvine, I, p.6.

Shāhjāhānpur on March 26, 1707, and waited in the neighbourhood of Ujjain for one month and twenty days, when he was ordered by Azam to start for Gwalior.[1]

Azam's march through Mālwa.

Azam left Burhānpur on April 15, and instead of following the route by the Akbarpur ferry, adopted the shorter but the more difficult route across Pāndher to the Tumāri pass, long, narrow and entirely waterless. The suffering of the army, due to heat and want of water, was terrible. The Grāssiāhs[2] too, were a source of great trouble on the way, for they plundered every man they could lay their hands on. When the army was camping at Durrāhā (twenty-four miles N.-W. of Bhopāl) Azam connived at the escape of Shāhu to the Deccan.[3] On

---

[1] Azam, pp.135-7, 148-50, 166; Kāmrāj, fol.69a, 84; M. U., III, pp.658-9; *Iradat*: Scott, II, 4, pp.16-18; Kāmwār; Kushal Chand, 367a; Irvine, I, pp.14-15.

[2] Irvine wrongly terms them as jungle tribes (I, p.14). Many of these Grassiahs were Rajputs, who lived the life of outlaws, their chief source of livelihood being the exactions made from the landholders and others who would buy them off by paying up their dues. Malcolm, I, pp.508-14.

[3] Bhimsen, II, fol.163a. This view is accepted by Sir Jadunath also (*Aurangzib* V, p.207). Bhimsen was with the army during the march and must have known the facts from his patron Dalpat Bundelā, who was a confidential adviser of Azam. Khāfi Khān says, that Shāhu was released at the suggestion of Zulfiqār Khān, who was intimate with Shāhu

May 4, Azam reached Sironj. Here he heard that Muazzam Shāh had reached Lahore. He sent Zulfiqār Khān, Rām Singh Hādā of Kotāh, Dalpat Bundelā of Datiyā, Khān Alam and others to reinforce Bidār Bakht, now moving towards Gwalior. These combined forces moved ahead and Bidār Bakht crossed the Chambal against the advice of Zulfiqār Khān and awaited Azam's arrival at Dholpur.[1] Azam was hastening towards Gwalior. He had appointed Nejābat Khān governor of Mālwa. Abdullāh Khān now came to Azam and joined his forces.[2] While at Sironj, Gopāl Chaudhāri appeared before Azam and offered to join his forces. He was, however, killed by Bādshāh Quli Khān to whom he had been handed over for his sensuality and oppression of his subjects.[3] The armies now hurried to Gwalior.

Nejābat Khān made Governor of Mālwa. April, 1707.

---

and was interested in his affairs also. (II, 581-2). Duff, Sardesai and Irvine accept the version of Khāfi Khān (Duff : Oxford, I, p.314; Irvine, II, p.162; Sardesai : *Madhya*, I, p.2). Sardesai adds that Jai Singh was also interested in the release, which is wrong, Jai Singh joined the forces of Bidār Bakht in Mālwa (Irvine, I, p.15). Duff goes on to add that there was signed a treaty between Azam and Shāhu (Oxford, I, p.314). The statement of Khāfi Khān is not acceptable in the light of Bhimsen's view.

[1] Bhimsen, II, p.163, *Iradat*, pp.16-18, 20-26; Kāmrāj, fol.84; Irvine, I, pp.15, 17-19.

[2] Azam, pp.193-4, 200; M.U., II, 871.

[3] Azam, pp.215-221.

On the way Gaj Singh, son of Rājā Anup Singh of Shivpuri, joined the forces of Azam. Anup Singh was with Prince Muazzam on Imperial service. To manage the affairs at home, Khānde Rai, the general of the forces at Shivpuri, was left behind.[1] This journey of Azam too, was full of sufferings from heat and bad water. He crossed the boundaries of Mālwa only to hear of Agra having fallen into the hands of Prince Muhammad Azim, second son of Prince Muazzam.

The two forces met on the battle-field of Jājau on June 8, 1707, in which Azam and his two sons were killed fighting. Prince Muazzam Bahādur Shāh was victorious and became the Emperor of India. In this battle Rām Singh Hādā of Kotāh was killed, and his death left his rival, Budh Singh Hādā, who fought for Muazzam, supreme. Dalpat Bundelā was also killed. Jai Singh of Amber deserted the cause of his patron and went over to the side of Muazzam, although he was not well received by the latter. Muazzam continued to favour his younger brother Bijay Singh, who was already with

---

[1] Khānde, fol.194-6, 543-546.

him.[1] Soon after the battle, Raja Anup Singh of Shivpuri called upon his son and introduced him to Muazzam. Gaj Singh had not taken an active part in the battle and with due regard to the services of his father he was pardoned. Anup Singh was granted the districts of Narwar and Shāhbād.[2]

Prince Jahān Shāh made governor of Mālwa : 1707-1712 A.D.

Immediately on his succession Bahādur Shāh made numerous appointments. Prince Khujista Akhtar, the fourth son of the Emperor, was given the title of Jahān Shāh Bahādur and along with his three brothers his rank was raised to 30,000 *zat* and 20,000 horsemen. He was made governor of Mālwa with permission to nominate anyone his deputy in the province.[3] Lack of provincial records make it difficult to find out the names of the deputies of Jahān Shāh Bahādur.[4] The chief events of the

---

[1] Irvine, I, pp.22-35; Bhimsen, II, 165a; *Iradat,* p.37; Kāmrāj, fol.27; Yāhyā, 113b; Tod (Oxford), III, pp.1495-96; *Vamshbhaskar,* IV, pp.2972, 2993-2999.

[2] Khānde, fol.197, 551-3.

[3] Irvine, I, p.36.

[4] In foot-note of page 65 in his *Memoirs,* Malcolm (Vol. I) asserts that Jai Singh of Amber was the Nāzim or governor of Mālwa during the years 1710-11. There appears to be the same mistake in converting the date of the document, on the basis of which he makes this statement. Jai Singh was in Mālwa only after 1713 A.D.

governorship were the visit of Bahādur Shāh to Mālwa on his way to and back from the Deccan, the formation of the triumvirate at Udaipur, which tried without any success to intervene on behalf of Gopāl Singh Chandrāwat of Rāmpurā, and, lastly, the Bundi Kotāh tussle which continued for more than forty years with varying fortunes for either side.

Bahādur Shāh passes through Mālwa: April-May 1708 and Dec. 1709, May, 1710.

In 1708, after the affairs of Jodhpur had been satisfactorily settled, the Emperor returned to Ajmere, whence he started towards Chitor and Ujjain. On the way, while presents were received from the Mahārānā, it was reported that he had fled to the jungles; but the Emperor decided that the affairs of Kāmbakhsh needed immediate attention and moved on.[1] Early in Safar the Imperial army reached the town of Mandleshwar,[2] where on April 20, news was received that Mahārājāh Ajit Singh of Jodhpur, Jai Singh of Amber and Durgādās

---

[1] Bahādur, 64-94; Bhimsen, II, 172a; Kāmwār; Irvine, I, pp.48-9.

[2] Irvine gives the name as 'Mandeshwar', which is Mandsaur, now in Gwalior State. (I, p.49, p.67, p.347). Ojhā corrects it as Mandleshwar on the river Narmadā (*Rajputana*, II, p.913) *Vir Vinod* and *Vamsh Bhaskar* support this view (*Vir.*, II, p.834; *Vamsh*, IV, p.3010-11). The authorities speak of their return from the bank of the Narmadā; hence the view of Irvine appears to be incorrect.

Rāthor, who were with the Imperial army, had fled away.[1] The Emperor, more intent on going to the Deccan, passed through the Naunahra pass on May 1, 1708, and crossed the Narmadā on May 7.[2]

On his way back the Emperor crossed the Narmadā on December 15, 1709, and marched by way of Māndu and Nālchhā. On January 9, he was at Dipālpur, and camped at Kāliyah Dāh in Ujjain on January 28. From Ujjain he thought of returning by the same route by which he had come, but the revolt of the Sikhs in the Punjab made him anxious to go there. He moved to the Mukund-Durrāh pass in Hādoti and, on his way to Ajmere, received Mahārājāh Ajit Singh and Jai Singh, who had submitted on the mediation of Prince Azimush-shān :[3] The affairs of Mālwa did not receive any earnest attention during this governorship.

In February 1712, Bahādur Shāh died at Lahore. All the four Princes were with the

---

[1] Bahādur, 96-7; Bhimsen, II, 172b; Khush-hāl, fol.376b; Irvine, I, pp.49-50-57.

[2] Bahādur, 100-101; Bhimsen, II, 172b; Irvine, I, p.50.

[3] Bahādur, fol.183; Kāmwar, 67-8; *Iradat,* 57-61; K.K., II, pp.660-61; *Vir Vinod,* II, pp.780-1; Irvine, I, pp.67, 71, 73.

The War of Succession: The Final success of Jahāndār Shāh: Feb.-March 1712 A.D.

Emperor, and there began the war of succession at Lahore. At first, Jahāndār Shāh, Jahān Shāh and Rafiush-shān combined to oppose the forces of Azimush-shān, and the last named was killed. The three victorious brothers now quarrelled among themselves. On March 17, Jahān Shāh was killed fighting just when his forces were showing signs of victory. Rafiush-shān was defeated and killed on the next day and Jahāndār Shāh succeeded to the Imperial throne.[1]

Amānat Khān, Governor of Mālwa: July 1712. Feb., 1713.

The new Emperor started for Delhi on April 21, 1712. On May 19, when the Imperial camp was at Sarai Daurāh,[2] Sarbuland Khān, brother-in-law of the late Prince Azimush-shān, who was then the *faujdār* of Kārā Mānikpur, presented himself to the Emperor with five or six thousand men. He also presented the collected revenues of the province, which amounted to some 10 or 12 lakhs. In lieu of his loyalty to Jahāndār Shāh and for not joining Prince Farukhsiyār, the son

---

[1] Irvine, I, pp.158, 185.

[2] Date of encamping at Sarai Daurāh is that given by Ketelaar (date corrected to O.S.) Ketelaar like Valentyn differs about the date of the start from Lahore. *Jour. Punjab. His. Soc.*, Part I, Vol. X, pp. 35 and p.40; Valentyn, 297; Irvine, I, pp.190-191.

of Azimush-shān, then in revolt in Bihar, he was made governor of Gujrāt. Amānāt Khān, who had been governor of Gujrāt before Sarbuland Khān, was made governor of Mālwa on the recommendation and responsibility of Khān Jahān Kokaltās Khān. Zulifiqār Khān, the prime minister, was not consulted in the matter.[1] The new *subahdar* ruled over the province till February, 1713. He had to fight against Ratan Singh or Islām Khān of Rāmpurā, who had rebelled and opposed Amānat Khān. Amānat Khān was created Shahmat Khān after this victory.[2]

Jahāndār Shāh was defeated and Farukhsiyār succeeded to the Imperial throne. Shahmat Khān (Amānat Khān) was created Mubāriz Khān and sent back to Ahmadabad as its governor. Mālwa was given in charge to Sawāi Jai Singh of Amber, who was ordered to march straight from his capital to his new government.[3] Patronized by the Saiyyads, who now dominated the affairs of the Empire, Bhim

Sawāi Jai Singh, Governor of Mālwa: Feb. 1713, —Nov. 1717.

---

[1] K.K., II, p.715; Farukh., 49a; M.U., III, pp.730-1; *Mirat*, I, p.391; Irvine, I, pp.191-2; II, p.138.

[2] M.U., III, p.733; Irvine, II, p.138.

[3] Mirzā Muhammad: *Ibrat.*, fol.174; Irvine, I, p.262. *Vamsh.* adds that it was obtained on the recommendation of Rājā Bahādur of Rupnagar (Kishangarh), IV, p.3042.

Singh of Kotāh was emboldened to come to grips with Bundi and take his vengeance on Budh Singh. On his way to Ujjain, Jai Singh visited Bundi a few days before its invasion by the Kotāh house.[1] Gopāl Singh Chandrāwat once again occupied the Rāmpurā State and Jai Singh connived at this, especially because he was a party to the treaty of Udaipur, in which he had stipulated to help him.[2] In May, 1715, Saiyyad Hussain Ali passed through Mālwa, but Jai Singh avoided meeting him, which made the Saiyyad angry. In reply to the complaint of the latter, the weak Emperor said that the Saiyyad had the power to dismiss Jai Singh. Jai Singh, however, was not removed.[3] The same year marks the renewal of the Maratha raids into Mālwa,[4] but, before they could be attended to, Jai Singh was summoned to the Court to join the Emperor in the conspiracy to overthrow the Saiyyads. An urgent messenger was sent on March 20, 1716, to bring Jai Singh from Mālwa. On May 24, he was

---

[1] Jai Singh left Bundi on January 31, 1714: Bundi was attacked on February 2, 1714. *Vamsh.*, IV, pp.3042-3.

[2] Tod, I, p.466; *Vir Vinod*, II, p.989.

[3] M.U., III, p.326.

[4] Mandloi Daftar: Athalye Collection (Unpublished): Letters No. 8, 9, 13; Sardesai, *Madhya*, I, p.317.

reported to be at Sarai Alāhwardi Khān and two days later he was conducted to the Emperor's presence.[1] Day after day he steadily rose in the estimation of Farukhsiyār, and on September 15, 1716, he was entrusted with the task of putting down the Jāt rebel Churāman. Rājā Gaj Singh of Narwar, Rāo Budh Singh of Bundi, now once again in favour, and Rāo Bhim Singh of Kotāh were sent with Jai Singh. He was kept busy by this expedition for the next two years.[2] The affairs of Mālwa were naturally neglected. His absence from the province gave the Marathas a chance to enter the province and make exactions. They tried to obtain a footing in the province and granted *mokāsās* in Mālwa to various officers in their army.[3]

In the meanwhile, the relations between the Emperor and the Saiyyads had become strained. The Emperor thought of sending some powerful noble to oppose the return of Saiyyad Hussain Ali Khān, then in the Deccan, because the power of his brother,

---

[1] Kāmwār, p.140; M.U., II, p.82; Mirza., fol.293; *Vamsh.*, IV, pp.3051-2; Irvine, I, pp.324, 333.

[2] Irvine, I, p.324 *et seq;* p.333 *et seq:* Qānungo: *Jats*, I, p.51, p.21; Kāmwār, p.140, p.168; Shiv., 11b; *Vamsh.*, pp.3052-3, 3056.

[3] K.K., II, p.781; S.P.D., XXX, 17A, 17B.

the Vazir Qutub-ul-Mulk, mainly depended on him. The occurrence of another Maratha invasion in 1717 made Farukhsiyār appoint Muhammad Amin Khān governor of Mālwa.[1] The new governor spent much time in making preparations and did not seem in readiness to start early, which made Farukhsiyār impatient. Murād was ordered to induce him to go, but he failed to make him leave; then on his recommendation, the Emperor dismissed Muhammad Amin Khān from the office of second *Bakshi*, which he then held, and appointed him permanent governor of Mālwa. This trick succeeded and Muhammad Amin Khān at last started for Mālwa on November 19, 1717; he was secretly given the *farman* of his appointment on the day he started.[2]

Muhammad Amin Khān, Governor of Mālwa: Nov. 1717—Dec. 1718.

When Muhammad Amin Khān left Delhi, he bragged of the aid he hoped to get from Dost Muhammad Khān (afterwards the founder of Bhopāl). But when he reached Sironj, he found that his boast would come to nothing. Soon he wrote to Delhi demanding impossible reinforcements in men and artillery and extravagant advances in

Muhammad Amin Khān in Mālwa.

---

[1] Irvine, I, pp.339-40, p.365; *Madhya*, I, p.88; M.U., I, pp.329-30.

[2] M.U., I, p.339; Irvine, I, pp.339-40.

money, which were all rejected.[1] At the capital it was taken for granted that he meant to beat a hasty retreat. In the meanwhile, rumours were afloat in Mālwa that Muhammad Amin Khān was going to the Deccan with a force of 60,000 experienced horsemen and able fighters to fight against Hussain Ali, then in the Deccan. Hussain Ali was greatly perturbed, and finally on Novmber 13, it was reported to the Emperor that Hussain Ali Khan had started from Aurangābād the previous month. On December 4, 1718, Hussain Ali left Burhānpur and crossed the Narmadā. When it was reported to Hussain Ali that Muhammad Amin Khān had collected men and was preparing to fight, he sent Nasuruddin Khān Irāni to Muhammad Amin Khān to discover his intentions, when suddenly it was reported that Muhammad Amin Khān had started on a return journey to Delhi. Hussain Ali moved down to Ujjain. On his way, when he passed the skirts of Māndu, Marhamat Khān, son of Amir Khān, did not come to meet Hussain Ali on the pretext of illness, which enraged the latter. Near Māndu Hussain Ali met Ikhlās Khān, who was supposed to have great influence with the Saiyyads,

---

[1] *Dastur-ul-Insha*, p.53 in Irvine, I, p.361 *n*.

and was sent to dissuade Hussain Ali from going to Delhi. Ikhlās Khān, however, acquainted Hussain Ali with the real facts and the struggle then raging at the Delhi Court. Hussain Ali reached Ujjain on December 16 (according to Khāfi Khān, 26), 1716. Thence he decided to move on to Delhi *via* Mandsaur.[1]

Return and dismissal of Muhammad Amin Khān : Dec. 1718—Jan., 1719.

Muhammad Amin Khān had not received any help from Delhi and when he heard of the return of Hussain Ali Khān, he was put in a fix. Neither were his forces strong enough to check the progress of Hussain Ali, nor could Muhammad Amin Khān think of avoiding to meet him, as it would smack of cowardice. "Luckily", says Irvine, "the orders came for his return to the capital and he set out at once". It was rumoured in Mälwa that he had returned without any orders, which was evidently set afloat by the weak and vacillating Emperor to hoodwink his dominating minister, who was, however, too clever to be so easily deceived.[2] And by

---

[1] Khāfi Khān, II, pp.794-97; Kāmrāj, *Ibrat.*, fol.65a *et seq;* M.U., I, p.349; Irvine, pp.357, 360, 365-7, 368. Irvine writes Mandeshwar which is same as Mandsaur. See Thornton's *Gazetteer*, p.645-6.

[2] K.K. (II, pp.800-802) mentions the rumour. It is repeated in M.U. (I, p.349). Irvine, I, p.361 *n.*, p.366 *n.*

the time Muhammad Amin Khān reached Agra, the Emperor had changed his mind once again. At the suggestion of the Vazir he sent orders to Muhammad Amin Khān to return to Mālwa. But these orders did not suit the plans of that noble and he refused to return. The Emperor now grew furious and deprived Muhammad Amin Khān of his *jagirs* and rank.[1] Mālwa remained without a governor for some months.

With the arrival of Hussain Ali Khan in Delhi the Saiyyad at last got the upper hand. All the opposing forces had either been won over by them or estranged by the Emperor. Jai Singh and Budh Singh were the only two exceptions and the Vazir secured orders for both to return to their capitals. Budh Singh had to fight a skirmish with the forces of Bhim Singh Hādā of Kotāh before he could leave Delhi.[2] On February 18, all was ready for the final event, Farukhsiyār was deposed and Prince Rafi-ud-dārājāt, the youngest son of Prince Rafi-ush-shān, was placed on the throne.

Deposition of Farukhsiyār: Accession of Rafi-ud-dārājāt: Feb. 18, 1719.

With the accession of this boy king the supremacy of the Saiyyads was assured, who now

---

[1] Irvine, I, pp.366-7-387.

[2] K.K., II, p.806; Irvine, I, p.371, p.376; *Vamsh*, IV, pp.3065-66.

took up the work of reorganizing the government. All those who had helped the Saiyyads were to be rewarded for their loyalty to them with offices and high posts. The Nizām was considered a dangerous person and the best way to remove him from Delhi was to send him away to some province. He was granted the governorship of Mālwa on the understanding that it would not be revoked.[1] With the appointment of the Nizām to the governorship of Mālwa, the history of the province enters upon a new phase. The Nizām-Saiyyad tussle later merged in the Emperor-Nizām tussle and the whole question became further complicated by the entry of the Marathas.

The Nizām is made the governor of Mālwa : February 20, 1719.

There was nothing remarkable in the administrative history of the province during this period save the fact that it was not being properly attended to. Mālwa became the bone of contention for the furtherance of one's own interests. This disregard by the Central Government made the various *zamindārs* and grantees careless about the Empire. Again, the governors did not care to impose all the demands and requirements of the Empire on the

Condition of the administration.

[1] Irvine, I, pp.386-89, pp.405-15; K.K., II, p.817; Kāmwār, fol.188, Shiv., 26b; Wārid, 157b; *Ahwal-ul-khawaqin,* 14b, 146, 152 in Irvine; Khush-hāl, fol.413b, 414a.

grantees, which only helped them in the creation of their States. The administration was declining and the machinery was weakening with the result that its breakdown before the Maratha onrush seemed but natural. The Maratha forces had entered the province and were making attempts to obtain a footing there. The governors did not mind this small beginning, which was to grow into the greatest danger in the following decade.

SECTION 3.—THE MARATHAS REACH MALWA: LEGALIZATION OF THEIR TITLE IN THE DECCAN. (1707—1719)

Aurangzib's death meant a revolution in Maratha affairs. Shāhu's return to the Deccan and that of the Emperor to the North changed the whole situation. The civil war among the Marathas kept them busy for some years and the opposition of the junior line at Kolhāpur was always a danger to be dreaded by Shāhu. The position of the new Maratha king and the condition of his kingdom were too weak to allow him to adopt a vigorous policy of opposition to the Empire. Hence Shāhu followed a policy of co-operation with the Imperial authorities. This policy of peaceful settlement was also favoured

The Maratha power in 1707. Its weakness.

by Zulfiqār Khān, who was governor of the Deccan during the reign of Bahādur Shāh, and, under his instructions, Daud Khān agreed to allow *chauth* to all the leaders who acknowledged the suzerainty of Rājā Shāhu; the money was to be collected and paid through Mughal officials. Soon after the execution of Zulfiqār Khān, Daud Khān was sent away to Gujrāt and this settlement ended.[1] This peaceful settlement, combined with the weakness of the Maratha power, can alone explain the absence of Maratha invasions of Mālwa.[2]

The peaceful settlement of Daud Khān Pani : 1700-13.

In 1713, the Nizām was appointed to the charge of the Deccan, and he continued to hold the position till he was superseded by Hussain Ali Khān himself. The Nizām was himself opposed to the policy of conciliation with the Marathas. The struggle commenced once again and continued till 1718, when Hussain Ali Khān was forced to come to terms. During this period of struggle the newly installed Peshwā, Bālāji Vishwanāth, did all he

The Nizām in the Deccan : the rise of Bālāji Vishwanāth.

[1] *Madhya,* I, pp.23-68; Irvine, II, pp. 162-3; Duff, I, p.319, p.321; Rājwāde, VIII, pp.54-56. According to Sardesai their dates are incorrect.

[2] Malcolm explains this absence by attributing it to the influence of Sawāi Jai Singh, which is incorrect (Malcolm, I, p.63*n*.)

could to strengthen the Maratha power and to give it unity, strength and, above all, vigour. He thus made it possible for his son Bāji Rāo to follow an aggressive policy when the latter came to the helm of affairs after his father's death in 1720.

The Marathas in Mālwa. 1715-1719.

The renewal of the Mughal-Maratha struggle in the Deccan coincides with the recurrence of Maratha invasions of Mālwa. Early in 1715, Dāwalji Somvanshi led an invasion into Mālwa and harassed the people. Nand Lāl Mandloi, who was in charge of Kampel district, arranged to pay Rs. 25,000 to the invaders, upon which they returned to the Deccan.[1] They seem to have come again soon afterwards, and in January, 1717, Shāhu granted a *mokāsā* to Kānhoji Bhonsle in the districts of Mālwa, north of the Narmadā.[2] In 1718, Hussain Ali made peace with the Marathas, and for the time being the invasions of Mālwa also came to an end. The penetration into Mālwa made by the Maratha generals, however, could not be undone.

[1]Mandloi Daftar: Athalye's collection: 13, 8 and 9. The sum of Rs. 25,000 was paid by the Emperor by setting it off against the dues to be paid to the Imperial authorities. Also *Madhya*, I, p.317.

[2] S.P.D., XXX, 17A and 17B. *Mokasa* of Nemad and Handiā districts was given. *Deshmukhi* was given from Ujjain and Bhilsā dist. (January 24, 1717).

Hussain Ali's Treaty, 1718.

The settlement with Hussain Ali was the result of the mediation of Shankarji Malhār. The treaty not merely gave the Marathas a right to levy *chauth* and *sardeshmukhi* in the six *subahs* of the Deccan but also confirmed Shāhu in his own possessions, now termed as *Swarāj*. The Emperor refused to ratify the treaty, but in practice the treaty was accepted in the Deccan.[1]

The Marathas go to Delhi with Hussain Ali: November, 1718.

In November, 1718, when Hussain Ali started from the Deccan for Delhi, he arranged to take with him a Maratha contingent. Bālāji Vishwanāth went with the forces and he took with him his son Bāji Rāo also. Shāhu sent the Maratha forces with generals of promise and repute. Udāji Pawār, Phānde Rao Dabhade and Kānhoji Bhonsle were prominent among them. In addition to other things, Hussain Ali had promised to get the treaty ratified by the Emperor.[2] It was really a God-sent opportunity. The Maratha statesmen and generals hoped to gain a thorough knowledge of the internal state of the Empire by this visit to Delhi.

---

[1] Duff, I, pp.332-5; Irvine, II, pp.163-4; *Main Currents*, pp.110-111; K.K., II, p.781, 790; *Madhya*, I, pp.82-115.

[2] Grant Duff adds that the Peshwā was asked by Shāhu to try for the grant of tributes from Gujrāt and Mālwa also (I, p.336).

Soon after the accession of Rafi-ud-dārājāt, the Marathas received three *farmāns* (March 3, 14, 1719) which granted them *chauth* and *sardeshmukhi* over the six *subahs* of the Deccan and the hereditary grant of the lands by Sivāji in 1681, with slight modifications.[1] The Maratha forces received their dismissal on March 10, and the Peshwā returned with the Maratha position in the Deccan legalized and their exactions in the Deccan recognized by the Empire. The Marathas thus reached the borders of Mālwa, and with the few outposts already established and the *jagirs* that Rājā Shāhu enjoyed in the district of Bijāgarh,[2] their encroachment on Mālwa was naturally the next step in their scheme of expansion.

In Delhi: grant of *farmans*. March, 1719. A.D.

---

[1] Irvine, I, pp.382-4, pp.406-7; Kāmwar, fol.199; Duff, I, pp.337-40. His date is wrong. See Irvine, I, p.407*n*.

[2] Land was granted by Aurangzib to Rājā Shahu most probably to meet the expenses of his maintenance. It does not appear to have been resumed after Aurangzib's death. The management of the same was vested in the Peshwā. His orders to the *Muqaddams* of the village Ketāre (Khargon dist.) and for management of the safety of the village were acts of management only. Vād, I, p.93; S.P.D., VII, p.32.

SECTION 4.—MALWA AND THE PRINCES OF RAJPUTANA: (1707—1719).

The death of Aurangzib definitely marks a change in the position and importance of the Princes of Rājputānā. With the accession of Bahādur Shāh there began a policy of courting their co-operation, which necessarily made them feel their own importance. They now thought of interfering with the affairs of Mālwa, which introduced an additional complication in the politics of the province. The Princes who could command general respect were three, the rulers of Mewād, Mārwād, and Jaipur. Jai Singh of Amber had his own ambitions as regards Mālwa, and his relationship by marriage with the Rajput families of Mālwa and the high position that he enjoyed at the Court raised him in the esteem of the people. His governorship in Mālwa gave him an added importance. The Rajput element of Mālwa was an important factor in provincial politics, and greatly influenced it. Sardesai rightly terms Rajput politics as "an important factor in the political situation in India in the early part of the 18th century",[1] more specially as the future

Mālwa and the Princes of Rāj-putānā.

[1] *Main Currents*, p.109; *Madhya*, I, pp.77-80.

of Maratha aggression in north India depended on their success in Mālwa and Rājputānā.

The battle of Jājau gave rise to the rivalry between the two Hādā houses of Kotāh and Bundi. It also embittered Jai Singh against Bahādur Shāh, and this feeling made him sacrifice the interests of the Empire for his own.

Kotāh-Bundi struggle: 1707-1719.

The rivalry between Kotāh and Bundi was not merely that of two houses siding with two opposing parties in the war of succession, but, according to Tod, it arose from the desire of Rām Singh Hādā to become the head of the Hādā clan in place of Bundi.[1] Budh Singh was favoured by Bahādur Shāh, who on his accession granted him the title of *Rāo Rājā* and fifty-four forts including Kotāh, which had been confiscated.[2] But the forces of Budh Singh could not capture the fort of Kotāh,[3] which was being guarded by Bhim Singh, son of Rām Singh

[1] Tod, III, p.1495.

[2] Tod, III, p.1496; *Vamsh.* (IV, pp.2998-9) says that the title was *Maharao Raja.*

In *Vamsh.* the following twelve forts are named :—

1. Kotāh. 2. Jhālarapātan. 3. Gāgron. 4. Shāhbad. 5. Shergadh. 6. Bārod. 7. Chechat. 8. Chhābada. 9. Gugair. 10. Pachpād. 11. Pādap. 12. Dag. They are all in Mālwa and practically extend over the territories of Kotāh State (IV, p.2999).

[3] *Vamsh.*, IV, pp.3008, 3022-24.

Hādā of Kotāh. Budh Singh soon gave himself up to pleasures and became unmindful of the affairs of State.

With the coming of the Saiyyads into power Bhim Singh gained considerable importance, as he sided with them. Budh Singh did not respond to the call of the Emperor Farukhsiyār on his succession, and the latter granted the State of Bundi to Bhim Singh of Kotāh. Budh Singh became a refuge with Jai Singh, then in Mālwa. In 1716, on Jai Singh's recommendation he was taken into favour and Bundi was restored to him, the Kotāh Rāo retaining the districts of Bārān and Mau.[1] In the campaign against the Jāts, both Budh Singh and Bhim Singh served under Jai Singh.[2] In 1719, when Hussain Ali returned to Delhi and planned to depose Farukhsiyār, Budh Singh with Jai Singh was trying to uphold the cause of the Emperor, but they were both ordered to retire to their principalities. Budh Singh had to fight out his way through the forces of Bhim Singh, who thought of taking advantage

---

[1] *Vamsh.*, IV, pp.3030-1, 3039.

[2] *Vamsh.*, IV, pp.3040-34, 3043-48, 3052-56, 3058-59; Tod, III, pp.1496, 1524; Irvine, I, pp.333, 326; Kāmwar, pp.140-168; Shiv., 11a.

of the situation and killing Budh Singh.[1] The Saiyyads had their vengeance on Budh Singh when they settled the State affairs after Farukhsiyār was deposed.[2] These disturbances in Hādoti disturbed the neighbouring parts of Mālwa.

The other question raised by the battle of Jājau was of far greater importance. Jai Singh had betrayed Azam's cause and had come over to Bahādur Shāh, but the Emperor went on favouring his younger brother Bijay Singh and on April 20, 1708, Bijay Singh was given the kingdom of Amber and the title of Mirzā Rājā.[3] Jai Singh was kept by the Emperor in the Imperial camp, more or less under surveillance. After the campaign against Mārwād, Mahārājā Ajit Singh also came into the Imperial camp. By the time the Imperial armies reached the banks of the Narmadā, the hopes of their restoration were shattered and Jai Singh, Ajit Singh and Durgādas fled away from the Imperial camp and went to Udaipur. There a triple treaty

Jai Singh dissatisfied: The triple treaty of 1708.

[1] *Vamsh.*, IV, pp.3065-67; Tod, I, pp.473-4; III, pp.1496, 1527; Irvine, I, p.376; Shiv., p.236; Mirzā., p.449; K.K., II, pp.805-806; Kāmwār, p.191.

[2] Irvine, II, pp.5-6.

[3] Bahādur, 110; Tod, I, p.465*n*.3; *Iradat*, 58; Irvine, I, p.67; *Vamsh.*, IV, pp.3000-06; *Vir Vinod*, II, pp.769-774.

was signed, which restored peace among the three princes. Jai Singh married the daughter of the Mahārānā and agreed to do away with the law of primogeniture so far prevalent in Amber. The three princes decided to act together. The restoration of Jai Singh and Ajit Singh was the first aim of the triple treaty. They, however, decided to act in concert in matters which concerned them, as well as in those which they thought to be essential for their land.[1] For once the racial unity was restored, but the treaty was full of grave dangers and ominous in its future results.

The triple treaty was very successful in the beginning and the restoration of the two Princes was achieved. The Emperor, too, became pliant, and on the intervention of Prince Azimush-shān, accepted their submission on June 11, 1710.[2] Soon, however, the triumvirate decided to interfere

---

[1] *Vir.*, II, pp.769-70, 772-74, 775-78; Tod, I, p.465, 466; II, pp.1014-5; III, p.1341; Irvine, I, pp.67-71; Ojhā, *Rajputana*, II, p. 914-7.

[2] Bahādur Shāh pressingly wrote to the Mahārānā to bring about a peaceful settlement with Jai Singh and Ajit Singh. *Vir.*, II, pp.773-6; Irvine, I, pp.71-73. The restoration of the two Princes, Jai Singh and Ajit Singh, was made on Sept. 26, 1708, but they were received in audience only in June 1710.

in the affairs of Rāmpurā in Mālwa. At the time of Aurangzib's death, Ratan Singh, the convert to Islām was still the master of Rāmpurā, while his father was a fugitive. Gopāl Singh joined the forces of Azam Shah and fought for him.[1] The defeat of Azam Shah ended all the hopes of Gopāl Singh, whose cause was now taken up by the Māhārāna who acted on behalf of the triumvirate. The forces of the Mahārānā attacked, but Ratan Singh repulsed the attack and the latter was rewarded by the Emperor for his success.[2] The Mahārānā did not make any further effort for his protégé.

The Rāmpurā affair and the triumvirate.

Ratan Singh, however, was emboldened now and thought of taking advantage of the disorders prevailing after the death of Bahādur Shāh. He took Ujjain and hoped to enlarge his own principality. When Amānat Khān was appointed governor of Mālwa, he asked Ratan Singh to withdraw from Ujjain, but the latter paid no heed to this request. Amānat Khān then sent one of the *thānedārs*, named Rahim Beg, to get hold of Sārangpur, but Ratan Singh defeated him and dispersed his men. Amānat Khān prepared for a fight. Ratan Singh also

Defeat and death of Ratan Singh: Battle of Sunerā, 1712.

[1] Azam, pp.159, 252-3.

[2] *Akhbarat*, August 28, 1709; Tod, I, p.466.

collected a big army of 20,000 men and had with him Dost Muhammad Khān, the Rohilā leader. A battle was fought at Sunerā (10 miles S.-W. of Sārangpur),[1] in which Ratan Singh was killed. Dost Muhammad Khān and the rest of the army dispersed and melted away. Amānat Khān went to Rāmpurā and the widows submitted. Jahāndār Shāh was greatly pleased at his success and Amānat Khān was created Shāhmat Khān.[2]

The loss of Rāmpurā to the province: It reverts to Mewād: 1713-1718.

Gopāl Singh took advantage of this development and with the help of the Mahārānā occupied Rāmpurā. The Mahārānā gave only a portion of the whole district to Gopāl Singh, the rest being annexed to the Mewād State. Durgādas Rāthor, who could not get along with Ajit Singh, left Mārwād and took over the charge of the newly

---

[1] K.K. mentions that the battle was fought near *Nālā* Sārangpur (II, p. 694). Ketelaar, who passed the scene of the battle on January 6, 1713, some months after the battle, definitely states that it was fought at Sunerā, a village on the high road between Sārangpur and Shāhjahānpur. *J.P.H.S.*, X, Pt. I, p.87.

[2] K.K. says that some rumours attributed this revolt to the secret instigation of Zulfiqār, who wanted Amānat Khān to be disgraced, as he was appointed without his advice. K.K., II, pp.693-697; M.U., II, pp.147-8; III, pp.730-1; Irvine, II, p.138.

acquired districts.[1] Later in 1718, at the request of Jai Singh, Farukhsiyār formally granted the *parganāh* of Rāmpurā to the Mahārānā.[2] Thus, the territory of the State of Rāmpurā, which had been included in the *subāh* of Mālwa since the days of Akbar, was once again lost to it. The agreement which was signed by Gopāl Singh and his grandson Sangrām Singh on August 29, 1717, once for all reduced this full-fledged State into a *zamindari*, paying a tribute and owning obedience to the Mahārānā of Udaipur.[3]

Mālwa princes and Ajit Singh.

In 1717, there was a good gathering of Mālwa princes in Delhi, when many of them were present with the party of Ajit Singh of Mārwād, the most notable of these being Keshodās, ruler of Sitāmau, Kunwār Mān Singh of Ratlām, Rāo Gopāl Singh Chandrāwat of Rāmpurā and Rājā Kishan of

---

[1] Tod, II, p.1034; *Vir.*, II, pp.957-62, 989-90; Ojhā: *Rajputana*, II, p.926.

[2] On the basis of *Vir Vinod* (II, p.989), Ojhā puts the grant of the *farman*, prior to the agreement with Gopāl Singh in August 1717 (*Rajputana*, II, p.928, p.1378). *Vamsh.* puts it only after May, 1718, (IV, pp.3063-4). The latter view seems to be correct. *Vir Vinod* mentions the existence of the original grant of Rāmpurā to Mewad by the Emperor Farukhsiyār but does not give it (II, 989).

[3] *Vir.*, II, pp.957-9.

Khilchipur.[1] This was probably the last gathering of such magnitude. But the influence of the house of Mārwād in Mālwa was now not as great as that of Jai Singh of Amber. Jai Singh's star was, of course, in the ascendant and Ajit Singh had to be more concerned with the affairs of Gujrāt only.

Re-imposition of *Jaziya*: 1717-1719.

By the close of this period, the triple treaty had practically ceased to be of any great influence. It could not save the Hindu population from the odious *Jaziyā*, which was re-imposed in 1717 at the instigation of Ināyetullah. That it would not continue long was abundantly clear, yet it was there till its final abolition in 1719 by Rafi-ud-dārājāt in his first audience.[2]

SECTION 5. THE DEVELOPMENT OF MODERN MALWA. (1707—1719).

This period marks a stage further in the development of modern Mālwa and that of its States. It was a period of general disregard of internal provincial affairs, which allowed the States to crystallize into political entities. Again, the

---

[1] Tod, II, pp.1023.

[2] Irvine, I, p.246, p.334, p.404; Ojha, *Rajputana*, II, pp.924-5; Tod, I, p.469; *Vir.*, II, pp.954-5.

increased importance and influence of the Rajput princes of Rājputāna made it possible for these newly-sprung States of Mālwa to strengthen their own position and to try to raise their own political status. There was none at the capital, wise or strong enough to observe and check these tendencies of the States; the junior officers of the province were benefited by humouring the wishes of the States than by asserting the rights of the Empire. Except this main tendency, which was working more or less unseen, there were very few events of political or historical significance.

States of Mālwa take shape.

The fall of the independent State of Rāmpurā, the tussle and the varying fortunes of Kotāh and Bundi, and the renewal of Maratha attacks on Mālwa have already been dealt with. There are left three main events of provincial importance which need be discussed at length; they are the expansion of the principality of Shivpuri (Narwar), the beginning of the modern State of Bhopāl and the disruption of Ratlām State.

Expansion of Narwar State.

The State of Shivpuri held by the Kachhāwāh ruler, Anup Singh, benefited from the battle of Jājau. Though Gaj Singh, son of Anup Singh, was with Azam, Anup Singh continued to support Bahādur Shāh. For his previous services and this help Bahādur Shāh granted the districts of Narwar and Shāhbād to Anup Singh.[1] Anup Singh died in 1710 and was succeeded by his son Gaj Singh. Soon after the new grants, the father and son concentrated their efforts in bringing the newly granted territories under their control. In their attempts they were greatly helped by their commander, Khanderai. Gaj Singh was on active service in the campaign against the Jāts, led by Jai Singh.[2]

Beginning of the State of Bhopāl: Dost Muhammad Khān.

While this Hindu State was expanding in the north of Mālwa, Dost Muhammad Khan Rohilā was laying the foundations of a Muslim State in the southern tract of Mālwa. Dost Muhammad was an Afghan adventurer, who came to India in the last years of Aurangzib's rule. After serving another Afghan named Jalāl Khān, he joined the Imperial service and was detached with a party of soldiers to Mālwa, where he attracted the attention of the provincial authorities by his brave and daring nature. In 1712, he fought for Ratan Singh of Rāmpurā against Amānat Khān. About this time Dost Muhammad Khān was given the management of the

[1] Khande, fol.197-9, 551-3.
[2] Khande, fol.202, 290, 468-9.

Bersiāh district, which had a revenue of Rs. 15,000.[1] By the year 1717, he had gained much importance and had come to be looked upon as a notable chief. When Muhammad Amin Khān came to Mālwa, he had hoped to receive much help from Dost Muhammad. But the Saiyyads appear to have made friends with Dost Muhammad, which relation he maintained until their fall.[2] He tried all means fair and foul to strengthen his own position, power and principality; he was slowly building up the modern State of Bhopāl; in 1719 he was known as 'Zamindar of Bhākra' only.[3]

The Rāthor State of Ratlām was the scene of much bloodshed during the closing years of the period. Chhatra Sāl Rāthor had left behind him two sons and one grandson from his eldest son, killed at Panhālā. Strangely enough, he had divided the State into three equal divisions and given one portion to each with an equal status.

---

[1] Malcolm, I, pp.349-50; K.K., II, p.694.

It is not certain when Dost Muhammad got the district of Bersiāh. The fact that he is not referred to as *zamindar* of Bersiāh in K.K. gives rise to the doubt that it was granted only after 1712.

[2] *Dastur-ul-Insha*, p.53 in Irvine, I, p.361*n*.

[3] Irvine, II, 28; *Burhan-ul-futuhat*, fol.168a; Malcolm, I, pp.351-352.

The division was very complex. Soon, however, Beri Sāl, the grandson, left Mālwa and went to his sister, who was married to Jai Singh of Amber: he had evidently not much interest in his holdings in Mālwa. Now, the two sons of Chhatra Sāl quarelled for the portion of Beri Sāl. The elder one, Kesari Singh, who occupied the seat of the principality, took hold of his nephew's share. The younger brother, Partāb Singh, killed Kesari Singh and became the sole master of the whole State (1717). Mān Singh, the elder son of Kesari Singh, was then at Delhi, while the younger son, Jai Singh, was at Ratlām, who now fled from there, gathered together forces, called up his relatives from the estates of Narwar (one near Ujjain), Lālgarh etc., and marched on to Ratlām with the additional help of the Imperial forces at Māndu. Jai Singh had informed his elder brother, then at Delhi, of the happenings at Ratlām. Partāb Singh took refuge in the small fortress of Sāgod, which was besieged. One day Partāb Singh tried to escape from the fortress in the early hours of the day, but his escape was detected and in the ambush that followed Partāb Singh was wounded and later killed. Jai Singh entered Ratlām in triumph. Mān Singh on his way back from Delhi took help from Amber, but

Troubles in Ratlām State. Founding of Sailāna, 1718.

it was no longer needed. Jai Singh went to receive Mān Singh, and the two brothers returned to Ratlām. Jai Singh succeeded to the possessions of Partāb Singh and thus founded the State of Sailānā in 1719.[1]

The condition of the province as a whole did not improve during the period. The journal of Ketelaar contains a vivid account of the conditions prevailing in 1712-3[2] and it can safely be asserted that from the very spirit of the times no improvement was possible; many fresh causes of disorder were coming to the surface. The poverty of the peasants forced them to rise in revolt. They harassed the travellers passing between Agra and Sironj and extracted money out of them. The high roads were infested with robbers. There was frequent private warfare between the various States which only

Condition of the province and its people.

[1] *Gazetteers* of Sailānā and Ratlām States are not exhaustive. The *Souvenir* of Sailānā State gives he facts of Jai Singh's succession as understood by that State. No other authorities of value can be quoted. The main dispute lies in the fact whether Jai Singh succeeded to the portion of Partāb Singh as divided and given by Chhatra Sāl or whether it was given afresh by Mān Singh out of the united State of Ratlām as Mān Singh found it on his return to Ratlām from Delhi. The agreement among the brothers has been the cause of much dispute between the two States.

[2] *J.P.H.S.*, X (I), p.77, 92.

rendered the tract more desolate. The weakness of a ruler encouraged his neighbours to encroach upon his territories, as was the case in Jhābuā.[1] The heir-apparent of the place was too turbulent to obey his father. In many cases the Princes also taxed the goods that passed through their territories.[2] It was, however, different in the case of strong rulers, *e.g.*, the State of Kotāh under Bhim Singh: the Bhils and other disturbing factors were ruthlessly put down, and in this work he engaged the rulers of the Umat States of Rājgarh and Narsingarh, who were willing to help Bhim Singh on payment of their expenses.[3] But, on the whole, Imperial authority remained intact and was generally respected;[4] but this too was to vanish in the coming decade, when the forces of disorder multiplied in the form of internal troubles, foreign invasions and the ultimate breakdown of Imperial rule.

---

[1] *Jhābua Gaz.*, p.3.

[2] *J.P.H.S.*, X (I), p.90.

[3] Tod, III, pp.1524-5.

[4] Partābgarh-Deoliā State makes the queer claim that its ruler, Prithi Singh (1708-17) was received by Shāh Alam Bahādur Shāh and was granted the right to coin money. This is, however, based on traditions only. In the absence of any authority, it can not be accepted. On the face of it, it appears to be unacceptable.

CHAPTER IV.

THE MUGHAL-MARATHA STRUGGLE THE FIRST STAGE (1719—1730)

SECTION I.—THE STRUGGLE FOR A FOOTING IN MALWA.

With the year 1719 the history of Mālwa enters upon a new and definitely more complex phase. The opposing forces, *viz.*, the Mughals and the Marathas, finally come to grips. After some raids and invasions the Marathas finally gained a footing in the province by the year 1730, and practically came to control the whole of southern Mālwa. The appearance of Muhammad Bangash to challenge the Marathas marks the second phase of the struggle, which ended in the cession of Mālwa from the Empire in 1741.

But this struggle was not a simple straight fight between the Mughals and the Marathas; many factors were involved in it. The decade opens with the Nizām as the governor of Mālwa, who later established his dynasty in the Deccan by making himself its permanent semi-independent viceroy. To him the office of the Vazir of the Empire was not as important as the maintenance of his domination in the Deccan. He, however, continued to be interested in the affairs of Mālwa not merely because it was a buffer province between his *subāhs* and the Empire in the North, but also because he felt that it would be a stroke of shrewd policy to divert the Marathas to Mālwa, who would otherwise have proved a thorn in his side. The *subāh* of Mālwa was a paying *subāh* too, and as such in the early years of the period it was considered a good prize for its governor.

The Marathas began with the old policy of invading Mālwa, when they were on bad terms with the Imperial authorities in the Deccan. With the establishment of the Nizām in the Deccan and the succession of Bāji Rāo to his father's office as Peshwā, there began the rivalry between the two, which continued for full twenty years. Bāji Rāo entered on a policy of active aggression which was only tempered by hostilities at home with the Nizām, and he included Mālwa in his own programme of conquest.

The third factor in the politics of Mālwa was supplied by the personality of Sawāi Jai Singh of Amber. An ambitious prince as he was, he desired to take advantage of the decadance of the Empire and to extend his own State from the Jamunā to the Narmadā. He was friendly with the Marathas, kept them informed of even the most confidential consultations and talks in the inner circles of the Emperor, ministers and other influential men at the capital. He even advised the Marathas on all crucial points and hoped to gain his own end if the Marathas became powerful enough to trouble the governors of Mālwa. He believed that if difficulties thickened there, he could get the province for himself from the Emperor and keep the Marathas either at peace or out of it by paying them the subsidy they might ask for. He was trying to dominate over the neighbouring States too and thus extend his own influence and control. The local princes and *zamindārs* naturally looked to Jai Singh for guidance as the most powerful, influential and enlightened prince in the neighbourhood. Jai Singh's advice was naturally such as would help him only to fulfil his own ambition.

There were other grantees, too, in Mālwa, who were more or less absentee landlords and whose only concern with the land was to get their money. Whenever there was any interference by the local authorities, they complained to their patron at the Court and clamoured for the removal of these officers from office. Their local agents in Mālwa followed the policy of least resistance, such as would pay in the end. They naturally made friends with the Maratha invaders and tried to save their own lands from devastation. Thus, these holdings naturally provided a good refuge and shelter for the rebels and the invaders.

The last, but not the least, important factor was the condition of the Empire itself. Whenever the Emperor sent as its *Subāhdār* anyone interested in its affairs, the latter only tried to further his own interests and cared least for the interests of the Empire. If a disinterested person like Girdhar Bahādur came down, he found his own position very precarious, partly because of lack of support and co-operation in the province and partly because very little aid could be expected from the Court also. Neither the money nor the forces, which were often promised, was forthcoming. Naturally, the interests of the Empire were least cared for.

SECTION 2.—THE NIZAM'S FIRST GOVERNORSHIP.

(FEBRUARY 20, 1719—AUGUST 29, 1722)

On Rafi-ud-dārājāt's accession, a reorganization of the whole administration was thought of. The distant provinces were left undisturbed. Mālwa and Kabul still attracted the attention of the Saiyyad regents. No one had been appointed to the governorship of Mālwa after the return and dismissal of Muhammad Amin Khān the previous year. The Nizām was still in Delhi. The government of Patna had been assigned to him on January 28, 1719, but apparently he was not anxious to go there.[1] The Saiyyads apprehended danger from the Nizām, and Hussain Ali proposed that he be assassinated. Qutub-ul-Mulk, however, thought that detached from his friends he would be weakened and, therefore, offered him Mālwa. The Nizām declined it at first, but later on accepted it on the solemn promise of irrevocation. He received his robe and dismissal to his government on the third day after the new Emperor's accession (February 20, 1719).[2]

The Nizām appointed permanent governor of Mālwa.

---

[1] Irvine, I, pp.371, 404-5; K.K., II, p.792; Kāmwar, p.188; Mirzā Muhammed, p.446.

[2] Irvine, I, p.405; Kāmwar, p.188; Shiv., p.26b; Ahwāl,

The Nizām left Delhi on March 5, and took away with him all his property and family and did not leave even his son to represent him at the Court. All the Mughals, who had been out of employment, went with him. At this time all sorts of rumours were afloat in Delhi; it was talked that the Nizām would combine with Jai Singh of Amber and Chhabilerām Nāgar of Allahabad against the Saiyyads. Mitr Sen, the prime mover in arranging the enthronement of Nekusiyār, met the Nizām at Agra. The Nizām gave no definite answer and moved on to Mālwa. Later when Mitr Sen and Chhabilerām sought his help, he gave them no encouragement. The Saiyyads were, however, convinced of his non-complicity only later, when some letters fell into Hussain Ali's hand.[1]

---

p.152a; KK., II, pp.817-9, 847-8; Elliot's translation of Khāfi Khān is wrong when it says "the *Subadari* of Patna was given to Nizām-ul-Mulk." (Elliot, VII, p.480); it should be "Nizām-ul-Mulk was given the *Subah* of Mālwa in place of the *Subadari* of Patna" (K.K., II, p.817).

[1] Irvine, I, p.408, 410-11, 414; II, p.2, 17. Tod gives a letter dated Bhādon, 4th Shuklā, 1776 (August 8, 1719) from Jai Singh to Bihāri Dās (of Udaipur) which says that the Nizām was marching rapidly from Ujjain to join Jai Singh. (Tod, I, p.475). It appears to be fabricated news of Jai Singh. Khāfi Khān definitely asserts that the Nizām went on even to hinder the revolt of Nekusiyār. K.K., II, p.827-8, 832.

The sickly puppet on the throne, Rafi-ud-dārājāt, and his equally powerless successor, Rafi-ud-daulā, ceased to exist by September 8, 1719. Prince Akhtar was enthroned on September 18, as Muhammad Shāh; and ruled till 1748. The Saiyyads continued to dominate the Empire, the king being a mere puppet in their hands.

The Nizām reached Ujjain by the middle of May, 1719, and the night following his arrival there was a heavy fall of rain. He spent the monsoon months at Ujjain, and set out to reduce the province only after the rainy season. He, however, found that the troubles with the Saiyyads had begun from the first day of his appointment. Marhamat Khān, son of Amir Khān, who was the *faujdār* of Māndu, had given offence to Hussain Ali Khān, when the latter was on his way to Delhi from the Deccan. At the time of the new appointments he was removed from the *faujdāri*, which was now given to Khwājā Quli Khān. When the Khwājā went down to Māndu, Marhamat Khān refused to leave the fort and prepared to resist. Later, on the mediation of Ghiyās Khān, a trusted officer of the Nizām took him into his own service and applied to

The Nizām in Mālwa. 1719-1720 A.D.

The Marhamat Khān affair.

the Vazir for Marhamāt Khān's pardon. It was, however, refused.[1]

The Amjherā affair.

Soon after taking charge of Māndu, Khwājā Quli Khan called Jairup Singh Rāthor, the *zamindar* of Amjherā, to Māndu and at the instigation of his younger brother, Jagrup Singh, deceitfully captured him. Jagrup Singh now became the master of Amjherā and Jairup's minor son, Lāl Singh, fled for his life to the Nizām, who sent Ghiyās with a force to Amjherā to chastise Jagrup Singh. Later on he himself followed. Jagrup had no chance of escaping and was captured.[2]

The Bundelās repulsed. Nov.-Dec. 1719.

Chhatra Sāl had once again become active at the instigation of Budh Singh Hādā, the dispossessed ruler of Bundi. In the south Jai Chand Bundelā, son of Chhatra Sāl,[3] captured the fort of Rāmgarh, near Sironj and Bhilsā. On receipt of a *farmān*, the Nizām entrusted the task of recapturing the fort

---

[1] Irvine, I, p.405; II, pp.17-8, 19; Ahwāl; K.K., II, p.800, 818-9.

[2] K.K., II, pp.849-50.

[3] Irvine reads this name as 'Jai Chānd' while in Khāfi Khān it is 'Gyān Chand'. Among the names of the sons of Chhatra Sāl there is only one 'Rāi Chānd' which is similar to either of these names. Irvine, II, p.18; K.K., II, p.850; *Nagari Pracharini Patrika*, Vol. XVII, p.135.

to Marhamat Khān and supplied him with a big army. On reaching Bhilsā and Sironj, Marhamat Khān gathered additional forces consisting of the Afghans and the Rohilas and took the fort with their help. When the new of the victory reached the Saiyyads it only irritated them the more.[1]

Troubles were brewing at this time on the north-western frontier of Mālwa. The Kotāh-Bundi dispute had not yet ended. At the time of Farukhsiyār's deposition, Budh Singh stood for Farukhsiyār and left Delhi after fighting his way through the opposing forces. He had joined Jai Singh then camping near Amber. The Saiyyads promised to give the principality of Bundi to Bhim Singh of Kotāh as a reward for his loyalty to their party. Budh Singh had been intriguing with Girdhar Bahādur, then in revolt at Allahabad and instigating the Bundelās also. Bhim Singh was sent to Kotāh from Delhi on November 7, 1719. He secured for Dost Muhammad Khān Rohilā (later of Bhopāl) a high *mansab*. Dost Muhammad was on unfriendly terms with the Nizām and hence was expected to help in opposing the Nizām. Dost Muhammad Khān was placed under Bhim Singh.

Bundi-Kotāh tussle. 1719-1720.

[1] Irvine, II, 8, 10, 18; K.K., II, p.850.

Saiyyad Dilāwar Ali Khān and Gaj Singh of Narwar were also ordered to joini him.[1] When Bhim Singh reached Mathurā and Gokul, on his way to Kotāh, he became a follower of the Vallabhāchāri sect, and lived in seclusion for a fortnight. Rumours were soon afloat that Bhim Singh had died. Budh Singh was still at Amber and the affairs of Bundi were in the hands of Sālim Singh, who now hoped to take advantage of the situation. He began to plunder the territories of Kotāh. Bhim Singh now left his retreat and came down to Kotāh, and the next day there ensued a battle between the forces of Bundi and Kotāh in which the former were completely defeated. Later, Bhim Singh attacked and took Bundi on March 2, 1720.[2]

The Saiyyads had instructed Bhim Singh and Dilāwar Ali Khān to keep in readiness on the north-western frontier of Mālwa. Bhim Singh was promised the title of Mahārājā, a seat next to Ajit

---

[1] Irvine, II, p.5-6; K.K., II, p.844, 851.

[2] The report of the battle reached Delhi on February 2, 1720. K.K. says that Sālim Singh was captured, while Kāmwar says that he died, but here Kāmwar is wrong. K.K., II, pp.851, 877; *Vamsh.*, IV, p.3074; Irvine, II, p.6. *Vamsh.* does not mention the name of Dilāwar Ali Khān as having fought at Bundi.

Singh only in the *darbār*, a *mansab* of *7-hazāri* and the "fish standard", if he took part in a successful campaign against the Nizām in Mālwa. Finding that all opposition to them had been put down, the Saiyyads now decided to deal with the Nizām. Their plans against him were already formed; in the meanwhile he had also irritated them by fresh actions. The reports of the enlisting of men and collecting of war material by the Nizām in excess of the provincial requirements had also reached the ears of the Saiyyads.

The Nizām and the Saiyyads. Feb.-April, 1720.

Hussain Ali now called upon the Nizām, through his agent in Delhi, to explain the various points on which he had grievances against him. The favour shown to Marhamat Khān, the removal of a *zamindār* in *parganāh* Nālam (Tālam in Sārangpur?) and some other land disputes were specially stressed. In reply, the Nizām wrote direct to Hussain Ali acknowledging the letter of his own agent. He complained of the enmity of the official news-reporter and hoped that though others might not understand the situation in Mālwa, Hussain Ali would, as he had lately passed through it. To save Mālwa from the Maratha invasions it was essential to keep a well-equipped and large army. He added that he meant no harm to the Saiyyads, as was evident from his attitude towards Nekusiyār's rebellion.[1] This, however, only added fuel to the fire. Hussain Ali broke out in strong language. After long consultations the Saiyyads despatched mace-bearers with a *farmān* to recall the Nizām from Mālwa. Alam Ali Khān, then in the Deccan, was warned, while Dilāwar Ali Khān was ordered to cross the Chambal on the pretence of bringing the members of the family of the Saiyyads from the Deccan. The Saiyyads hoped that if the Nizām submitted all would be well; if he did not submit they could still fight or negotiate as the situation developed.[2]

The Nizām, on the other hand, was receiving letters from the Emperor and his mother, sent to him through Muhammad Amin Khān, depicting their own helpless condition due to the usurpation of all authority by the Saiyyads and informing the Nizām that they expected him to espouse their cause and effect their deliverance. Muhammad Amin had himself informed the Nizām that the Saiyyads were only waiting for the right opportunity to destroy him. The Nizām, who had already become suspicious of

---

[1] K.K., II, p.851; *Tarikh-i-Muzaffari,* p.174; Irvine, II, pp.17-8.

[2] Ahwāl in Irvine, II, pp.19-20; K.K., II, p.851, 860.

the intentions of the Saiyyads, was confirmed in his doubts by the movements of the forces of Dilāwar Ali Khān, Bhim Singh and others on the frontier. He was at Mandsaur in April, when he heard from his agents of the despatch of the mace-bearers to recall him. The war-like preparations of the Nizām were well advanced, and no sooner did the news of the advance of Dilāwar Ali reach him than he hastened to complete the same. He first decided to go to Ujjain and there to await the receipt of the *farmān*.[1]

The *farmān* recalled the Nizām from Mālwa, on the plea that for the protection and settlement of the affairs in the Deccan it was essential that Hussain Ali should take charge of Mālwa and stay there. In return for this he was offered the choice of any of the four provinces, *viz.*, Agra, Allahabad, Multān and Burhānpur. It was a distinct breach of faith. The Nizām stood in great need of money. The north-western portion of Mālwa had been devastated by the forces of Bhim Singh and his associates. He refused to leave the province. The *rabi* crops were soon to be harvested and much of

[1] K.K., II, pp.850-2; Kāmwar, p.221; *Ibrat.*, p.307 in Irvine, II, pp.19-20.

The Nizām leaves Mālwa: Struggle in the Deccan, 1720.

the revenue was to be collected forthwith. He left Mandsaur about April 13, and decided not to go to Ujjain nor to wait for the *farmān*. He talked of going to Sironj and moved upto Mukund-Durrāh, whence he turned back, went as far as the village of Kāyath (near Ujjain), and from there made straight for the Narmadā. He crossed the river at the Akbarpur ferry on April 28, the news of which event reached Delhi on May 6.[1] Immediately, Bhim Singh Hādā, Gaj Singh of Narwar and Dost Muhammad Khān Rohilā and others already near Mālwa, were ordered to proceed against him without delay. On June 19, 1720, there was fought a battle near Khandwā in which the Imperial forces were defeated by the Nizām. Bhim Singh, Gaj Singh and Dilāwar Ali Khān were killed in the battle; Dost Muhammad Khan with his friends and surviving followers made good his retreat into Mālwa, pursued and plundered by the Maratha auxiliaries of the Nizām.[2]

---

[1] K.K., II, pp.851-2, 859-60; *Ibrat.*, pp.307-8; Kāmwar, p.221; Irvine, II, pp.18, 22.

[2] K.K., II, pp.876-882; *Ibrat.*, p.318; Ahwāl asserts that Dost Muhammad Khān turned and fled away fol.162a, 157b; Kāmwar, p.221-3; Irvine, II, pp.22-23, 28-34.

The news of this defeat put the Saiyyads into a state of consternation. Hussain Ali sent a *farmān* to the Nizām in the name of the Emperor inquiring about the cause of his leaving Mālwa. It also gave the Nizām the six *subahs* of the Deccan. There was a personal letter from Hussain Ali also. The Nizām diplomatically asserted in his reply that he had left Mālwa due to the disturbances caused by the Marathas, which had led him to fear for the safety of Burhānpur and even of Mālwa, and still more for the safety of the family of the Amir-ul-Umrā. The great distance precluded him from taking Imperial sanction beforehand.[1]

The fall of the Saiyyads: Sep.-Oct. 1720.

The struggle with the Nizām was not yet at an end. On July 30, 1720, another battle was fought in the Deccan in which Alam Ali Khān was killed. This ensured the supremacy of the Nizām in the Deccan for the time being. The Saiyyads were greatly alarmed. After much discussion and difference of opinion Hussain Ali Khān began his march to the Deccan to put down the revolt of the Nizām. He took the Emperor also with him, and the complete establishment of Mālwa

[1] Shiv., p.33b, 39a, 40b, 41a, 42b; *Ibrat.*, p.327 in Irvine, II, pp.45-7, 35-37.

with those of many other provinces accompanied the Emperor. On the way Hussain Ali Khān was murdered on September 28, 1720. This closed the fate of the Saiyyads. Muhammad Amin Khān, who was with the army, was made the Vazir, and the Imperial army returned towards Delhi. Qutub-ul-Mulk surrendered after fighting a battle and was imprisoned. Muhammed Amin Khān enjoyed the office for four months only. On his death the office was given to the Nizām who was still in the Deccan (February 4, 1721).[1]

Mālwa during the absence of the Nizām: April 28, 1720—Aug. 30, 1722.

The province of Mālwa continued to be in charge of the Nizām even after he had left for the Deccan on April 28, 1721. When Muhammad Amir Khān became the Vazir, the Nizām proposed that Zāhir-ud-daulah, brother of Muhammad Amin Khān, who had rendered great services to the Nizām, be made governor of Mālwa. The Vazir did not agree to this proposal and the Nizām continued to be the governor,[2] till he was replaced by Girdhar Bahādur on August 30, 1722. The Nizām was then in Delhi working as the Vazir of the Empire.

---

[1] Irvine, II, pp.47-50, 51-54, 58-60, 67-8, 72-74, 85-93, 95, 103-105.

[2] M.U., II, p.332.

When the affairs of the Empire were in a state of disorder and internal troubles and revolts were weakening it, the Maratha power was definitely becoming stronger. Bāji Rāo, the new Peshwā (1720—40) was for a vigorous policy in northern India, and though many people opposed this policy, he carried with him Rājā Shāhu's confidence and support. Some grants had already been made to the Marathas in Mālwa as early as 1717,[1] many of their generals had been invading some of its territories off and on and establishing a few outposts also, but the Peshwā could not think of the North at this time. These early years of his Peshwā-ship kept him engaged at home in settling the affairs of Konkan, strengthening his own position, and trying to understand the new situation which had arisen on the establishment of the Nizām in the Deccan. In 1721 the Nizām left for the North making Mubāriz Khān his own deputy in the Deccan. The absence of the Nizām, the policy of Mubāriz Khan to oppose the Maratha demands in the Deccan,[2] and, lastly, the strengthened position of the Peshwā made Bāji Rāo burst into activity once more after the rainy

Bāji Rāo I the new Peshwā: His new policy.

[1] S.P.D., XXX, 17A, 17B.

[2] *Madhya*, I, p.163.

season of 1722 had come to an end; but by then the Nizām was no longer the governor of Mālwa.

SECTION 3.—FIRST GOVERNORSHIP OF GIRDHAR BAHADUR.

(AUGUST 30, 1722—MAY 15, 1723)

Muhammad Shāh appointed Girdhar Bahādur governor of Mālwa on August 30, 1722. He was a Nāgar Brāhman and was the nephew of Chhabilerām of Allahabad. Lately he had been the governor of Oudh, whence he was removed to make room for Sādāt Khān.[1]

Girdhar Bahādur's arrival in Mālwa coincided with the renewal of the Maratha activities in the South. After the close of the rainy season of the year 1722, Bāji Rāo decided to lead an expedition into Mālwā. Immediately after the *Dasherā* celebrations (Oct. 8, 1722), he left Satārā and reached Burhānpur on January 18, 1723. When the Peshwā was camping at Jalgāon, he granted to Udāji Pawār half of his *mokāsā* in Gujrāt and Mālwa (Dec. 3, 1722).[2] From Burhānpur the Peshwā moved down

Bāji Rāo's expedition into Mālwa. Feb., 1723.

---

[1] Kāmwar, p.254; *Siwanih-i-Khizr* in Irvine, II, p.123 (Date N.S.); Shrivāstava, p.30 (Date N.S.).

[2] Vād, II, p.223; *Dharcha Pawara*, pp.20-22.

to Makadāi district, and after spending about a week there he entered Mālwa near Handiā (Feb. 1). Thence he started for Dhār, and reached Gardāwad (9 miles N. of Dhār) on February 10. He crossed the Māhi river and camped at Badakshā (Bolāsā in Jhābuā State)[1] on February 12. Here he awaited the arrival of the Nizām, who on his way to Gujrāt had decided to meet him.[2]

The Nizām in Mālwa: His meetin with the Peshwā: Feb. 13, 1723.

On assuming the office of Vazir, the Nizām found that it was a very difficult task to carry on the work. Haidar Quli Khān, the governor of Gujrāt, was a great favourite of the Emperor and the Nizām decided to remove him from the capital. Haidar Quli left for his government, but immediately on reaching there he began to interfere with the lands assigned to various nobles. The Nizām decided to go to Gujrāt to remove Haidar Quli Khān from Gujrāt also, and the Emperor was with great difficulty induced to sanction it. On his way to Gujrāt the Nizām passed through Mālwa. He camped at

---

[1] Badakshā can be identified with village Bolāsā (about 7 miles S.-E. of Rāipuriā). It is just mid-way between Rāipuriā and the Māhi. The difference in name appears to have arisen due to mistaken reading from the notes in 'Modi' script.

[2] Vād, II, pp.222-224; S.P.D., XXX, p.266.

Sārangpur (Dec. 30, 1722), at Dhār (Feb. 3, 1723), and started for Ahmedābad three days later. On his way he met the Peshwā at Badakshā (Bolāsā) on February 13, 1723.[1] It was an important meeting and was to be the forerunner of many more. The Nizām, then, moved on to Gujrāt, and probably the Peshwā accompanied him upto the next stop at Raipuriā (in Jhābuā State). There the Peshwā stayed for two days. On February 19 he took leave of the Nizām and returned to Badakshā. Bāji Rāo started for Khāndesh and, passing in the neighbourhood of Amjherā and Dhār, climbed down the Pāyā Ghāt near Māndu and crossed the Narmadā at the Akbarpur ferry on February 25, 1723.[2]

Jhābuā affairs: Jan.-Feb., 1723. At this time many of the Peshwā's generals were busy collecting the Maratha dues with the arrears of previous years, especially on the western border of Mālwa; the chief of these were Kanthāji Kadam, Udāji Pawār and Pilāji Gaikawād. Kanthāji Kadam was summoned by the Peshwā to meet him at Dharampuri, on his way back to Khāndesh. Early in January, 1723, Kanthāji was

---

[1] Irvine, II, p.127-9; K.K., II, p.946; Kāmwar, 256-61. Ghulām Ali, p.45a; S.P.D., XIII, p.3; S.P.D., XXX, p.266; *Mirat.*, II (34), pp. 45-7.

[2] S.P.D., XXX, p.266; Vād., II, p.223.

at Ali (now under Ali-Rajpur State), whence he went down to the Jhābuā State, stayed at Sheogarh (13 miles north of Jhābuā) and demanded *chauth* and *sardeshmukhi*. Khush-hāl Singh then ruled Jhābuā; he was a weak and incompetent ruler, but he prepared to resist; Kanthāji, however, suddenly left Sheogarh without realizing the dues in order to meet the Peshwā at Dharampuri. Khush-hāl Singh died soon after leaving the State to his son Anup Singh.[1]

The Nizām back in Mālwa: The Bhopāl expedition.

The Nizām did not meet with any opposition in Gujrāt, Haidar Quli Khān having fled away to Delhi. The Nizām had obtained the province of Gujrāt for himself or his son, and now he appointed his own uncle Hāmid Khān, nicknamed Jangli Shāhzādā to be the deputy governor of Gujrāt and returned to Mālwa by March 13.[2] As he was free from any trouble, he decided to wreak his vengeance on Dost Muhammad Khān of Bhopāl, who had fought against him in the battle of Khandwā in 1720. A force was sent against Dost Muhammad Khān,

---

[1] S.P.D., XIII, p.1, 3. Jhābuā (pp.3-4) puts this raid late in 1772, and says that Kanthāji left for Hindustan; both of these statements appear to be wrong.

[2] K.K., II, p.946-7; Kamwār, pp.256-61; *Mirat.*, II (34), pp.47-8; Irvine, II, pp.129-130.

who took refuge in the fort of Bhopāl. There was some fighting and later the Imperial forces took the small fort of Islāmgarh (8 miles north of Bhopāl). Dost Muhammad Khān now submitted, sent his own son Yār Muhammad Khān to offer excuses and make due submission to the Nizām's satisfaction.[1]

The Maratha forces in Bhopāl: March 18-April 5.

After crossing the Narmadā on February 25, the Peshwā went to Boregaum in Khāndesh, and thence to Makadāi. But soon he entered the Handiā district and crossed the Narmadā near Hushāngābād on March 18. He wandered about in these districts till April 5, 1723, when he finally left the province to return to the Deccan. During his stay in the Hushangābād district some of his troops were sent against Dost Muhammad Khān Rohilā and they gained a victory over him. In the plunder they obtained an elephant which was presented to the Peshwā.[2]

---

[1] Kāmwar, p.263; Rustam, p.251b; Wārid, p.12; Irvine, II, pp.130-131. These events were reported to the Emperor on March 14, 1723.

[2] The receipt of an elephant is recorded on April 16, 1723. S.P.D., XXX, p.267. Vād., II, p.224. It is clear from this that the forces of the Peshwā co-operated with those of the Nizām in the latter's campaign against Dost Muhammad Khān.

After settling his quarrel with the Rohilās the Nizām decided to return to Delhi. He had gone to Sironj, where on May 15, 1723, he took over the control of the province to himself and appointed his second cousin Azimullāh, son of Raeyat Khān, deputy-governor of Mālwa. Girdhar Bahādur's first governorship ended. The Nizām returned to Delhi leaving his artillery and heavy baggage at Sironj.[1]

The Nizām takes over Mālwa: Azimullāh appointed as his deputy: May 15, 1723.

SECTION 4.—AZIMULLAH'S DEPUTY GOVERNORSHIP

(MAY 15, 1723—JUNE 2, 1725)

When the Nizām left Mālwa appointing Azimullāh his own deputy, he took care to have there his own man to check the Rohilā chief; he appointed Chandra Bans, son of Rao Chand, to be the *faujdār* of Islāmgarh, recently conquered from Dost Muhammad Khān.

On reaching Delhi, the Nizām found himself quite helpless in restoring any order in the affairs of the Empire. The Emperor's ears had been poisoned against him, and his suspicions aroused. Moreover,

[1] Kāmwār, p.265; Rustam, p.251b; Wārid p.12; Irvine, II, p.131.

The Nizām decides to return to the Deccan : In Mālwa, April-May, 1724.

the political rivals of the new Vazir at the Court initiated the talk of transferring the six *subāhs* of the Deccan to the name of the infant Prince lately born to the Emperor; this alarmed the Nizām, who considered the six *subāhs* to be his own. He resigned the office of the Vazir in disgust and ceased to appear in the Court. A reconciliation was effected, but only a little over a month later the Nizām took leave (on Dec. 7, 1723) to go to his own *jagirs* in Oudh. In February, 1724, he was at Soron on the Ganges, when he submitted a report to the Emperor that the Marathas had invaded Mālwa and Gujrāt. As both of these provinces were under himself and his son, he proposed that he must march southwards to expel them. By rapid marches he passed through Agra and Narwar and reached Ujjain. Before this the Marathas had recrossed the Narmadā.[1] Hence he went down to Dost Muhammad Khān's country and camped at Sehore, near Sironj.[2]

---

[1] It may have been according to the orders of the Peshwā; Kanthāji Kadam reports on March 28, 1724, that immediately on receipt of the orders from the Peshwā, he left Kukshi and came over to the southern bank of the Narmadā, where he awaited further orders. S.P.D., XIII, p.2.

[2] Kāmwār, p.263; K.K., II, pp.947-950; M.U., III, p.739; *Burhan.*, p.169a in Irvine, II, pp.134-7.

The Peshwā in the meanwhile had once again decided to invade Northern India (Nov.—Dec. 1723). He sent his generals ahead and followed them later. Leaving Satārā on January 27, 1724, he reached Khāndesh in the beginning of March, and then roamed about in Nemād for two months. On May 8, he crossed the Narmadā at the Akbarpur ferry, and went to Rājā Sabal Singh of Barwāh.[1]

Bāji Rāo's expedition into Mālwa; May, 1724.

The contest for the Deccan *subāhs* now began in full swing. Mubāriz Khān, whom the Nizām had left in the Deccan as his own Deputy, was made by the Emperor, governor of the whole of Deccan. Orders were at the same time sent to all the leading generals including Rājā Shāhu to help the Khān (Feb., 1724).[2] It was probably in reply to this request of the Emperor that Shāhu submitted a draft of his terms for helping Mubāriz; this draft is included in the terms the *farmān* granting the *chauth* and *sardeshmukhi* in Gujrāt and Mālwa to the Marathas.[3] Mubāriz Khān accepted the governorship of the Deccan and began preparations to oppose his rival. The Nizām came to know of these preparations when

The preparations for the final struggle in the Deccan: The Maratha alliance.

---

[1] S.P.D., XXX, pp.268-9; Vād., II, pp.224-225.

[2] Kāmwar, p.267; Wārid, pp.13-14; Khush-hāl, p.1044a in Irvine, II, pp.137-8.

[3] S.P.D., X, p.1.

he was at Sehore, from a report sent by Ināyet Khān (at Aurangābād) and it was confirmed by an intercepted letter to Mubāriz Khān from his agent at Delhi.[1] All pretences were now given up. As the Peshwā was in Nemād, the Nizām decided to meet him and secure his help in the coming struggle. The Peshwā hurried down to Nālchhā from Barwāh *via* Maheshwār and Jahāngirābād (near Māndu). The Nizām also went to Nālchhā and on May 18, 1724, they once again met. The draft treaty with the Emperor, proposed by Rājā Shāhu had not been accepted so far; Bāji Rāo was not willing to let this chance go, and so the Nizām had to win him over to his cause by acceding to his demands.[2]

After the interview the Nizām made all haste for the Deccan and reached Burhānpur late in *Ramzān* (May-June, 1724). He took away with him to the Deccan Yār Muhammad, son of Dost Muhammad Khān, more or less as a hostage lest Dost Muhammad should once again join his enemies.[3] The Peshwā too recrossed the Narmadā on May 22, and started for the Deccan.[4]

---

[1] M.U., III, p.178; K.K., II, pp.949-51; Irvine, II, pp.140-1.

[2] S.P.D., XXX, p.269, 271; Vād., II, pp.224-5.

[3] Malcolm: Report, p.156; Rustam in Elliot, VIII, p.59.

[4] S.P.D., XXX, p.269; Vād., II, p.224.

Immediately after the departure of the Nizām for the Deccan, Azimullāh also left Mālwa for Delhi (June, 1724), leaving that province in charge of his assistants.[1] All eyes were now fixed on the struggle between the Nizām and Mubāriz Khān in the Deccan which ended in the defeat and death of the latter on October 1, 1724. The Emperor found that the Nizām, instead of being destroyed, had become all the more powerful. He took away the province of Mālwa from him, removed Azimullāh and appointed Rājā Girdhar Bahādur its governor. Eight days later the Emperor covered the failure of his own plans by restoring the Nizām to favour once again; he was pardoned; Mālwa, however, was not restored to him.[2]

Girdhar Bahādur appointed governor of Mālwa: June 2, 1725.

SECTION 5.—GIRDHAR BAHADUR'S SECOND GOVERNORSHIP: HIS DEFEAT AND DEATH.

(JUNE 2, 1725—NOV. 29, 1728)

Girdhar Bahādur was appointed to the governorship, and he brought with him his cousin Dayā

[1] Irvine, II, p.170; *Mirat.*, II (34), p.55, 56, 57; Kāmwar.

[2] Irvine, II, pp.152-3, 242; Kāmwar, p.199; K.K., II, p.962, 973; *Ajaib*, No. 174; fol.646.

Bahādur, son of Chhabilerām of Allahabad; both the cousins set out to restore order in the province.

Grants to Udāji Pawār in Mālwa.

The neglect of the affairs of Mālwa after the departure of the Nizām for the Deccan, and the treaty of Nālchhā on May 18, 1724, between the Peshwā and the Nizām, gave the Marathas a golden opportunity to push further into Mālwā. Udāji Pawār's star was already in the ascendant. The Peshwā had granted half of his own dues of *mokāsā* in Mālwa to him on December 3, 1722, and in December, 1723, he further ordered that all the territories, the dues of which had been granted to him, should be passed over to his charge; but this order could not be carried into effect by the Peshwā due to his short stay in Mālwa during the campaign of 1723-24. Hence, in July, 1724, a definite grant was made to Udāji for the year 1724-25, which included the *mokāsā* dues of the Dhār and Jhābuā districts.[1]

Jhābuā affairs: April, 1725.

In April, 1725, and the months following, Ambāji Pant Trimbak Purandare was actively collecting the dues in Mālwa. On April 21, 1725, he came to Jhābuā State from Jhālod (Panch Mahal), encamped at Parnāliā (about 8 miles north-west of

---

[1] *Dharchya Pawār.*, pp.10-12; Malcolm, I, 73-4*f.n.*; S.P.D., XXX, p.273.

Thāndla) and stayed in the State for wellnigh a week. Jai Singh of Sailānā joined Ambāji's forces, hoping to take advantage of the situation. Anup Singh of Jhābuā, who had succeeded his father Khush-hāl Singh in 1725, was called upon by Ambāji to pay Rs. 1,40,000, being the arrears of the dues that were imposed on the State. Anup Singh refused to pay anything, but later agreed to pay Rs. 1 lakh only, which was accepted in full satisfaction of the claim on the mediation of Mahant Mukandji of Sheogarh.[1] Ambāji collected the dues from the districts of Amjherā and Shājahānpur also.[2]

Grants in 1725.

In the months immediately following the appointment of Girdhar Bahādur, the Peshwā was busy with the affairs of the Deccan. Victorious over the opposing forces of Mubāriz Khān, the Nizām

---

[1] *Jhabua Gaz.* (p.4) says that in 1725 Vithoji Rāo Boliā, a *subah* of Holkar entered the Thāndla district and camped at Bordi. This is incorrect. Jhābuā was given to Udāji Pawār in July, 1724 and continued to be with him till 1726. Holkar had not yet become an important figure. The event and other details appear to be correct, the mistake in names is here corrected. S.P.D., XXX, p.272. The account given in *Jhābuā Gaz.* is based on Bule's *Bakhar*, which is mainly traditional.

[2] The grantees of these districts had to pay the cost and other expenses incurred in the expedition by Ambāji Pant. S.P.D., XXX, p.279.

once again began his old game of fomenting divisions among the Maratha ranks and harassing the Peshwā and his forces. Yet the push in Mālwa continued. The footing of the Marathas in Mālwa was becoming stronger. They had established relations with the leading men of the province; Nandlāl Mandloi, of Kampel had begun to carry on his transactions with the Maratha leaders, and had agreed to pay the Maratha dues in the province. The Peshwā went on granting the right to collect the *mokāsā* dues in Mālwa even in 1725. Amjherā was granted to Gojāji Devakāte, an assistant of Chimāji, while Udāji Pawār was continued in his right over Jhābuā and Dhār: Krishnāji Hari, Trimbak Gangādhar, Kesho Mahādev and Jānāji Bhonsle were in charge of Indore (which was with the Peshwā) and other districts of Mālwa. Details of the division of dues were being decided upon. The Peshwā appointed Kesho Mahādev and Kesho Vishwanāth to keep accounts and carry on the work of the collection of his dues and other administrative work in Mālwa and for the various grantees respectively. Their pay too was fixed by him.[1]

The Peshwā first thought of going down to Mālwa himself and of reducing the province and

[1] S.P.D., XXX, pp.272, 273, 275.

establishing his own posts.[1] But he could not go. After the Dasherā celebration in October, 1725, other generals were sent from Punā to collect the dues and to carry out the orders and grants made in July last. Ambāji Pant Purandare went ahead and penetrated as far as Mandsaur by February, 1726. Another force was sent under Santoji Bhonsle, while a third force followed under Kesho Mahādev, a *sardar* of the Peshwā; other generals from Berar were ordered to join Kesho Mahādev. This third force entered Mālwa by the Akbarpur ferry.[2]

Maratha forces in Mālwa, 1725-26.

Dayā Bahādur set himself to reducing the province with all vigour. And when these invading Maratha forces entered Mālwa, he interfered with the collection of their dues. Kesho Mahādev reported the fact to Rājā Shāhu, who wrote to Girdhar Bahādur (about March 4, 1726) not to interfere. Girdhar Bahādur, however, turned a deaf ear to all such requests. Dayā Bahādur pursued them with such rapidity that the Maratha forces had to surrender and come to terms. The internal dissensions among the Maratha generals helped Dayā Bahādur. He kept the Maratha force under Kesho Mahādev and his associates practically under

Dayā Bahādur drives them out of the province: March 1726.

1 S.P.D., XII, p.7.
2 S.P.D., XIII, 5.

surveillance for one month and a half. The Maratha generals could escape from his vigilant watch with great difficulty only after March 7, when they knew that Ambāji Pant was not far off from them. Soon after this, dissensions again broke out among them, and the whole force split into a couple of hostile parties. Some went even as far as Bundi and Kotāh and thence moved towards Sironj and began to plunder the country between Sironj and Alamgirpur, while others returned to the vicinity of Ujjain and began to disturb the country around. But so vigilant and active had the Mughal forces become that the whole expedition failed and the Maratha generals were driven out of Mālwa. They could not collect even a single rupee in spite of all their efforts and wanderings.[1] Ambāji Pant had, however, moved from Mālwa to Gujrāt and he made some collections in the months of May and June, 1727. It was possible only because of the peaceful settlement arrived at by Ambāji Pant with Sarbuland Khān in March, 1726, for allowing the Marathas to collect the *chauth* dues in Gujrāt and the lands of Mālwa situated on the river Māhi.[2]

---

[1] S.P.D., XIII, 6-9; *Ajaib,* No. 180, ff.66b-67a.

[2] On the authority of *Mirat* (II, pp.92-3) Irvine mentions (II, pp.192-3) the settlement with Kanthāji Kadam in October,

This failure did not discourage the Maratha leaders, and soon after the rains they started on their expedition to Mālwa. Shāhu made a settlement with Udāji Pawār for the dues assigned to him in Gujrāt and Mālwa. Sakho Mahādev was sent to Mālwa to look after the accounts, and Rāmchandra Malhār was sent as his clerk. Grants of dues in the lowlands south of Māndu were made, and orders were given to recover from Nandlāl Mandloi the money which he had promised to Ambāji Pant in previous February.[1] Letters were written to Sarbuland Khān, Girdhar Bahādur and the *faujdārs* of Māndu, Sārangpur, Ujjain and Mandsaur to help the cause of Udāji Pawār. But at this time the attention of the Maratha leaders was centred on the affairs of Gujrāt and in the Deccan.

Grants to Udāji Pawār in Mālwa, 1726

The Maratha fortunes in Mālwa reached their lowest ebb between the months of October, 1726 and June, 1727. The dues could not be collected, and Sakho Mahādev (the officer in Mālwa) had to

Girdhar Bahādur's administration in Mālwa.

1726, which was only the confirmation and execution of an earlier settlement with Ambāji Pant Purandare. Vād gives an order (dated April 22, 1726—Ramzān I, A.H. 1138) which mentions this settlement and states the division of the Maratha dues. It mentions the grant in Mālwa too, which probably refers to those areas only which were near the Māhi, Jhābuā, Amjherā, etc. Vād., I, p.105.

[1] *Dharchya Pawara.*, pp. 13-15; S.P.D., XXX, p. 278.

ask for remission of his payments to the Peshwā.[1] Girdhar Bahādur did all he could to strengthen the Mughal administration in the province. He even tried to restore the Mughal control on Rāmpurā. But he was greatly handicapped for want of money. The soldiers clamoured for the arrears of their pay and often revolted against their officers. The *zamindārs* too were oppressing the people and when Girdhar Bahādur tried to restrain their high-handedness, they became hostile to the governor.[2]

During the summer of 1727, Hamid Khān, uncle of the Nizām, known as the 'Jangli Shāhzādā' who had to retire to the Deccan from Gujrāt, tried to secure the aid of the Marathas to conquer the province of Mālwa and thence to recover Gujrāt, but his overture went unheeded.[3] On the occasion of the Dasherā (September 13, 1727) elaborate military preparations were made. The Nizām was completely beaten on the battle-field of Pālkhed in February, 1728 and had to accept the terms dictated by the Peshwā. Thus the Peshwā was temporarily freed for some years from any imminent danger from

[1] S.P.D., XXX, p.281-2.

[2] *Ajaib,* Nos. 175, 176, 180, 181, 204; ff.65a-b, 64b-65a, 67a-b, 81b-82a.

[3] Irvine, II, p.189; S.P.D., X, p.37, pp.31-32.

the side of the Nizām, and was free to think of the conquest of Mālwa.

Early in 1728, the Marathas once again led their forces into Mālwa. The district of Bakāner and the lowlands south of Māndu were taken and the whole country was settled. Their forces could not go northwards, as Dayā Bahādur had marched down to Jhābuā and had been joined by Santāji Bhonsle. The Marathas could, however, collect their dues in the district of Māndu, as the Muslim officer at Māndu gave writs ordering his assistants to pay the *chauth*.[1]

Udāji Pawār and Malhār Holkar get grants in Mālwa. May, 1728.

The effects of the victory of Phālkhed were soon apparent. On May 26, 1728, the Peshwā issued a series of letters calling upon the rulers of various principalities in Mālwa and those on its border, as well as upon the various officials at the headquarters of the different districts, to pay the dues to the persons named by the Peshwā. Udāji Pawār got a big share, while in many cases he shared equally with Malhār Holkār, who rose to prominence in Mālwa for the first time in 1728.[2] Holkar's appointment was evidently intended to check the growing

[1] S.P.D., XIII, 11.

[2] *Dharcha Pawar*, pp.27-38; Malcolm, I, 146-7

importance of Udāji Pawār, whose field of activity was expanding. The Peshwā did not want Udāji to become the sole master of Mālwa, even though it was only as a subordinate to himself.

These continuous Maratha inroads in Mālwa had caused great consternation at the Mughal Court. Jai Singh was summoned to the capital, while arrangements were made to send big armies to Mālwa and Gujrāt. Jai Singh, however, preferred to stay at home and asked Dādo Bhimsen, the Peshwā's agent in the north, (in August 1728) to request his master to send the Maratha armies to Mālwa at an early date, for without such a display of force the Emperor would not yield.[1]

The Emperor concerned about Mālwa.

The Peshwā took up the hint. Early in October, 1728, he arranged a settlement with Santāji Bhonsle for the leadership. Soon after, the Maratha army advanced from the Deccan. Chimāji was put in supreme command, and Udāji Pawār and Malhār Holkar accompanied him. The Maratha army reached the southern bank of the Narmadā on November 24, 1728. The next day they crossed the river and camped near Dharampuri. Thence they marched rapidly northward, crossed the *ghat*

Chimāji Ballāl leads Maratha forces into Mālwa; Nov. 1728.

---

[1] S.P.D., XIII, 10.

near Māndu, and on November 27, halted at Nālchhā.[1]

The battle of Amjherā: defeat and death of Girdhar Bahādur; Nov. 29, 1728.

The Mughal forces were led by Girdhar Bahādur, the governor, and his cousin Dayā Bahādur who seems to have acted as his chief executive officer and military commander.[2] Hearing of the approach of the Maratha armies he prepared to oppose them when they would begin to climb the *ghats*. Girdhar Bahādur believed that the Marathas, thinking the pass near the fort of Māndu to be well-guarded, would ascend the *ghat* near Amjherā, and he marched with his army to the latter place and there took up a strong position.[3] But as the Marathas did not appear on that side, he suspected that they might have climbed up the hills near Māndu, and hence on November 29, 1728, he set out for Dhār.

---

[1] S.P.D., XXX, 55; XXX, p.326, pp.283-284; XXII, p.8.

[2] *Vamsh.* (IV, pp.3125-6) says that Durjan Sāl Hādā of Kotāh was with the forces sent by the Emperor to help Dayā Bahādur. Durjan Sāl did not stay long in Mālwa and returned to Kotāh leaving behind him his own forces to fight against the Marathas.

[3] It is probable that Nandlāl Mandloi might have informed the invading forces of the movements and position of the Imperial army. But even if Nandlāl had desired to oppose the Marathas, he could not have been successful as his forces, horses and foot, numbered 2,000 only. Malcolm, I, pp.82-4, *n.*

He had not moved more than a few miles when he found the Maratha horsemen coming towards him. The agile light troopers of the South did not give the Mughal governor much time to array his forces. Immediately a terrific battle ensued, in which Girdhar Bahādur and Dayā Bahādur were both killed.[1] The disaster was complete. The Mughal forces fled away, leaving everything behind, and their camp was plundered. In addition to guns, standards, kettle-drums and other booty, the Maratha forces captured eighteen elephants.[2]

The news of the victory soon spread throughout northern India and reached the ears of the Peshwā, then marching towards Bundelkhand, much earlier than the official couriers, whom Chimāji had despatched on November 30, could carry it. Messages of congratulations poured upon Chimāji, and Rājā Shāhu too expressed his satisfaction.[3] The

---

[1] S.P.D., XIII, 23, 25, 27, 17; *Ajaib*, No. 182, 201, ff.3a, 69a, 79b. For the discussion of the date and details of the battle of Amjherā, see Appendices I and 2 of this Chapter.

[2] S.P.D., XXX, 59; XIII, 25, 26.

[3] S.P.D., XIII, 15. The unofficial information reached the Peshwā on December 9, 1728. The official couriers reached him only about December 20, 1728. S.P.D., XXX, 278; for Shāhu's satisfaction see XIII, 17; Bāji Rāo, XIII, 23.

effect of this victory was great. The Mughal offensive ended, and the Marathas found Mālwa totally defenceless. The moral effect of this defeat was disastrous and the local princes, *zamindars* and others felt the utter weakness of Mughal rule.

SECTION 6.—GOVERNORSHIP OF BHAWANI RAM: NOVEMBER 29, 1728—NOVEMBER, 1729.

After the death of both Girdhar Bahādur and Dayā Bahādur in the battle of Amjherā (November 29, 1728), Bhawāni Rām, the son of Girdhar Bahādur, naturally assumed the control of the province. The Emperor wrote to Bhawāni Rām expressing his sympathy in his sad bereavement and further requesting him to remain at Ujjain and to defend Mālwa against the invaders. He was created a Rājā with the title of Chimnā Bahādur and was given the *jagirs* of his father. He was further the recipient of a sum of two lakhs of rupees. The Emperor also ordered Saiyyad Najmuddin Ali Khān, the Mahārānā (through Sawāi Jai Singh) Durjan

S.P.D., XIII, 16, 25, 26, 27, 28, 31, 32, 35, 38, 43, all contain messages of congratulations from various other Maratha generals, bankers, officials and private persons.

Sāl Hādā and Muhmmad Umar Khān to march to his aid.[1]

Maratha forces in Mālwa: The siege of Ujjain.

Immediately after the battle of Amjherā, Chimāji Ballāl encamped at Amjherā, and for the following three days allowed rest to his forces. He was also watching the new situation that arose in Mālwa consequent upon the defeat and death of the two cousins. On December 3, Chimāji resumed his march, reaching Ahu (10 miles N.-E. of Amjherā) at the end of the day, and Depālpur three days later. On December 13, 1728, he was in the vicinity of Ujjain, where he halted for four days. But an advance Maratha force, led by Udāji Pawār, probably moved towards Ujjain and besieged it on December 9, 1728. Chimāji, however, joined him at Ujjain only on December 19. Girdhar Bahādur had already enclosed the city with a rampart. Now, on hearing of the advancing Maratha forces, Bhawāni Rām hurriedly recruited fresh troops, collected provisions and prepared to defend Ujjain. After a siege of one (lunar) month and five days

[1] *Ajaib*, Nos. 182, 184, 189, ff.69a, 69b-70a, 71a-b; S.P.D., XIII, 51. The news of the appointment did not reach Mālwa till after the second week of January, 1729. S.P.D., XIII, 30 was evidently written in the last days of January or after.

Bhawāni Rām made a sally on January 13, 1729. In the hand-to-hand fight which ensued both sides lost heavily. But the Marathas had to retreat to Kaliyādah and halted there for two nights. The Emperor was pleased to hear of the success of Bhāwāni Rām and expressed his appreciation and satisfaction by sending presents to him and his brothers, who all had defended Ujjain so bravely.[1]

Exactions from Ujjain and the neighbouring districts.

On December, 12, 1728 Chimāji had received a letter from Bāji Rāo instructing him to settle the affairs of the province and then to go down to collect money. He had further added that a large sum must be exacted from the city of Ujjain, and after confiscating all the lands belonging to Girdhar Bahādur, the dues from the same were to be collected. During the siege of Ujjain, Chimāji arranged to send a portion of his army to the surrounding territories and the dues were collected from Nolāi, Dhār, Ratlām and Badnāwar. The *kotwāl* of Ujjain also paid Rs. 5,000. Chimāji's officers found it difficult to collect their dues even in southern Mālwa. Nandlāl was summoned by Chimāji to settle a few questions regarding the

[1] *Ajaib* is definite about the duration of the siege, *i.e.*, 1 (lunar) month and 5 days. It ended on January 13, 1729. Hence it must have begun on December 9, 1729.

adjustments of accounts and also to instruct him to arrange for the payment of the dues from the various villages. He visited the Maratha camp on January 2, 1729, and later paid a large sum.[1] But no big collections could be made.

The Maratha forces move on to Rājputānā.

Leaving Kaliyādah on January 15, 1729, the Maratha forces marched on to Sārangpur by way of Kāyeth and Shāhjahānpur. At Sārangpur the *faujdār* could not oppose the Maratha hordes, which plundered and devastated the town (January 18, 1729). Thence they moved towards Sironj and Ahirwādā. Najmuddin Ali Saiyyad, who had been sent to help Bhawāni Rām, was at Sironj by this time. Hearing that the Marathas were moving towards the place, the Emperor instructed Bhawāni Rām to go to the help of the Saiyyad, if it was necessary. He was also ordered to make friends with Rājā Durjān Singh of Chanderi and take his help in putting down the Marathas. The Marathas, however, turned towards Bundi and Kotāh, when they learnt that Najmuddin Ali was strongly entrenched at Sironj. On February 5, they were in the territories of Bundi and Kotāh States. For

---

[1] S.P.D., XXX, p.284 (=XXII, 8, 9); Malcolm, I, 72*n.*; *Ajaib*, Nos. 183, 188, 190, 198, 203, 204, 187, ff.3a, 69b, 71a, 71b-73b, 77b, 80b, 81b, 70b.

twelve days they wandered about in the neighbouring country, realized their dues from the Umat Rājā of Rājgarh and encamped at Bhānpurā on February 20, 1729. They were advancing by short marches; on February 23, they passed Rāmpurā, while a week later we find them in Jāwad in the territories of Mewād. During these days Pilāji Jādav's forces were sent to Dhār and Amjherā to keep up the Maratha hold on that area.[1]

Breakdown of Mughul administration in south-western Mālwa.

The breakdown of the Mughal administration of southern Mālwa was complete. The province was assigned by Rājā Shāhu to Bāji Rāo and his brother Chimāji. Other Maratha officers and generals, however, wanted to plunder these lands and collect money. In the middle of February, Siyāji Gujar crossed the Narmadā and plundered the lowlands south of Māndu, and the districts of

---

[1] S.P.D., XXX, pp.284-5 (=XXII, 9); XIII, 30; Rājwāde, VI, 604; *Ajaib*, Nos. 190, 191, 201, 196; ff. 72a, 72b-73b, 79a-b, 75b.

Expecting that a new governor might be appointed and sent to Mālwa with forces to drive the Marathas out, Bāji Rāo had promised to join and help Chimāji, if necessary. But the need did not arise. S.P.D., XIII, 30.

Though Najmuddin Ali neither fought any battle with the Marathas nor helped Bhawāni Rām, he informed the Emperor that he had driven the Marathas from Sironj side, which was all false. *Ajaib*, Nos. 195, 204, ff. 75a-b, 82a.

Maheshwār, Dharampuri, and collected about Rs. 10,000 in all. In April, Rāghoji Kadam Rāo and Sawāi Kat Singh Kadam Rāo attacked southern Mālwa and levied contributions on Dungarpur, Bānswādā and Jhābuā, and on their way they devastated the district of Māndu. Rājā Shāhu took these intruders to task.[1]

Bhawāni Rām's financial difficulties. Immediately after the Marathas had left Ujjain, Bhawāni Rām began to strengthen the defences of Ujjain; but he soon discovered that he did not command sufficient financial means to carry out the design. The salary of the additional forces raised by Girdhar Bāhadur had not yet been paid. The sum of two lakhs paid by the Emperor was insufficient and no additional money was forthcoming. Again, though the Emperor had promised to restore the *jāgirs* of Girdhar Bahādur to Bhawāni Rām, no orders for restoration had yet been issued, and evidently no money could be had from those lands.[2]

Bhawāni Rām and Saiyyad Najmuddin. Reinforcements were also promised, but they too were not forthcoming. Saiyyad Najmuddin Ali Khān had been sent by the Emperor to help Bhawāni Rām, but his arrival only added to his difficulties.

---

[1] S.P.D., XIII, 42; Vād, I, 214; *Ajaib*, No. 185; ff. 70a-b.

[2] *Ajaib*, Nos. 185, 190, 191, 203; ff. 70a, 72a, 73a-b, 80b.

After the Marathas had marched towards Rājputānā, he wrote to announce that he had been appointed governor of Mālwa, and ordered (?) Bhawāni Rām to keep the revenues collected by the latter in trust till he reached Ujjain, to collect some miscellaneous dues and to send them to him. In spite of the repeated orders from the capital not to interfere with the affairs of Bhawāni Rām and to return to his *faujdāri* of Dhāmuni, the Saiyyad went to Kaliyādah and raised all sorts of troubles (April, 1729). Finding persuasion useless, Bhawāni Rām threatened Najmuddin. For one day the men on both sides stood armed and ready for action. Durjan Sāl Hādā and Umar Khān did their best to persuade the Saiyyad and at last left him. Najmuddin now found himself in a maze, and eventually marched away, plundering the *mahals* on the way, taking away cattle and corn and burning what remained. Najmuddin Ali was later ordered to pay for the damage thus caused and to refund the rent and other dues collected by him in Mālwa to Bhawāni Rām. The latter in his turn was ordered to submit his *rāzināma* (document of conciliation) with the Saiyyad. Thus, much time was lost in private quarrels between the Imperial officers and nothing could be done either to strengthen the Imperial authority in the province or to restore the Imperial rule in southern Mālwa.[1]

Troubles of Bhawāni Rām at Ujjain.

The rumours set afloat by Najmuddin Khān of his having superseded Bhawāni Rām made the position of the latter in Mālwa impossible. The *zamindārs* refused to pay revenue to his officials. Though Najmuddin Ali was informed more than once that the governorship of Mālwa and all the *jāgirs* of Girdhar Bahādur had been given to Bhawāni Rām, the official order of appointment and grant was received only on May 19, 1729. But the troubles of Bhawāni Rām with the Saiyyad were also causing reaction against the former at the Court. On May 27, another letter from the Court followed, which informed Bhawāni Rām of the confiscation of his *jāgirs* in the districts of Mandsaur and Todā (?). With the confiscation of these *jāgir* lands Bhawāni Rām found it impossible to pay the soldiers, who were clamouring for the arrears. His soldiers, thinking that Bhawāni Rām would not be able to pay their arrears, mutinied. They were joined by the neighbouring *zamindārs* and lawless people from the city of Ujjain, and the huge mass

[1] *Ajaib,* Nos. 192, 193, 195, 202, 204, 205, 196; ff. 6a-6b, 73b-74a, 74a, 74b-75a, 80a, 81b-82b, 82b-83a, 75b.

of rebels surrounded and attacked Bhawāni Rām, then at Kaliyādah. But he got together the forces still loyal to him, fought and put the rebels to flight.[1]

The Maratha forces had moved on to Rājputānā, but many of the other generals and bands were disturbing southern Mālwa. The Emperor proposed to send Abhaya Singh of Jodhpur against them, but nothing came of that proposals and the Maratha officers encamped in southern Mālwa during the rains of 1729. In collecting their dues these officers did not hesitate to arrest and keep Nandlāl Mandloi interned until he paid some money. Udāji Pawār went on reminding Mandloi to try for the realization of the dues.[2] On September 16, 1729, the grants made to Udāji Pawār and Malhār Holkar in the previous year, were continued.[3]

Bhawāni Rām's dismissal and reinstatement.

The position of Bhawāni Rām was, however, getting weak during the rainy season; he was removed from the office of governorship of Mālwa and his remaining *jāgirs* were also confiscated. But it was not possible to appoint any one else to the

[1] *Ajaib,* Nos. 185, 191, 203, ff. 70a, 73, 80b, 6b-8a.

[2] *Ajaib,* Nos. 193, 203, ff. 74a, 80b; A.M.D., 66, 67, 70. Sardesai gives A.M.D., 67 in his *Madhya,* I, pp.324-5.

[3] S.P.D., XXX, pp.293-4.

governorship just then. The affairs of the province were going from bad to worse. The Marathas were expected immediately after the rains. Najmuddin Ali Khān and Rājā Durjan Singh of Chanderi were oppressing the people. Jai Singh had not yet moved out of his capital, nor was he expected to start for Mālwa before the end of the rains. Hence on the recommendation of Jai Singh, Bhawāni Rām was reinstated in his high office of governorship, given his *jagirs* back and ordered to co-operate with Jai Singh, when the latter went to Mālwa. Jai Singh was ordered to proceed to Mālwa at an early date, and for the maintenance of his cavalry, he was granted the districts of Mandsaur and Todā (?). Jai Singh's general, Zorāwar Singh, stationed at Rāmpurā, sent only 700 horsemen to Ujjain to help Bhawāni Rām.

Marathas in Mālwa : Sept.-Nov. 1729.

The Maratha danger was again becoming menacing. The rains were soon coming to an end. Kanthāji Kadam had invested Khargaon and levied a blackmail of Rs. 50,000. The Maratha forces then crossed the Narmadā at Barwāhā into Mālwa. Malhār Holkar and Udāji Pawār were stationed at Chikaldā and were awaiting the arrival of the Peshwā and other generals. The Peshwā did not come and soon after they plundered and devastated the district of Dharampuri and marched on to Māṇdu. An order had, however, been sent from Delhi to Bhawāni Rām to send provisions, lead and gunpowder to the fort of Dhār, so that it might hold on against the Maratha invaders till Jai Singh arrived in Mālwa.

Bhawāni Rām finally replaced by Jai Singh: Nov., 1729.

Though restored to the high office, Bhawāni Rām was not pleased. He did not get a pie to pay off his debts and the arrears of pay. The *jāgir* too was not fully restored. His money and credit were both exhausted. The horsemen sent by Jai Singh were too few to be of any real help. Moreover, the appointment of Jai Singh to drive the Marathas out of Mālwa did not appear to be a very happy decision. He submitted to the Emperor, "On the arrival of Jai Singh a number of disloyal rājāhs will roam about in the province. The Rājādhirāj (Jai Singh) will not stay here for all the twelve months of the year". Hence, he went on submitting that if he was granted even half of what would be granted to Jai Singh, he could drive the Marathas out of Mālwa. He further requested that Mahārāo Durjan Sāl of Kotāh and Rāja Durjan Singh of Chanderi might be sent to Mālwa to help him in his campaign against the invaders from the Deccan.

In response to all these requests Bhawāni Rām was first of all informed that Rāo Ramchandra of Datiyā and Rājā Udāwat Singh had been ordered to go to his help, and as Rājā Jai Singh too had started for Mālwa, he (Bhawāni Rām) was asked to make a bold stand till Jai Singh reached Mālwa. Finally, he received a letter from the Amir-ul-Umrā intimating that the confiscation of the two districts could not be undone. He was further informed that as the Marathas wished to plunder Hindustan and to take possession of Patna and Allahabad, it was thought desirable to appoint 'the best of the Rājās' (Rājā Jai Singh) to the governorship of Mālwa. It was expected of Bhawāni Rām that he would obey and accompany Jai Singh as long as he stayed in Mālwa.[1] Thus ended the short but the most eventful governorship of Bhawāni Rām in Mālwa.

---

[1] *Ajaib*, Nos. 196, 199, 200, 197; ff. 75b-76b, 77b-78a, 78a-79a, 76b-77b; S.P.D., XXII, 31.

It appears that as Bhawāni Rām was not willing to serve as a deputy of Jai Singh. He left the province immediately on hearing of his supersession.

SECTION 7.—SECOND GOVERNORSHIP OF JAI SINGH

(NOV. 1729—SEPT. 19, 1730)

At the end of November 1729, Sawāi Jai Singh of Amber became the governor of Mālwa for the second time.[1] He had been trying all these years to further the interests of the Marathas and thus to gain the governorship of Mālwa for himself and extend his own control and influence upto the Narmadā. Now he was ordered by the Emperor to go down to Mālwa to drive the Marathas out and to open negotiations with Rājā Shāhu for a peaceful settlement. The Emperor paid Jai Singh

Jai Singh and the Marathas.

[1] According to Sir Jadunath Sarkar he was sent there this time not to act as governor, but "to drive the Marathas out with his own forces." (Sarkar, I, p.246. n.).

But a letter from the Amir-ul-Umrā to Bhawāni Rām definitely informs the latter—"The best of the Rājās (Jai Singh) has been appointed; you should obey and accompany him as long as he stays there (in Mālwa)." *Ajaib*, No. 197, f. 77a.

S.P.D., X, 66 also throws some light on the question. The Nizām told Dip Singh not to interfere with the affairs of Bhawāni Rām.

This statement shows that Mālwa was in charge of Jai Singh at this time.

Rs. 13 lakhs to equip an army, which would not be friendly to the Marathas.[1]

Jai Singh left his capital on October 23, 1729. When he was still on his way to Ujjain, the Marathas had entered Mālwa. On October 17, 1729, Rājā Shāhu had assigned the dues of Mālwa to Bāji Rāo. Udāji Pawār, had once again been granted the dues of many districts there, and Holkar shared them with him in some. Both of them led the invading forces and sometimes during the last week of November, 1729, they captured the fort of Māndu and appointed Desoji Bāgh as its *qiledār*.[2]

The Marathas take Māndu: Nov., 1729.

When Jai Singh was encamped at Bārod on the Kāli Sind, he was joined by the various princes of Mālwa. On reaching Ujjain, when he heard that Māndu had been taken by the Marathas, he hastened to that place. A skirmish was fought between the Maratha forces and the troops led by Jai Singh. But peace was made, and Māndu was handed back to the Mughal forces. The Marathas were at Nolāi on January 18, 1730, whence they retreated to the Deccan.[3]

Māndu given back to Jai Singh.

---

[1] *Vamsh*, IV, 3133-4; S.P.D., X, 66.

[2] Pārasnis, p.127; S.P.D., XXII, p.31 (=XXX, p.297), XXX, p.293; Rājwāde, VI, p.600.

[3] According to *Vamsh* (IV. pp.3187-9), Jai Singh entered

Jai Singh was personally more concerned with the affairs of Bundi, especially because the opportunity of turning it into a vassal State had at last arrived. Immediately after taking Māndu, he returned to Ujjain and thence started for his capital.[1] On this journey he crowned Dalel Singh Hādā as the Rāo Rājā of Bundi (May 19, 1730). The affairs of Mālwa were left to his deputy, and were naturally neglected by him specially as peace negotiations were opened with the Marathas.[2]

Jai Singh returns to Jaipur.

The Emperor had asked Jai Singh to bring about a peace with the Marathas and to see that no Maratha invaders crossed the Narmadā. The

---

Māndu long before the Marathas came to Mālwa. The Marathas besieged the fort, but Jai Singh made friends with them and gave Māndu to them. This, however, does not seem to be correct. According to Marāthi sources, the fort was taken by the Marathas late in November, or early in December, 1729. It appears impossible that Jai Singh, starting from Jaipur on October 23, should reach Māndu within a month.

A.M.D., 78.

The formal order for the transfer of Māndu to Jai Singh was given by Rājā Shāhu only on March 18, 1730.

[1] From a letter of the Nizām to the Bangash we learn that Jai Singh drove Udāji Pawār out of the fort of Chikaldā at this time, but Udāji regained it soon after. *Khajista*, ff. 336-7.

[2] *Vamsh*, IV, 3192-3231.

Peace negotiations with Rājā Shāhu.

Peshwā, on the other hand, was also anxious to continue his hold on the province. He wanted that the dual control of the Mughals and the Marathas might go on side by side, and the subjects might be allowed to enjoy peace. The Peshwā wrote letters to Jai Singh with the same object (October, 1729) and also ordered Kusāji Ganesh to go to Ujjain (January, 1730). On March 18, 1730, Rājā Shāhu informed Chimāji Ballāl, Udāji Pawār and Malhār Holkar that "Jai Singh has come to the Ujjain province. You should treat him with respect, in view of the old hereditary friendship between the two Royal families. Give him the Māndu fort if he asks for it." He thus set his seal of approval on the transfer of Māndu, which had already been made (in January, 1730).[1]

Jai Singh also sent Dip Singh as his ambassador to Rājā Shāhu. The envoy promised the Marathas a subsidy of Rs. 11 lakhs a year for Mālwa, but before this agreement could be ratified, Jai Singh was replaced by Muhammad Bangash as governor of Mālwa (September 19, 1730). The Rājā had already returned to Jaipur and now lost all his

[1] S.P.D., XXX. pp.300-1; Vād, I. 198; Rājwade, VI, 599 (A.M.D., 72 is same as this but the date as given there is October 1, 1729); A.M.D., 7.

interest in Mālwa. Before long the Peshwā called upon Malhār to go to Mālwa again.[1]

With the appointment of the Bangash all possibilities of any peaceful settlement with the Marathas ended, and the struggle was renewed in which the Mughal forces were badly beaten and all hopes for the continuance of Mughal control over Mālwa vanished.

SECTION 8.—OTHER INTERNAL AFFAIRS OF MALWA DURING THE PERIOD: (1719—1730)

During this period public attention was mostly centred on the struggle between the Marathas and the Mughals. But many other forces also were active, and they had their own influence on the political history of the province.

First, the efforts of Jai Singh for domination over Bundi continued and in 1730, he succeeded in putting his nominee on its throne. He thus fulfilled his great ambition to turn Bundi into a vassal State. Jai Singh's engrossment in Bundi affairs was mainly responsible for his neglect of the administration of Mālwa during his second governorship. Vigilance

Bundi affairs.

[1] S.P.D., X, 66; XXX, p.300.

and active policy on his part might have greatly influenced the coming events.

Rāmpurā affairs.

Secondly, the affairs of Rāmpurā were still unsettled. Sangrām Singh, a grandson of Gopāl Singh Chandrāwat, who still held a portion of the district of Rāmpurā as a feudatory of the Mahārānā of Udaipur, had grown very turbulent. Girdhar Bahādur's efforts to restore Mughal control over Rāmpurā ended with him.[1] In December, 1728, a son was born to Jai Singh of the princess of Udaipur. Jai Singh grew anxious, as the newcomer was to be the cause of much trouble to his State. According to the triple treaty of 1708, the new-born prince, Mādho Singh, was to be the master of Jaipur State on the death of Jai Singh, while there were two elder sons of Jai Singh, Shiv Singh and Ishwari Singh, who would certainly claim by the right of priority of birth. To avoid future trouble, and at the request of Jai Singh, the Mahārānā assigned the district of Rāmpurā to the infant prince Mādho Singh (March 26, 1729), Jai Singh standing surety for his son that the latter would remain a loyal feudatory of Mewād like the other 16 nobles. Jai Singh, however, took up the control and manage-

[1] *Ajaib*, No. 175; ff. 64b-65a.

ment of the district, which practically meant the loss of the district to Mewād except in name.[1]

In the meanwhile some misunderstanding between Sangrām Singh of Rāmpurā and Durjan Sāl of Kotāh resulted in the latter plundering Rāmpurā. Soon after, Rāmpurā was occupied by the officers of Jai Singh, and Sangrām Singh went to Delhi to ask for the grant of Rāmpurā in his own name. At this time the Emperor dared not irritate Jai Singh, and therefore Sangrām Singh failed to achieve anything. On his way back to Mālwa, he was killed. His descendants continued to hold a few villages near Rāmpurā.[2]

---

[1] Authorities differ as to the date of Mādho Singh's birth. Ojha puts it in 1727, apparantly on no definite authority. *Vir Vinod* dates it as December 17, 1728 (II, 973), while *Vamsh.* (IV, p.3121) gives it as December 19, 1728. Of these three the one given by *Vir Vinod* should be relied upon.

Vamsh says that the district was given to Jai Singh (IV, 3108-3110). *Vir Vinod* states that it was given to Mādho Singh. The deed of grant and the bond of service signed by Jai Singh are printed in *Vir Vinod*. Hence, the statement in *Vamsh.* must be rejected. *Vir Vinod*, II, 973-7.

[2] *Vir Vinod*, II, 990. But *Vamsh.* (IV, 3116-20) states that Sangrām Singh got a deed of grant, which appears improbable. It also alleges that Jai Singh arranged to get Sangrām Singh killed.

While disturbances were rampant on the north-western frontier of Mālwa, its south-western corner too was not free from them. The States of Jhābuā and Amjherā were the scenes of various disorders. In Amjherā Jairup was the ruler of the State, but his more ambitious younger brother Jagrup was desirous of becoming its master. The latter's efforts were foiled in 1719 by the intervention of the Nizām, but his ambition did not leave him and the civil war continued in the State.[1] The Marathas naturally took advantage of this war and imposed their tribute.

Affairs in south-western Mālwa: Amjherā.

In Jhābuā, Raja Khush-hal Singh was greatly harassed by Jai Singh of Sailānā. The Maratha forces invaded Jhābuā early in 1724, but as the Peshwā was then returning to the Deccan, Kanthāji Kadam had to leave Jhābuā. Soon after this, Khush-hal Singh died and his turbulent son succeeded to the throne. In 1725, Ambāji Trimbak came to Jhābuā and encamped at Parnuliā. He was joined by Jai Singh of Sailānā, who hoped

Jhābuā.

---

[1] K. K., II, 849-50. A.M.D., 40, the letter dated August 8, 1725, mentions a skirmish having taken place between the two rival forces in which ten men from Jagrup's side were killed, while the other side lost thirteen men.

to profit by the situation. Anup Singh paid 1 lakh in cash and it was accepted by Ambāji. Mahant Mukundgir of Sheogarh helped the State in negotiating this settlement. Jai Singh did not gain anything this time and he arranged to get Anup Singh murdered, which was done in 1727. Jai Singh also occupied the district of Thāndlā, but it was recovered from him by Thākur Ratan Singh of Bori. A posthumous son was born to Anup Singh six months after his death, and the affairs of the State were managed by the mother of the infant Rājā in consultation with the nobles. The Marathas took advantage of this situation and by helping the State against Jai Singh of Sailānā, they established their control over it, which could not be removed for the following forty years and more.[1] Through Jhābuā lay the shortest route to Gujrāt and Bānswādā.

The weakening of the States of Amjherā and Jhābuā, and the pro-Maratha tendency of Mohan Singh of Barwāni, practically lost that portion of Mālwa to the Empire, and with the defeat and

---

[1] *Jhabua State Gaz.*, pp.314 are based mainly on 'Bule's *Bakhar*'. The details have been corrected from the Marāthi material. See Section 5 *ante*.

death of Girdhar Bahādur in November, 1728, these States became the strongholds of the Marathas.

Other States: Condition of the people of Mālwa.

The affairs of the other States went on uninterrupted and the course of events at these courts was uneventful. The condition of the people and the land went from bad to worse, and the revenues which were estimated at 90 lakhs in 1720, fell to 40 lakhs in 1724-5. The Nizām started for the Deccan in 1724, leaving behind him an empty treasury and a poor people. The Marathas invasions and the exactions by Girdhar Bahādur completed the ruin of Mālwa and its people.[1]

SECTION 9.—THE REAL CAUSE OF THE MARATHA INVASIONS ON MALWA.

The various reasons assigned by various writers.

Various reasons have been assigned for the invasions of Mālwa by the Marathas and for the wonderful success they met with in that province. Writers from the Marāthi-speaking country generally say that the ideal of the Peshwā was to establish *Hindu-pad-Pādshāhi* (Hindu paramountcy over the whole of India). According to Sir John Malcolm too, it was a kind of holy war against the Empire, which appeared to be the embodiment of the anti-

[1] Chahār, 79b in *India of Aurangzib;* S.P.D., X, 66.

Hindu policy and spirit of Aurangzib. He explains the easy success of the Marathas in Mālwa thus :

"Thus invited by weakness and provoked by injury, we are not surprised to find that the Rajput princes and chiefs of Jeypoor, Marwar, Mewar, and Malwa, so far from continuing to be that defence they had before proved themselves of the Empire, were either secretly or openly the supporters of the Maratha invaders, to whose first invasion of Malwa, we are told by every Persian or Hindu writer that notices the subject, hardly any opposition was given; and we possess many testimonies to show that they chiefly attributed their success on this occasion to the action of religious feeling." [1]

A close study of history and the fresh light thrown on the affairs of Mālwa by the vast mass of contemporary records in Marāthi, recently made available to the public, do not support these old theories.

During the period 1698-1707, the Marathas were fighting against Aurangzib for their existence, and they first thought of invading Mālwa just to divert the attention of that Emperor. But the idea of raiding a rich province like Mālwa continued to

---

[1] Malcolm, I, pp.53-4,67.

attract the imagination of the Maratha statesmen even when the pressure of Aurangzib had ceased. The newly invigorated Maratha power which, thanks to the genius of the first Peshwā, was bubbling with energy, wanted fresh fields for expansion. By the year 1719, they had gained their right to levy dues on all lands south of the Narmadā. The invasion of Mālwa was the next logical step; and when a new Peshwā, who had not only seen the weakness of the Empire with his own eyes but was full of ambitious schemes, came to control the destiny of the Maratha State, an expansion of the field of activity was but natural, and the province of Mālwa had to meet the new rushing tide.

The desire for expansion.

There was a primary cause of the invasions on Mālwa. The Peshwā was deep in debt and he wanted money to pay it off. It was not possible for him to realize huge sums at home or in the Deccan, Because the Nizām would not easily allow further encroachments on his own territories. Thus, the provinces of the Mughal Empire appeared to be the only places whence money could be forthcoming. Gujrāt and Mālwa were nearest to the Deccan, but the former had been dominated by the Maratha general, Dābhāde, which left Mālwa alone to the Peshwā.

The economic cause for invading Mālwa.

The early inroads of 1723-26 had given the Maratha generals, working under the Peshwā, some footing in Mālwa and some dues were collected everytime the Maratha armies went to the province. But Girdhar Bahādur, the governor (1725-28), and his cousin Dayā Bahādur interfered with the realization of these dues. In March, 1726, Rājā Shāhu wrote to Girdhar Bahādur requesting him not to interfere with the collection, but with no result. The Maratha forces sent to Mālwa during the campaigning season 1725-26 were driven out of Mālwa. But as the Peshwā and the main Maratha forces were then busy opposing the Nizām, nothing could be done at that time.[1] Peace with the Nizām was made in February, 1728, and hence when the invasion of Mālwa was undertaken in the cold weather of 1728-29, the main idea of the Peshwā and his brother was to collect huge sums of money. Therefore, the main cause of the invasion was economic. The letters of Bāji Rāo, Chimāji and other Maratha officers written during the campaign amply prove this point.

At the end of October, 1728, Bāji Rāo was anxious to pay off the debts incurred by Rājā Shāhu

[1] S.P.D., XIII, 5,9, XXX, pp.280-1.

Clearing of the debts the main question: Money required very badly.

in the late struggle with the Nizām. Bāji Rāo and Chimāji planned to realize the *ghās-dānā* dues very strictly.[1] Chimāji having left Punā ahead of him, the Peshwā clearly states the chief aim of the expedition thus, "the sum and substance of the whole thing is to follow a policy by which debts may end and permanent arrangements be made for the future." He advised Chimāji to keep this fact in view and to send money at an early date.[2]

Bāji Rāo's instructions to his brother during the campaign in Mālwa, 1728-29.

Immediately after Bāji Rāo had heard of the victory of Chimāji over Girdhar Bahādur, he ordered his brother to make heavy exactions from the city of Ujjain, and after settling the affairs of the province, immediately to hasten to a rich country to collect money and thus to refurnish the army. Lastly, he added that a policy which would result in the defeat of the enemy and the clearing of the debts should be followed.[3] The need for money was greatest at Satārā, and in reply to his despatch of victory, Chimāji was asked to give details of the monetary gains in the battle.[4]

---

[1] S.P.D., XIII, 13.
[2] S.P.D., XIII, 14.
[3] S.P.D., XIII, 15.
[4] S.P.D., XIII, 17.

Later, as the details of the victory and further movements of the Maratha army reached the Peshwā, he instructed Chimāji to immediately send money to the Deccan through a banker at Aurangābād.[1] He ordered that the sums due from Nandlāl Mandloi in connection with expedition of Ambāji Pant in the year 1725-26, be exacted.[2] He further asked Chimāji to confiscate all the *jāgir* lands belonging to Girdhar Bahādur and then to exact their dues from the same.[3] The one all-absorbing thought with Bāji Rāo was the clearing of the debts and he definitely wrote to his brother, 'Go roaming about wherever you like, but bring money somehow or other.'[4]

Soon, however, it became evident that no large sum would be forthcoming from Mālwa, and also that the local people, hoping that help would be forthcoming from Delhi, were preparing to offer resistance. Bāji Rāo, therefore, asked his brother not to create trouble in Mālwa for money, but to go

---

1 S.P.D., XIII, 18, 19.

2 S.P.D., XIII, 20, 21.

3 S.P.D., XIII, 22, 23.

4 S.P.D., XIII, 29. In letter No. 33 (Vol. XIII) to Chimāji Bāji Rāo again repeats the same urgent demand for money.

to some other province whence money would be more easily had. For the lands, which had been conquered, he advised Chimāji to let the former peasants and landlords continue if they promised to pay the revenue. Lastly, he added, 'Be very cautious; execute such plans as will yield money. Use discretion and be alert, without considering your personal ease and comfort.'[1]

Chimāji himself was involved in debt and the news of his victory only made his creditors press him to pay off their loans.[2]

The Peshwā not keep on bringing Mālwa under his control if the Maratha dues would be regularly paid.

Even after this successful invasion of Chimāji, the Peshwā did not appear very keen on having full control over the province, if he could be assured of the smooth payment of the Maratha dues.[3] The Maratha statesmen hoped to get their subsidy regularly from Rājā Jai Singh, and therefore Rājā Shāhu ordered the surrender of the Māndu fort to Rājā Jai Singh. In 1730, when by the order of the Emperor Jai Singh opened peace negotiations, Rājā Shāhu promised not to allow his generals and army to cross the Narmadā if Rs. 10 lakhs in cash

---

[1] S.P.D., XIII, 30.
[2] S.P.D., XIII, 25.
[3] Rājwāde, VI, 599.

were regularly paid to him.[1] Such a policy could not be consistent with the idea of establishing *Hindu-pad-Pādshāhi,* nor could it be expected of men leading a holy war against the Muslim Empire.

The causes of the great success of Chimāji in Mālwa during 1728-9.

The success of the Maratha forces in Mālwa was in no way due to reasons of religious affinity. The completeness of the Maratha victory at Amjherā was rather unexpected and more or less accidental. To assign the success of Chimāji to any help from the local chieftains and landlords would be going against historical evidence. The Maratha forces were too strong to be checked by Nandlāl Mandloi with his 2,000 wretched militia horsemen, even if he had wished to oppose them. On the other hand, a letter from the Peshwā clearly shows that the local chieftains and landlords did not readily submit to the Maratha invaders, nor did they easily agree to pay their contributions.[2]

It is probable that the relations between the Imperial governor of Mālwa and the land-holders and the grantees of the province were not very cordial, but this, again, was not due to any religious animosity. A full generation had grown up since

[1] Vād, I, 198; S.P.D., X, 66.
[2] S.P.D., XIII, 30.

the death of Aurangzib. With its first abolition in 1713, the *Jaziyā* had practically ended; all attempts at renewing it later were fruitless and foredoomed to failure. By 1728, the *Jaziyā* had been finally abolished and no hope of its renewal existed. The governor of Mālwa was also a staunch Hindu and his lieutenant, Dayā Bahādur, was also one of those, who had tried their utmost to get the *Jaziyā* abolished with success. Under such circumstances there was no inducement to the people of Mālwa to welcome the Marathas on religious grounds.

Why Jai Singh favoured the Marathas?

The policy of Jai Singh to favour the Maratha cause was also not dictated by any religious motive, but mainly by self-interest and love of personal gain. He wanted to become the governor of Mālwa and thus extend his dominion from the Jamunā to the Narmadā. He hoped that he could keep the Marathas out of the province by paying them their dues regularly and thus he would perpetuate his hold on the province. But he could hope to become the governor of Mālwa only if the Marathas made the position of every other governor untenable there.

With this aim in view he helped the Marathas, and advised the Hindu princes of Mālwa not to oppose the invaders from the South. Forced by circumstances, Girdhar Bahādur had to be very regular in exacting the State dues; thus alone could he hope to get the necessary money. The princes of Mālwa thus grudged the heavy burden of taxes and they hoped that the Marathas would not be so exacting. Thus, for economic reasons they became favourably inclined towards the Marathas. They, however, went on to join the Marathas openly only after December, 1730 and not before that year.

Dissatisfaction in Mālwa due to economic pressure.

APPENDIX 1.

THE LETTERS OF THE MANDLOI DAFTAR.

During recent years much controversy has raged over the authenticity of certain letters in the Mandloi *Daftar*. Nandlāl was the *Mandloi* (or *Qānungo*) of the district of Kampel near Indore from 1694 to 1731. Though not a very prominent man, his monetary transactions with and leanings towards the Marathas had given him great importance in the history of the Maratha conquest of Mālwa. This importance has been admitted without question from the account given by Sir John Malcolm in his *Memoir*, which is mainly based on a statement supplied by a descendant of Nandlāl (Malcolm, 1, pp.82-5*n.*). Much of the account is exaggerated and has given an added importance to the Mandloi family, which is not supported by the Marāthi papers from the *Daftar* of the Peshwā.

Nandlāl Mandloi and the Marathas.

Practically all the important and genuine papers in the Mandloi *Daftar* have been printed by Rājwāde at the end of his sixth volume. (The dates of many of these need correction). These letters do not contain anything startling. Sardesai, however, published seven Hindi letters in the *Madhya Bhag*, Vol. I, of his *Marāthi Riyāsat* (pp. 325-329). He received these from Mr. Bhaskar Ramchandra Bhalerao of Gwalior. They were said to be copies of letters printed in a pamphlet by Mandloi, which in their turn were said to have been copied from originals in the Mandloi *Daftar*. These letters contained many startling facts, *e.g.*, defeat and death of Girdhar Bahādur in 1724. Sardesai based his historical account on these letters. Later, on the authority of Sardesai, Sir Jadunath Sarkar used these letters while editing Irvines *Later Mughals*, Vol. II, though he did not accept many of the dates as given in these Hindi letters.

Seven Hindi letters published by Sardesai.

Since the publication of these letters in the work of Sardesai, a controversy had been raging over their authenticity. Mr. S. V. Athalye of Shiposhi had examined the whole *Daftar* some thirty years back, long before this controversy was raised; he also took copies of all the important letters. Even at the outset he had warned Sardesai that these letters were unauthenticated and no originals of these ever existed in the Mandloi *Daftar*. Now, the descendant of Nandlāl Mandloi (Rāo Chhatrakaran) also disowned these letters in 1927. (*Madhya*, I, pp.321-2; *B.I.S.M.Q.*, IX, 1, pp.40-44).

No originals of these letters ever existed in Mandloi *Daftar*.

These letters should be rejected.

These seven Hindi letters have to be rejected by the critical historian. The internal evidence unmistakably points out that they are not genuine. The course and cause of events as given in them are not supported by the vast mass of contemporary State papers recently published. Their language also looks quite modern. The high-flown epithets and titles applied to Nandlāl also arouse suspicion, as being far above the due of a mere *qānungo* of Mughal times. So, I have come to the conclusion that these seven letters in Hindi are merely later fabrication (most probably during the last quarter of the 19th century) to establish the historical importance of the family and thus to prop up its a claim to high honour.

After the rejection of these letters, the Mandloi *Daftar*, ceases to throw much light on the history of Mālwa. Save a few letters all the papers here are merely receipts for payments made by the Mandloi.

APPENDIX 2.

THE QUESTION OF THE DATES OF THE DEFEAT AND DEATH OF GIRDHAR BAHADUR AND DAYA BAHADUR.

Historians have so far believed that the two cousins, Girdhar Bahādur and Dayā Bahādur, were killed in two different battles. *Siyār-ul-Mutākherin* and similar works gave currency to this belief, and Sir John Malcolm confirmed it by making statements in support of it, which were mainly based on traditional accounts. This belief has taken root.

Historians believe that they were killed in two different battles.

Prior to the publication of the *Selections from the Peshwā's Daftar*, the interval between these two battles was supposed to have been one of two years. The records published in Vol. XIII of this series prove that Dayā Bahādur was also killed in 1728, and the latest historians have reduced the interval between the two battles to 4 days or at the most a week. But Sir Jadunath Sarkar rightly did not accept this as the final solution of the long-drawn controversy.

We shall here examine all the original contemporary authorities on the point. After reject-

The original authorities on the question.

ing the seven famous but forged Hindi letters of the Mandloi *Daftar*, the contemporary authorities which deserve attention are only two.

1. *Ajaib-ul-Afāq*, the letter-book of Girdhār Bahādur and his family (Br. Museum. MS. Or. 1776), and

2. *Selections from the Peshwā's Daftar*, Vols. XIII, XXII and XXX.

Of these the former does not mention anything about Dayā Bahādur;[1] it throws no light, therefore, on the question of the battle with him, nor does it give any details of the battle in which Girdhar Bahādur was killed. The few letters which simply mention the fact of Girdhar Bahādur's defeat and death (Nos. 182, 186, ff. 3a, 69a, 70b) are not dated. Therefore *Ajaib-ul-Afāq* is not very helpful to us. This leaves the volumes of the *Selections from the Peshwā's Daftar* as the only contemporary

[1] In letter No. 204 (ff. 82a) of *Ajaib* there is a reference to the uncle of Bhawāni Rām, wherein Turebaz Khān writes to Najmuddin Ali; "The Emperor knows about the honesty and fidelity of his (Bhawāni Rām's) uncle and that of his father, Rājā Girdhar Bahādur. The Rājā gave up his life in doing his duty." It can be guessed that Dayā Bahādur is the person referred to as Bhawāni Rām's uncle. But the writer does not add anything further than the above-quoted remark.

authority, on the basis of which the question can be settled.

The battle with Girdhar Bahādur was fought near Amjherā. Chimāji sent the despatch of his victory over Girdhar Bahādur to the Peshwā from Amjherā on November 30, 1728. (It was acknowledged by the Peshwā in his letter dated December 27, 1728, Vol. XIII, 23). The itinerary of Chimāji shows that the Marathas first encamped at Amjherā on November 29, 1728. Letters Nos. 15 and 23 (Vol. XIII) give details of the battle with Girdhar Bahādur. He, according to the Marāthi report, had taken post with his army at Amjherā, evidently wishing to block the pass leading due south of Amjherā, by the Ambikā Devi caves to Manāwar, Bakāner and the Narmadā, by which he expected the Marathas to come, as the alternative route by the Māndu fort was more circuitous and exposed to attack from that famous fort. But suspecting that the invaders might have followed this undefended alternative route, and were coming to cut off his rear, he in alarm (*wahami* in Marāthi) faced round, *i.e.*, north-eastwards, and descended to the plain between Amjherā and Tirlā, where he met the Marathas, just arrived. A severe battle immediately followed, and in it Girdhar

Defeat and death of Girdhar Bahādur in the battle of Amjherā, Nov. 29, 1728.

Bahādur with many of his leading officers was killed. His army and camp were plundered and a vast amount of booty fell into the hands of the Marathas. These letters do not name the exact site of the battle. It is, however, certain that it was fought near Amjherā on November 29, 1728. We know from the Maratha records that Chimāji was near Dharampuri on the north bank of the Narmadā on November 25, at Nālchhā on the 27th and on the 29th encamped at Amjherā, where he halted for four days and then set off northwards to Ujjain. He reports his victory in a letter dated November 30 from Amjherā. The language of Chimāji's despatch shows that the battle was a sudden collision, and continued for a long time; therefore it took place on the 29th immediately on the arrival of the Maratha horse at the place; after six hours' fierce fighting and the plundering of the Mughal camp, the victors pitched their camp at Amjherā only when they were free from all alarm.

Description of the battle in which Dayā Bahādur was defeated and killed.

The course of the supposed second battle in which Dayā Bahādur was killed can thus be summarized from the details given in letters Nos. 17, 26 and 27 (Vol. XIII). It is stated therein that Dayā Bahādur took up his position at Amjherā and lay guarding the pass near that place. The

Marathas, however, climbed the *ghat* of Māndu and hastened towards Dayā Bahādur, who suspecting (the very word *wahami* is repeated here) that the Marathas might be coming that way, left Amjherā and moved towards Dhār. When the two opposing armies came into contact, a severe battle ensued and continued for six hours. Dayā Bahādur and two of his leading officers were killed. His camp was plundered and a vast amount of booty fell into the hands of the Marathas, which included 18 elephants, many horses, various banners and kettle-drums.

These details establish two facts so far as this second battle is concerned, namely,—

1. Dayā Bahādur was stationed at Amjherā and the Marathas were coming from the Deccan.

2. The battle was fought somewhere between Amjherā and Dhār.

On consulting the itinerary of Chimāji we find that during this campaign, the Marathas climbed the *ghat* of Māndu only once and that was on November 27, 1728. The route as given in his itinerary is the same as indicated in the letters reporting the battle with Dayā Bahādur. Thus, the routes followed by the Marathas in their attack upon Girdhar Bahādur tallies with the route followed by them when going against Dayā Bahādur. But it is impossible to assign any other year than 1728 to these letters referring to the battle with Dayā Bahādur. Hence the only solution of the question is to hold that one, and only one, battle was fought. It is thus proved beyond doubt that Girdhar Bahādur was killed in the battle of Amjherā on November 29, 1728, and Dayā Bahādur also was killed in the same battle. The evidence in support of this conclusion is overwhelming.

Only one battle was fought at Amjherā, and both the cousins were killed in it; November 29, 1728.

No second battle could have been fought at Amjherā within a week of the first, because immediately after the defeat and death of Girdhar Bahādur and the utter route of his army the Marathas encamped at Amjherā, which would not have been possible if Dayā Bahādur had remained unbeaten in the same place. Moreover, the Marāthi letters are definite on the point that Dayā Bahādur did not know about the approach of the Marathas, and that he made a move from Amjherā towards Dhār on the mere suspicion that the invaders might turn his eastern flank. It is incredible that if Dayā Bahādur had survived Girdhar Bahādur by even a few days, he should have known nothing of the battle fought between Girdhar Bahādur and the Marathas, even when the latter had come and encamped in that very vicinity after their victory.

There is some negative evidence as well, which refutes the theory of a second battle having been fought. The news of the defeat of Dayā Bahādur reached the Peshwā on December 20, 1728 (XXX, p.278), and yet in his letter dated the 27th of that month (XIII, 23) he refers to the battle with Girdhar Bahādur and adds: "After defeating Girdhar Bahādur, you (Chimāji) moved towards Ujjain." If a second battle with Dayā Bahādur had been fought and won, the Peshwā would surely have referred to it, at least in his letter of January 4, 1729 (XIII, 29), where, too, he merely refers to the victory of Chimāji over Girdhar Bahādur. The reason for the Peshwā's omission of the name of Dayā Bahādur is that to him the death of Girdhar Bahādur was the only significant fact. The governor of the province was defeated and killed, and that was sufficient. To him the death of Dayā Bahādur (the governor's lieutenant) was only one of the various incidents in a great battle and he (I believe) referred to it by saying that several of his (Girdhar Bahādur's) generals were also killed. The close similarity between the accounts of the relative position of the two armies, the movements of the two cousins, and lastly the results, is noticeable.

Thus, all these facts go to prove conclusively that only one battle was fought near Amjherā on November 29, 1728, and in this battle both the cousins, Girdhar Bahādur, the governor, and Dayā Bahādur, the chief commander of his army, were killed. The battle was fought near Amjherā, in the plains between Amjherā and Tirlā, because the Maratha light horse was strung out in wide formation and not concentrated at Tirlā itself.

Why do many letters refer to the defeat and death of Dayā Bahādur alone and do not mention Girdhar Bahādur?

One question alone remains to be answered. How is it that the letters of congratulation from Satārā and the different Maratha generals do not contain any reference to Girdhar Bahādur and mention the death of Dayā Bahādur only? To the public at large and to the Maratha generals Dayā Bahādur was much better known than Girdhar Bahādur. Dayā Bahādur had shown great activity in pushing the Marathas out of Mālwa during the winter of 1725-26, and as long as he lived he did not allow them to collect the dues (XIII, 9, 11). Thus, they were pleased to know that their arch-enemy was killed. Their ignorance of the real office of Dayā Bahādur in Mālwa was so great that in one letter (XIII, 25) he is referred to as the governor of Ujjain. They did not, therefore, care to note the death of

Girdhar Bahādur, but rejoiced at the death of his cousin. Another instance of the admitted confusion of the names of the two cousins is given by Malcolm (I, p.79*n*.) and this confusion was made by the people of Ujjain themselves!

CHAPTER V.

THE MUGHAL-MARATHA STRUGGLE: SECOND STAGE. (1730—1749)

SECTION 1.—THE LOSS OF MALWA TO THE EMPIRE

The appointment of the Bangash to the governorship of Mālwa meant the breakdown of all peace proposals. The settlement effected by Jai Singh's agent, Dip Singh, with Rājā Shāhu was at an end. The struggle for Mālwa continued and the time was really very critical for the Maratha cause. Dābhāde's defection and Udāji Pawār's dissatisfaction made matters worse. But fortunately for the Peshwā, his new lieutenants in Mālwa, Holkar and Sindhiā, were capable of carrying the struggle to a successful end.

The greatest help to the Maratha cause came from the Mughal Court itself. A regular tussle was going on at the Court, between the pro-Maratha and the anti-Maratha factions. Jai Singh and Khān Daurān favoured a peaceful settlement, and they carried out the expedition of 1734-35 against their own convictions. The anti-Maratha party was headed by the Vazir, Qamruddin Khān, and it counted among its leaders Sādāt Ali of Oudh, Muhammad Bangash, Turebāz Khān and Abhaya Singh of Jodhpur. Every defeat of the Imperialist forces and failure of the Imperial generals, even though temporarily convincing the Emperor of the futility of his anti-Maratha policy, soon caused a reaction and fresh expeditions were planned. With every defeat and with every move for conciliation on the part of the Imperialists, the Maratha demands rose higher and higher, and every such rise in their demand increased the reaction against the Marathas and helped the anti-Maratha party.

Though Jai Singh, the last real Imperial governor of Mālwa, was driven out of the province and the province was occupied by the Marathas, all hope was not lost, and the Nizām was at last summoned from the Deccan. He too joined the anti-Maratha group and a fresh expedition was planned. It was only after his defeat at Bhopāl in December, 1737, that the Mughals felt the hopelessness of the situation and recognized the futility of any further efforts to recover Mālwa. The invasion of Nādir Shāh temporarily postponed the "cession of Mālwa" from the Mughal Empire, but it made it all the more inevitable; the weakened Mughal Empire could no longer resist the Maratha demands, and they were finally granted on July 4, 1741, when the Emperor bestowed its *Naib-Subāhdari* on the Peshwā.

Mālwa thus finally passed into Maratha control, and its loss to the Empire was complete. The foreign Rajput factor also disappeared from the politics of Mālwa soon after; all the plans of Jai Singh to strengthen his hold over it had come to nothing. On the other hand he was driven out of Mālwa and the Maratha forces entered Rājputānā. All efforts to make a united stand failed and when his nominal governorship was taken away from him, the last point of contact was also lost. After his death on September 21, 1743, there was left none else in Rajputana, who could think of meddling with the affairs of Mālwa. The various States of Rājputanā had to face the Marathas and to solve their own problems. The principalities and States of Mālwa were left to themselves to fight it out or to purchase their own renewed existence by paying heavy dues.

Though the struggle between the Mughal and the Maratha forces continued throughout the period, the breakdown of Imperial rule in Mālwa was complete quite early. As the Maratha forces advanced in the province and their hold increased, they began to consolidate their power. With the disappearance of Udāji Pawār from Mālwa, Malhār Rāo Holkar was left supreme. Soon after Rānoji Sindhiā came to his side. It was during these early years after 1732 that the foundations of the modern Maratha States in Mālwa were laid. Chimāji's settlement of 1733 marks an epoch in the internal history of the province. By the time they secured the *farmān* from the Emperor, they had also come to terms with various rulers in the province. These settlements were, however, of a temporary nature, the real consolidation of the Maratha hold in Mālwa occurred only after 1741.

SECTION 2.—MUHAMMAD BANGASH IN MALWA: HIS FAILURE:

SEP. 19, 1730—OCT. 12, 1732.

Muhammad Khān Bangash received the rescript of his governorship of Mālwa on September 19, 1730; it was secured for him by Roshan-ud-dowlāh and Koki Jiu, both of whom had been heavily bribed. Muhammad Khān was also promised an advance of Rs. 60 lakhs, but in reality very little

His appointment.

money could be obtained. On November 5, he reached Agra, where he obtained some guns and other equipments for his army. The military officers, *zamindārs* and Rājāhs of Mālwa were ordered to join him at Narwar. Leaving Agra on the 6th, he reached Gwalior on November 11; there he made a halt. Before leaving Delhi, Bangash had asked for the *faujdāri* of Gwalior; it was then promised to him, but the grant was not yet made. Now Bangash again pressed for it.[1]

The Marathas in Mālwa: Rise of Holkar.

The Marathas began their activities soon after the close of the rains in 1730. They found Mālwa without a governor and began to make plans for occupying it. The peace talks, which were being carried on by Jai Singh's agent, Dip Singh, on behalf of the Emperor, had been brushed aside.[2] This time the Maratha forces were led by Malhār Holkar. Udāji Pawār, who had played a prominent part in the previous campaigns in Mālwa, did not agree with

---

[1] *Khajista*, 312-314; *J.A.S.B.*, pp.304-8; Irvine, II, p.249. This section is based on W. Irvine's "The Bangash Nawābs of Farukkhābād" (*J.A.S.B.*, IV, 1678), supplemented by additional information from the Marāthi authorities. *Khajista Kalam* has also been examined and the corresponding references are given.

[2] S.P.D., X, 66.

the Peshwā and his brother about the terms of the *saranjām*. The Peshwā now made terms with his younger brother, Anand Rāo Pawār, who was granted a *saranjām* in Mālwa from the year 1732-3.[1] Udāji's withdrawal from Mālwa left Holkar supreme. On October 3, 1730, he was granted a *saranjām* of 74 *parganahs* in Mālwa with all rights pertaining to it. The administrative arrangements were made and Kusāji Ganesh was appointed *vakil* at Ujjain.[2] Holkar entered Mālwa and, while at Depālpur, summoned Nand Lāl Mandloi to settle the affairs of the province (November-December, 1730).[3]

When the Bangash was still at Gwalior, he received letters from Khān Daurān urging haste in proceeding against the Maratha invaders. Bangash sent three of his lieutenants by forced marches to Sironj, Mandsāur and Sārangpur, but he himself moved at ease and reached Sadhāurā (172 miles N. of Ujjain) in December, 1730; here he received a letter from the Nizām proposing their meeting at the Narmadā to concert common measures against the Marathas. In reply the Bangash promised to meet

---

1 S.P.D., XIII, 54-56; XXII, 54; Athalye's Dhār, 28.
2 S.P.D., XXII, 50; XXX, pp.300-1.
3 Rājwāde, VI, 605.

the Nizām and expressed the hope that the latter would close the ferries of the Narmadā against the Marathas and thus check their advance.[1] But the Marathas had already crossed the Narmadā.

The Bangash and the Marathas.

On January 15, 1731, Muhammad Khān reached Sārangpur. Holkar was then at Shāhjahānpur; on hearing of the approach of the Bangash he had already sent his heavy baggage across the Narmadā. As the Muhammadans were entering the camp at Sārangpur, the Marathas fell on them, but soon 'fled like crows on seeing a bow'. On January 17, the Bangash relieved Shāhjahānpur and three days later occupied Ujjain.[2] Now, the Marathas began to plunder the villages and towns of Mālwa, and the Bangash had to take the field again on February 8; he moved towards Dhār. Another force was sent under Ahmad Khān, his second son, to deal with Holkar in the direction of Sārangpur and Shāhjahānpur. Yār Muhammad Khān, son of Dost Muhammad Khān, who was with Ahmad Khān, turned traitor and asked Holkar to attack Ujjain, and he himself returned to Bhopāl. But Holkar failed to do much at Ujjain and turned

---

[1] *Khajista*, 135, 330-331, 320-22, 346; *J.A.S.B.*, p.309.

[2] *Khajista*, 135-6; *J.A.S.B.*, pp.309-10; Irvine, II, 249-50.

towards Dhār. The Bangash had reached Dhār on February 14, and, five days later, the Marathas appeared there. The fighting round about Dhār went on till February 26, 1731, when on hearing of the approach of the Nizām, the Bangash left for the Narmadā.[1]

When the Bangash had accepted the governorship of Mālwa, it was rumoured that he had promised to lead a compaign against the Nizām immediately after the Marathas had been dealt with. The rumour was believed in by the soldiers in the Nizām's army and hence, when the two nobles sat together to hold peaceful negotiations, they were greatly surprised. They met about March 17, and were together for twelve days. The letters of the Nizām give the only available clue to their negotiations which seem to have centred round the idea of taking advantage of the dissensions in the Maratha ranks. The Nizām proposed to favour Dābhāde, Gaikawād and Udāji Pawār, who were then opposed to the Peshwā.[2]

The Bangash and the Nizām.

From the Narmadā the Nizām went towards the territories of Mohan Singh of Awāsgarh, but had to

---

[1] *Khajista,* 104-07, 149-151; *J.A.S.B.*, 310-1; Irvine, II, 250.

[2] *Khajista,* 328-336; *J.A.S.B.*, 311-3; *Ahwal,* 199-200 in Irvine, II, 250-1.

The plans of the Nizām fail.

leave in haste, because his plans and hopes regarding the Marathas had failed. Bāji Rāo had defeated Dabhāde and his associates in the battle of Dabhoi. The Nizām grew anxious for the safety of his capital. He crossed the Akbarpur ferry, passed near the fort of Māndu and reached Surat by forced marches. Some three months later peace was made between the Nizām and Bāji Rāo, a secret clause of which left the latter free to pursue his own plans in the North.[1]

The Bangash and the Marathas.

The Bangash was indirectly benefited by this struggle between the Nizām and the Peshwā; Mālwa was saved from the full force of the Maratha depredations for the rest of the open season. He was busy reducing the Kākali and Chikaldā forts which belonged to Udāji Pawār. They were taken on April 1, and soon after some Bhil forts also fell. Just then he heard that Malhār Holkar was plundering the country near Mandsāur and Rāmpurā and that another Maratha leader, Anthu (Antāji Mānkeshwar), was ravaging the country round Kauth (Kāyeth, 17 miles E. of Ujjain). Other Maratha bands crossed the Narmadā and after plundering the country near Māndu retreated to the Deccan. Anthu

---

[1] *Khajista*, 336-344; *J.A.S.B.*, 313-4; Irvine, II, 251-2.

later began his plundering campaigns in the area round Shāhjahānpur. On May 9, 1731, the Bangash reached Ujjain. His armies were demanding their pay and showed signs of mutiny and no other help reached him; to make matters worse the Mahārāo of Kotāh and other Rājās refused to go against the Marathas. The Bangash had to take the field again on May 15, 1731.[1]

On June 3, he reached Kāyeth when Antu withdrew. The next day, the Bangash received summons from Sārangpur as Holkar was going to attack the place. By a forced march at night, the Bangash reached Sārangpur early in the morning, when soon the Marathas were on him. For the whole day a battle was fought and the Marathas took to flight only at sunset. Soon after, they re-crossed the Narmadā. After collecting some revenues near Rājgarh, Muhammad Khān went to Sironj, where he proposed to stay during the rains (1731). Sironj was farther from the Narmadā than Ujjain and nearer to his line of retreat, by way of Gwalior, to Hindustan. His foot-hold in Mālwa was too precarious for him to take any risk of being surrounded and cut off.[2]

---

[1] *Khajista*, 17-20; *J.A.S.B.*, 315-6.

[2] *Khajista*, 279-281; *J.A.S.B.*, 316-8; Irvine, II, 252-3.

He spent the rains at Sironj and employed himself in writing to Delhi for reinforcements, money and, above all, for forcing the Rājāhs (specially Chhatra Singh of Narwar) to co-operate with him.[1] The Marathas were strengthening their own forces, Anand Rāo Pawār was pacified and a grant was made to him from the next year. His cousins, Tukoji and Jivāji Pawār, were also associated with the affairs in Mālwa, and for their help they were granted 7 per cent of the dues realized from the province. Antāji was also rewarded for his campaign in Mālwa. Rānoji Sindhia, who was rapidly rising in the esteem of the Peshwā, was now closely associated with Holkar and was granted an equal share with Holkar in the dues realized in Māwa. Holkar got some additional grants outside Mālwa and was thus rewarded for his efforts. On November 2, 1731, the Peshwā entrusted the affairs on Mālwa to Holkar and Sindhiā, and gave them seals for the same. Nandlāl Mandloi, who was helping the Marathas, having died, his son, Tej Karan, was accepted by the Peshwā as the Mandloi.[2]

---

[1] *Khajista*, 124-6; *J.A.S.B.*, 318, 320.

[2] S.P.D., XXII, 38, 39; XIV, 48; XXX, 55, 303-7; Rājwāde, VI, 613, 614, 607.

The rains were over and the Bangash became exasperated with the disregard shown to his requests by the Court. He thought of going to Delhi, but later decided to undertake an expedition against Chhatra Singh of Narwar. In October-November, 1731, after reducing the other forts he invested Shāhābād. Chhatra Singh made terms but just then the Bangash heard of a fresh Maratha invasion on Mālwa. Chhatra Singh absconded at night and the Bangash was forced to return to Sironj to meet the Marathas. This expedition against Chhatra Singh completely antagonized the Emperor and the fall of the Bangash became inevitable.[1]

The Bangash and Chhatra Singh of Narwar.

After settling the affairs in Gujrāt, the Marathas turned to Mālwa with their full force. Fateh Singh and others were posted at Khimlāsā (24 miles E. of Sironj). Chimāji, Malhār Holkar and others were in Umatwādā.[2] Another force of 12,000 Marathas was still south of the Narmadā, yet another of 20,000 was approaching by way of Saugor. The various Rājāhs and *zamindars* made peace with the Marathas,

The Bangash and the Marathas: He makes peace with them, 1732.

---

[1] *Khajista,* 93-4; Khānde, pp.598-9; *J.A.S.B.,* 319-320; Irvine, II, 253.

[2] 'Umatwādā' is the tract where the Rajputs of Umat clan dominate. The States of Rājgarh and Narsinghgarh and the territories round about them comprise the Umatwādā.

paid their dues, and after settling their affairs, returned home. The Bangash received no help. He tried to open negotiations with Rājāh Shāhu, but was referred to the Peshwā as 'his sole and only adviser in all matters.'[1]

On reaching Sironj, the Bangash thought of attacking the forces at Khimlāsā, but soon he heard that Holkar with a force of 50,000 men was already as near as 15 or 16 miles from Sironj. He did not think it advisable to move eastward leaving Sironj, Bhilsā and other towns at the mercy of Holkar. Realizing that he was completely checkmated, the Bangash sent for the Maratha leaders, gave them presents and entered into an agreement with them. He, however, refused to put it on paper without the permission of the Emperor. Soon after, the Marathas evacuated Mālwa.[2]

The rains were spent by the Bangash at Sironj in writing to the Emperor for help in men and money. His own resources were exhausted, while his *jāgir* was in the hands of the Bundelās. If his reports were long-winded, he submitted that he was willing to serve under a new man who could abbreviate them.

---

[1] *Khajista,* 139-140; *J.A.S.B.*, 321-2.

[2] *Khajista,* 139-140; *J.A.S.B.*, 322-3; Irvine, II, 254.

Anyway, he implored that the Maratha advance be checked. No help came from the Court. The local chiefs were told that a new governor was about to be appointed. The Nizām too made no sign, even though appealed to by the Bangash. The only answer that Bangash received from the Court was a letter upbraiding him. Khān Daurān accused him of having allowed his agents to guide the Marathas and of conniving at their advance. Soon a rescript in the Emperor's own hand reached him informing him that Rājā Jai Singh was appointed his successor. He was directed to report himself at Agra. The news of his supersession had already reached him through his agents. After making over the charge of Ujjain and other towns to the officers of his successor, he left Mālwa and reached Agra on December 6, 1732.[1]

The Bangash replaced by Jai Singh in Mālwa, Oct. 1732.

With his return southern Mālwa was lost to the Empire. The breakdown of the Imperial power in Mālwa was complete. The failure of the Bangash clearly exhibited how the interests of the Empire were sacrificed to personal consideration. He had to face the difficulties arising out of scarcity of money and forces and lack of co-operation. The Court too was

Causes of his failure.

---

[1] *Khajista*, 21-3; *J.A.S.B.*, 323-4; Irvine, II, 254-5.

ill-disposed to him. The *jāgirdārs* complained against him. Hāfiz Khidmatgār was irritated because of his expedition against Chhatra Singh, and above all, the Emperor had grown suspicious regarding the friendship that had arisen between the Bangash and the Nizām. The courtiers knew that the Emperor was afraid lest another prince should be raised to the throne by some powerful combination of nobles and he deposed, and they did not hesitate to take advantage of this fear to further their own personal gains and advantages.[1]

SEC. 3.—SAWAI JAI SINGH'S LAST GOVERNORSHIP SEPT. 28, 1732—AUG. 3, 1737.

On September 28, 1732, the Emperor appointed Sawāi Jai Singh to be the governor of Mālwa. He started from Jaipur on October 20, and reached Ujjain in December. He had received 20 lakhs in all (13 as grant and 7 on loan) from the Emperor, on condition that he would raise an army and drive the Marathas out of Mālwa, but he preferred the peaceful method of buying them off.[2]

---

[1] *J.A.S.B.*, 324; Rustam Ali, 261a in Irvine, II, 255.

[2] *Khajista*, 314-5; *Vamsh*, 3212; Wārid, 115-6; Sarkar, I, 246-7.

After the rains of 1732 the Maratha leaders were once again active. Chimāji went to Bundelkhand (Nov.—Dec. 1732), while the Holkar and Sindhiā went to Gujrāt to capture Chāmpāner and provision Pāwāgadh. After settling these affairs, they went to Dungarpur and Bānswādā to settle the question of the payment of their dues. Thence they went towards Mandsāur. Anand Rāo Pawār and Vithoji Bule had already gone to Mālwa. (Dec., 1732). Udāji Pawār was summoned to Mālwa by Chimāji. Jai Singh was at Mandsāur in Feb., 1733. Holkar and Sindhiā left their heavy baggage near the Māhi, hemmed Jai Singh round and put his troops to great privations, by cutting off their grain and water supplies. Udāji and Krishnāji Pawār were tempted to join Jai Singh out of their jealousy for the Peshwā, but Holkar plundered a part of Udāji's baggage. Their mutual friends now intervened and severely rebuked the Pawārs, who then withdrew from the Mughal side. Jai Singh now sued for peace and offered six lakhs of rupees, but Holkar demanded more.[1]

The campaign of 1732-33 and the Marathas.

The Emperor, however, became anxious and desired to send forces to Mālwa to help Jai Singh.

[1] S.P.D., XXX, pp.307-9; XIV, 1-3; XV, 6.

But the various nobles, when called upon to proceed against the invaders, made excuses. Finally, though wedded to a life of ease and idleness, the Emperor decided to march in person. The tents were sent ahead and he left Delhi on Feb. 23, 1733, and moved by short marches. The news of the Emperor marching against the Maratha reached the forces of Jai Singh just when negotiations were afoot, and the Rajput captains, emboldened by the news, came forth to battle. In the battle which followed, the commander of Jai Singh's rear-guard was slain: Holkar lost some 15 officers and one or two hundred horses. Holkar fell back about 30 miles, while Jai Singh advanced 16 miles; the former, however, rapidly doubled back to Jai Singh's former position. Jai Singh found himself cut off and could not hold on; he made peace and promised to pay six lakhs in cash and to cede 28 *parganahs* in lieu of *chauth*. This occurred during the last week of February, 1733. Out of six lakhs only five lakhs were actually paid; three lakhs were paid on March 17, when the Maratha forces, led by Holkar, Sindhiā and Anand Rāo Pawār evacuated Mālwa and went to Gujrāt, and the remaining two lakhs were paid on May 4, when Chimāji, now on his way back to the Deccan, was about to leave Mālwa.[1]

The Imperial camp never got beyond Faridābād (16 miles S. of Delhi), and after camping on the Jamunā for a month, the Emperor returned to Delhi, when the Vazir had offered to undertake the campaign. At Agra, Muhammad Bangash joined the Vazir. It was reported that the Maratha forces under Chimāji were near Narwar, while other Maratha bands were plundering the Umat Rājāhs. An advanced guard was sent to Budhā Dongar (beyond Narwar). The Marathas were now returning to the Deccan. The news of the defeat of Jai Singh at Mandsāur was also known. Jai Singh had already left for his capital. The Vazir recalled his troops and started on his return march.[2]

The expedition of 1733-34.

Jai Singh's failure in Mālwa was great. Soon after he returned to his newly founded capital, Jaipur, and became quite unmindful of the affairs of Mālwa. His complicity with the Marathas was well

---

[1] S.P.D., XIV, 2, 7; XV, 6; XXX, pp.310-1; Irvine, II, 276-8; Wārid, 119-20; Sarkar, I, 247-8; *Vir Vinod*, II, 1218-20.

[2] S.P.D., XV, 6; XIV, 9; XXX, pp.309-11; Kushhāl, 1063b; Rustam Ali, 265; Wārid, 83; Ghulam Ali, 54b; Irvine, II, 276-7.

known to all, but the Emperor dared not remove him from the governorship, lest it should displease Khān Daurān. In the winter of 1733 it was Khān Daurān's turn to lead the expedition against the Marathas, but he spent three or four months in trying to persuade some one else to take his place. He was sending out and getting back his advance tents.[1] In the meanwhile the Marathas returned to Mālwā. The settlement of the year 1722 practically laid the foundation of the four Maratha States in Mālwa, *viz.*, those ruled by Holkar, Sindhiā, Anand Rāo Pawār and the two Pawār brothers, Tukoji and Jiwāji.[2] For full eight months the main Maratha forces had been concentrated at Janjirā where the Peshwā was busy fighting against the Siddis. In December Holkar and Sindhiā started for Mālwa and Pilāji Jādhav followed them. Pilāji had first planned to march into Mālwa, and leaving Narwar on the right to move to Kotāh-Bundi, to levy contributions there and to return by way of Orchhā and Datiyā, but all these plans had to be altered. He reached Nemād in December, 1733, and went

---

[1] Wārid, 119-20; Irvine, II, pp.278-9.

[2] S.P.D., XXII, 54, 82; Athalye's Dhar, 28, 31; Bhāgwat: *Purvardha,* I, 2.

straight to Datiyā and Orchhā, but he found the whole of the country desolate and had to fall back (April 8, 1734). He marched back to the Deccan leaving Chanderi on his left.[1]

The affairs of Bundi and Kotāh were left to Holkar and Sindhiā. On their way to Bundi, they reduced the fort of Barwāh (on the Narmadā) and settled its dues. Later they had a contest with Yār Muhammad Khān of Bhopāl in which many lives were lost (Dec. 1735).[2] When they passed through Ahirwādā, their help was sought by Surati Rām, son of Khānde Rāi, on a promise to pay the Maratha dues in return. After sending some forces to his help they moved on towards Bundi. Dalel Singh, the nominee of Jai Singh, was ruling over Bundi, while its former master, Budh Singh, a refugee at Begham, was sinking deeper and deeper into wine and opium. The latter, however, found a new ally in Pratāp Singh Hādā, the elder brother of Dalel Singh, who was jealous of his younger brother. Pratāp Singh was sent to the Deccan by Budh Singh's

Marathas in Bundi, 1734.

---

[1] S.P.D., XIV, 10, 11, 13; Sarkar, I, 248-9; also the correction-slip in II.

[2] S.P.D., XIV, 11, 18; XV, 1; Rustam Ali, 265b; Irvine, II, 279.

queen, with money for hiring Maratha aid against Dalel Singh. It was promised for six lakhs. Guided by Pratāp Singh, the Maratha army under Holkar, Sindhiā, Anand Rāo Pawār and Rāmchandra Bāwā attacked Bundi on April 22, 1734. After a severe fight the fort of Bundi was taken and the Marathas made captive of Sangrām Singh, father of Dalel Singh, who had been managing the affairs of Bundi as regent. Budh Singh's queen, hearing of the Maratha victory, hastened to Bundi and tied a *rākhi* thread, thus publicly accepting Malhār Holkar as her brother. After promising help in future the Maratha forces returned. Soon after a Jaipur force, 20,000 strong, came and restored Dalel Singh to Bundi.[1]

Muzaffar Khan leads the Imperial army in Mālwa: March-June 1734.

While the Marathas were ravaging northern Mālwa and leading their first expedition in Rājputānā, Khān Daurān had not yet left Delhi. At last in February, 1734, he summoned his brother, Muzaffar Khān, then in Mewāt, and sent him against the Marathas. Muzaffar Khān could leave Delhi only on March 20, 1734, and marched upto Sironj, even though the spies reported that the Marathas were

[1] *Vamsh.*, 3216-21; Sarkar, I, 251-2.

returning. Without coming into regular action he retraced his route on June 11, 1734.[1]

The Marathas retreated, but their first incursion into Rājputānā, at least for once, opened the eyes of the more thoughtful princes in Rājputānā, to the new danger. Jai Singh arranged a conference of all the princes of Rājputānā, who met at Hardā, near Agaunch (a village in Mewād) on July 17, 1734, to concert common measures for opposing the Maratha invaders. An agreement was signed by which all the princes pledged themselves to united action and to begin their campaign soon after rains; all the princes were to gather together at Rāmpurā with all their forces.[2] But the moral decay of the Rajput princes made it impossible for them to sink their tribal differences, to sacrifice their personal and private interests and to carry on a vigorous, united

The Treaty of Unity in Rājputānā, July, 17, 1734; Later efforts : Their failure.

[1] *Siyar,* 466-7; Ghulam Ali, 54a; Rustam Ali, 265b; Irvine, II, 279.

[2] On the authority of *Vamsh Bhaskar* (IV, 3227-28), Sarkar asserts that the conference was held in the second half of October, 1734, (Sarkar, I, 252). Tod dates it on August 1, 1734, (I, 482-83). *Vir Vinod* gives the date from the original document in the archives of Udaipur State and hence it should be accepted. The date given in *Vir Vinod* is Shravan, Vidi 13 (i.e. July 17, 1734). *Vir Vinod,* II pp.1220-21.

campaign against the Marathas. The treaty did not bear any fruit. Jai Singh himself knew this and, soon after the treaty he indirectly tried to open negotiations with the Peshwā.[1] Some years later, another effort was made to make the Rajput princes act in unison. It was also proposed that after driving the Marathas out of Mālwa, it might be partitioned among the Rajput powers of Rājputānā. But all these efforts brought no result and the fate of Mālwa as well as of Rājputānā was sealed.[2]

The Imperial campaign of 1734-5: The Vazir and the Marathas.

Immediately after the rains of the year 1734, the Maratha inroads into Hindustan were renewed. Pilāji Jādhav led an expedition to Bundelkhand and northern Mālwa. Bālāji, son of the Peshwā, accompanied him. After entering Mālwa from the eastern side near Kurwai in the first week of January, 1735, he began to rove about in the neighbourhood of Narwar. Vazir Qamruddin Khān decided to lead an expedition himself. He took leave as early as November 10, 1734, and moved by way of Agra. His forces numbered about 25,000. Early in February, 1735, two or three light engagements took place, in which the Imperial forces had the advantage.

---

[1] S.P.D., XXX, 108.

[2] *Vir Vinod,* II, 1225-6.

Pilāji then returned to Pāhori Shivpuri and Kolaras; these districts had been granted to him, by the Peshwā on December 3, 1734. Qamruddin Khān advanced upto Narwar, but his forces were completely immobilized and at last the Vazir offered a bribe of 5 lakhs to Pilāji. Pilāji then withdrew his baggage from Bundelkhand and set out for the Deccan. Leaving Mālwa on March 13, he crossed the Betwā and entered the Gadh district. The Vazir returned to Delhi on May 9, 1735.[1]

Khān Daurān and Jai Singh driven out of Mālwa by the Marathas.

While the Vazir was leading his forces in the eastern theatre of war, another Imperial force was sent to the western theatre, which was entrusted to Khān Daurān. Khān Daurān set out from Delhi on November 10, 1734, and was joined by Jai Singh on the way; Abhaya Singh of Jodhpur and Durjan Sāl of Kotāh also came out with their contingents. The combined forces were supposed to be 2,00,000 strong. They crossed the Mukundarā pass and reached Rāmpurā territory, where Holkar and Sindhiā were sighted (early in Feb., 1735). The Imperial forces were unwieldy and lack of organiza-

[1] Ashob, 104-6; Kush-hāl, 1066; Rustam Ali, 267; Ghulām Ali, 54b; S.P.D., XIV, 22, 21, 23; XXII, 102; XXX, pp.312-6; Irvine, II, pp.279-80; Sarkar, I, 253-255.

tion made it all the more difficult to manage them. The light Maratha forces could not be beaten by this unwieldy horde. For eight days the Marathas circled round the Imperial army, cut off its supplies, captured as many camels and horses as they could and on the ninth day made a sudden raid on Rājputānā. Leaving the Imperial forces behind them, they crossed the Mukundarā pass and went to Kotāh, Bundi, and thence into the defenceless territories of Jaipur and Jodhpur. The rich city Sāmbhar was plundered on February 28, and it yielded a rich harvest. The Imperialist forces came up toiling behind the invaders. Early in March, Khān Daurān was posted at Bundi. Jai Singh was near his new capital, while Holkar and Sindhiā were 20 miles from Jaipur. After some weeks of inactivity, Khān Daurān decided to accept Jai Singh's advice and make peace with Sindhiā and Holkar through his mediation. On behalf of the Emperor, Khān Daurān offered to the Marathas 22 lakhs as *chauth* of Mālwa and induced them to retire beyond the Narmadā. From this inglorious campaign Khān Daurān and Jai Singh returned to Delhi at the end of April, 1735. Holkar and Ramchandra Bāwā went to Kalabagh, while Rānoji retired to Ujjain by way of Sironj, Rājgarh and Pātan.[1]

Soon after, the mother of the Peshwā, entered Mālwa. She was proceeding to Hindustan on a long pilgrimage. She visited Udaipur (May 6), Nathdwārā, Jaipur (c. July 16), Mathurā, Kurukshetra, Allahabad, Benares and Gaya (November, 1735). It was a grand affair. She reached home only on May 2, 1736.[2]

The Emperor and the proposals to make peace with the Marathas.

When Bāji Rāo's mother was at Jaipur, Jai Singh began to negotiate with the Peshwā's agent about the Maratha occupation of Mālwa. On the other hand, the Emperor became furious at the disgraceful result of the Imperial expedition, which not only failed to crush the Marathas but ended in a promise to pay them a huge contribution as *chauth* for Mālwa. The Court blamed Jai Singh and Khān Daurān for this. Sādāt Khān told the Emperor,

---

[1] Ashob; Bayan, 532; Rustam, 266-7 in Elliot, VIII, 50-1; Khush-hāl, 1067a; *Siyar*, 467; S.P.D., XIV, 23, 21, 27, 29, 57; XXII, 284; Irvine, II, 280-1; Sarkar, I, 253-6. *Vamsh.* (IV, 3228-30) adds that Khān Daurān suggested and the Emperor agreed to hand over Mālwa to the Marathas; he confuses the events of the year 1736 with those of this year (1735).

[2] Sarkar, I, 256-7.

"Jai Singh has ruined the Empire by his secret support to the Marathas. Give me only the governorship of Mālwa and Agra. I do not ask for any monetary aid, Jai Singh may ask for 1 crore, but I do not need it. The Nizām is my friend, he will hinder the Marathas from crossing the Narmadā."[1] Sarbuland Khān and other nobles joined Sādāt Khān in denouncing Jai Singh. When the Emperor also joined in censuring Jai Singh and Khān Daurān for buying off the Marathas, Khān Daurān resumed his suit, "The Marathas cannot be effectually subdued by fighting. By friendly negotiations I shall induce either the Peshwā or his brother to come to meet Your Majesty. If his demands are accepted, there will be no disturbance in the Imperial domains in near future. If, on the other hand, Sādāt Khān and the Nizām combine, they would set up another Emperor." Some time later he further submitted, "I only promised the Maratha generals that they would be given as *jāgir* those *parganahs* of Mālwa which are in the hands of the refractory Rohilās and other brigands. Then they shall not disturb any district under the Emperor's rule. Bāji Rāo is obedient to Your Majesty in every way. He has

---

[1] S.P.D., XIV, 31.

brought his family from the Deccan on the plea of bathing in the Ganges."[1]

Jai Singh antagonized from the Emperor: Promotes the Maratha interests.

When this talk of removing him from the governorship of Mālwa reached Jai Singh's ears, it definitely antagonized him from the Emperor. He had always been an opportunist seeking his own interests, and now he definitely promoted the Maratha interests hoping, in his heart of hearts, that he would gain by the new move. He now called the Maratha agent at the Court to a secret council and told him, "I have hitherto guarded the prestige and interests of Bāji Rāo because I could not trust the Turks (*i.e.*, the Royal Mughal House). If the latter triumph over the Deccani forces, they will disregard us. Therefore, in every matter I shall follow the behest of the Peshwā." He then (Aug., 1735) sent a proposal to the Peshwā that he should come with Pilāji and other leading generals, at the head of 5,000 horsemen, to Jaipur and meet him. He, however, added that his territories on the way might not be disturbed. Jai Singh promised to pay the daily expenses of the Maratha forces (Rs. 5,000 a day) in addition to cash payment of the *chauth* for Mālwa and the rent of Pilāji's *jāgir* in northern

[1] S.P D., XIV, 47, 39, 31; Sarkar, I, 257-8.

Mālwa near Narwar. He assured the payment of the dues of Mālwa, Sironj, Datiyā, Orchhā and other States. Jai Singh further added that when the Peshwā arrived in Jaipur, they would take counsel together and later he would advise him to interview the Emperor only after assurances and oaths for his safe conduct were secured from the Emperor through Khān Daurān. If, however, it could not be secured, the Peshwā might return home from Jaipur.[1]

On the other hand, at the end of September, 1735), the Emperor began to plan another Imperial expedition against the Marathas during the coming open season. He reconciled Abhaya Singh to the Vazir. Then he proposed that Agra, Mālwa and even Gujrāt should be given in charge of the Vazir and urged that unless Jai Singh joined the Imperial forces, his country might be molested and he punished for his disloyalty. The Emperor himself proposed to take the field as soon as the rivers became fordable. Jai Singh and Khān Daurān were to be sent to the Deccan by way of Jaipur, while the Vazir, Abhaya Singh and Sādāt Khān would march by way of Gwalior.[2]

---

[1] S.P.D., XIV, 47; *Vamsh,* 3233; Sarkar, I, 258-9.
[2] S.P.D., XIV, 39, 32.

The Peshwā had also decided to march into Hindustan, visit the Rajput courts personally and impose the *chauth* by peaceful persuasion. Sindhiā, Holkar and the Pawārs got their forces ready. The Peshwā left Punā on October 9, 1735, and arrived close to the Narmadā on November 28, whence Holkar, Sindhiā, Anand Rāo Pawār and Bāji Bhimrāo, son of Pilāji, were sent ahead to Mālwa and Bundelkhand. After taking the fort of Kukshi on the Gujrāt frontier of Dhār, the Peshwā advanced through Lunāwādā and Dungarpur, arriving on the southern frontier of Mewād about January 15, 1736.[1] Bāji Rāo goes to Rājputānā.

Sādāt Khan was summoned to the Court to join the Imperial forces moving against the Marathas. He proposed various ways of distribution of the provinces, and once it was even remoured that he would be given the governorship of Mālwa, but nothing came true. On his way to Agra he had to encounter the *zamindār* of Adāru. In the battle that was fought, though Sādāt Khān succeeded in defeating and killing the *zamindār*, his own forces The campaign of 1735-36.

---

[1] S.P.D., XIV, 42, XXX, 144; Sarkar, 1, 260-1. Sardesai dates the letter No. 43 of S.P.D., XIV as December 10, 1735, which appears to be wrong. The Peshwā could be at Depālpur during these days only in the year 1736. Its correct date is November 29, 1736.

were considerably crippled.[1] The Bangash was also ordered to proceed to the defence of Mālwa. The Marathas had already crossed the Chambal but failed to take the fort of Gwalior. They advanced further on to Nurābād and other place near about. The Bangash reached Dholpur on January 14, 1736, and took up his position in the ravines of the Chambal and tried to guard every ford against the invaders, but dared not come out in the open to meet the Marathas. Mud walls had already been raised and guns were mounted to strengthen his own position. After spending many days in inaction (in February), the Bangash sent envoys to make terms with the Marathas. In the meanwhile, on March 1, Bhimrāo received orders from the Peshwā to cease hostilities as the Imperialists were inclined towards peace. The invaders withdrew soon after.[2]

In Bundelkhand, the Vazir advanced by way of Narwar towards Orchhā, where he entrenched and faced the Maratha generals. After many light skirmishes, on February 3, 1736, a pitched whole-day battle was fought in which the Marathas were

---

[1] S.P.D., XIV, 39, 40, 41, 42; XXX, 134, 143.

[2] *Khajista*, ff. 289-306; *J.A.S.B.*, 328; S.P.D., XIV, 55, 56; XIII, 48; XXX, 134; Irvine, II, 281-2; Sarkar, I, 267-9.

worsted. They rapidly retreated. The Mughals pursued the invaders upto Ujjain but at a great distance behind the Marathas.[1]

Khān Dāuran was sent to Rājputānā and was joined by Jai Singh on the way. The combined forces entrenched themselves in a strong position at the Todā tank. They were faced by Malhār Holkar and Pratāp Hādā. The Imperialist forces did not come out. The Marathas cut off their supplies. One day a party of 1500 Ahdi soldiers moved out of the trenches and was completely cut off, which greatly scared the Imperialists. Hostilities soon ended (Feb. 7). Peace negotiations were opened and Khān Daurān returned to Delhi.[2]

While this armed conflict was going on, the Peshwā was moving towards Udaipur and his agents

---

[1] Ashob, 105-07, is the only authority on this campaign. The Marāthi sources do not refer to this part of the campaign. Irvine, 11, 282-2. It appears to me that Ashob, who wrote his work in 1784, has confounded the years through lapse of memory and put them in 1736. The armistice was declared by February 7, and it appears improbable that the Imperial armies would have carried on the pursuit even after the armistice.

[2] Ashob, 108-09; Irvine, II, 283-4. S.P.D., XIV, 56, states that Khān Daurān would return from Delhi; he must have left Rājputānā during the second week of February to report to the Emperor on the situation.

had gone ahead of him. Mahādeo Bhatt Hingane went to Jaipur (January, 1736) and was introduced to Jai Singh by his minister Rājā Ayāmal. Jai Singh agreed to present the Peshwā with 5 lakhs in all, two lakhs in cash and the rest in jewellery, costly robes, five horses and one elephant. He further sent Ayāmal to invite Bāji Rāo to his own domain and promised to take him to Delhi, to introduce him to the Emperor and to arrange a lasting peace between the Marathas and the Empire. Jai Singh proposed a grant of 20 lakhs in cash and of a *jāgir* of 40 lakhs in Mālwa, adding that the subsidy might be assigned on Dost Muhammad Khān's principality. Dādāji Pant, another Maratha agent attended on Khān Daurān. The negotiations were carried on through Sindhiā and Rāmchandra Bāwā. Khān Daurān sent Nijabat Ali Khān from Delhi, to negotiate on his behalf; he sent money also to cover the expenses of Bāji Rāo. It was evident that the spirit of all were damped and the Emperor, too, became anxious to make peace with the Marathas.[1] Bāji Rāo's progress through Rājputānā was a glorious peaceful march. No sooner did he see that the Imperialists were inclined towards peace, than

The peace talks begin, Feb. 1736.

[1] S.P.D., XIV, 50-51; Sarkar, I, 265.

he ordered his generals (February 7) to suspend hostilities and to avoid all undesirable events.[1] From Udaipur the Peshwā marched to Jahājpur and Jai Singh hastened to meet him. They met at Bhambholāo, near Kishangarh (February 15). All the Maratha generals were presented to Jai Singh save Malhār Holkar, who did not come to the *darbār*, for Bāji Rāo had not asked Jai Singh to restore Bundi to Budh Singh as promised to Rājā Shāhu on the occasion of Pratāp's going to Satārā to beg the aid of the Marathas.[2]

Jai Singh advised the Peshwā to return to the Deccan, as the time was not suitable for an attack on Delhi.[3] When the peace negotiations opened, the Peshwā offered to Jai Singh his own terms which were noted thus in a memorandum : Bāji Rāo's peace terms.

"(1) The grant of the *subāhdāri* of Mālwa and that of its entire territories, excluding the forts held directly by the Emperor, the lands of *jāgirs* and old feudatories and grantees of rent-free lands and daily allowances.

---

1 S.P.D., XIV, 56; Sarkar, I, 266.
2 S.P.D., XIV, 52, 56; XXX, 160; *Vamsh*, 3238-40.
3 *Vamsh*, 3239; Sarkar, I, 264.

"(2) A cash payment of Rs. 13 lakhs for his expenses of war to be paid in three instalments :

Rs. 4 lakhs when Pilāji goes to the Court to settle the peace treaty;

Rs. 5 lakhs after the autumn harvest;

Rs. 4 lakhs after the spring harvest.

"(3) The *nazar* of 6 lakhs to the Emperor in return for the grant of *Sardeshpandyā* rights in the six Deccan *subāhs,* to be paid only after the country is brought under control."

Jai Singh promised to use his influence to secure for Rājā Shāhu the grant of *chauth* and the cession of Mālwa from the Emperor, as demanded by the Peshwā.[1] Soon after Jai Singh returned to Jaipur.

The Peshwā too started for his home. At Begham he met Budh Singh and spoke kindly to him. Then he went to Ahirwādā. He had now sent another Maratha envoy to Delhi named Bābu Rāo with the additional demand that Rs. 2 lakhs be given to Chimāji as a special reward for his devoted services to the government and for efforts to persuade Bāji Rāo to accept the policy of furthering the cause of the Empire.[2]

---

[1] S.P.D., XV, p.93; Sarkar, I, 273-4, 264.

[2] *Vamsh,* 3239-40; S.P.D., XIV, 58; XV, p.93; Sarkar, I, 264, 267, 274.

Bāji Rāo's demands are accepted and he is made deputy-governor of Mālwa: May, 1736.

The Emperor sent Yādgār Kāshmiri and Kirpārām in addition to Nijābat Ali Khān, sent by Khān Daurān, to Jai Singh (March 8). They carried back with them the memorandum of terms demanded by the Peshwā. At the request of Jai Singh, the Emperor went on writing 'granted' against each of the items of the demands put forth by the Peshwā.[1] The Peshwā was anxiously awaiting at Sironj till the beginning of June for the reply of the Emperor to his demands. Immediately on receipt of it he started for the Deccan. Thus, at the request of Jai Singh, the Emperor appointed Bāji Rāo the deputy-governor of Mālwa; Jai Singh, however, continued to be the nominal governor. "This was in fact, though not in form, a cession of the province."[2]

Demands of the Peshwā increase: Breakdown of the negotiations.

When Bāji Rāo's first demands were satisfied, he asked for further concessions. He knew through his agent that the Emperor and his advisers had secretly instructed Yādgār Khān and others to con-

---

[1] S.P.D., XV, p.93; Sarkar, I, 274; Irvine, I, 284; *Vamsh*, 3230 confuses the events of this year with those of the last year and dates the transfer of Mālwa in 1735, which is wrong. It occurred only in 1736.

Ashob, 110b; Ghulam Ali, 54b; Rustam Ali, 267-8; *Siyar*, 468, 473.

[2] Sarkar, I, 270-1; Irvine, II, 284-5.

cede to the Marathas authority to levy an annual tribute of Rs. 10,60,000 from the Rajput States, if it was considered necessary to satisfy them. The Emperor hoped that this would cause ill-feeling between the Rajputs and the Marathas. The Peshwā, however, realized that it only indicated the weakness of the Empire and he put forth another set of additional demands through Dhondho Pant to Khān Daurān, who submitted the same to the Emperor. The Emperor was willing to concede some of them. Khān Daurān, however, replied that the Vazir would soon be going to Mālwa as far as the Narmadā to settle all the affairs. Khān Daurān pressingly urged the Peshwā once again to go to Delhi and meet the Emperor. He even suggested that, if he could not come that year, he might promise to appear the next year. He promised that if the Peshwā came even as far as Ujjain, nobles would be sent from the Court to escort him to Delhi.[1]

Dhondho Pant had submitted the memorandum of the additional grants; Mahādeo Bhatt Hingane followed soon after, and submitted to the Emperor a petition and the present of a *Peshkash* from Bāji

[1] Irvine, II, 285; Duff, I, 391-2; S.P.D., XV, gives the list of such contributions on p.94; S.P.D., XV, pp.92-3, 87-8, 89; Sarkar, I, 274.

Rāo. On Sept. 29, 1736, Muhammad Shāh issued an Imperial *farmān* to Bāji Rāo granting him *jāgir*, a *mansab* of 7 *hazāri*, the *mahāls* of his *watan* and right to perquisites. He was also awarded robes of honour and jewellery. Chimāji was created a 5-*hazāri mansabdār*. Like other Imperial vassals, the Peshwā too was invited to the Court. It was promised that Bāji Rāo's demand for Rs. 15 lakhs would be met on his going to Delhi.[1]

Bāji Rāo and Chimāji granted Imperial *mansab*, etc.; Imperial *farmān* to the Peshwā, Sept. 29, 1736.

Having been appointed by the Emperor as the deputy-governor of Mālwa, the Peshwā went over to occupy the province. During the rains of 1736, the Maratha army encamped there. Rānoji Sindhiā, Pilāji Jādhav, Holkar, Anand Rāo Pawār, Tukoji Pawār and Jiwāji Pawār were in charge of the province and of the Maratha army. Anand Rāo, however, died in June, 1736 and was succeeded by his son Yeshwant Rāo Pawār, who was in Mālwa with his father. The Maratha generals tried to see

The Maratha camp in Mālwa, 1736.

[1] S.P.D., XV, pp.86, 88, 89; S.P.D., XIV, 62; its correct date is September 18, 1736, if the month given in the letter be correct; but it appears that the correct month is Jamadalakhir and the correct date is October 18, 1736. S.P.D., XV, 67; Rājwāde, VI, 17; its date as given by Rājwāde is wrong, the correct one being October 14, 1736.

that no land in the province should remain uncultivated.[1]

Bāji Rāo's final demands: 1736-7.

After the rains the Maratha activities were renewed. The Peshwā now sent in his final list of demands in which he claimed:

(1) That the governorship of the province of Mālwa, with all the States connected with it, to be given as *jāgir* to the Peshwā.

(2) Expulsion of Yār Muhammad Khān and Izzat Khān from their States with the aid of the Imperial forces and the grant of their principalities to Bāji Rāo.

(3) A *jāgir* of 50 lakhs a year in the six Deccan *subāhs* to the Peshwā. These *subāhs* should be transferred in the name of the Emperor's son and Bāji Rāo be asked to act for the absentee governor. Half of the dues collected by Bāji Rāo in the Deccan, for the Emperor, to be granted to Bāji Rāo.

(4) The kingdom of Tanjore be given to Rājā Shāhu.

(5) Grant of forts of Māndu, Dhār and Rāisin in Mālwa to Peshwā for keeping his family in them.

(6) All the territories south of the Chambal

---

[1] S.P.D., XXII, 331; XIV, 62; A.M.D., 104; Rājwāde, VI, 95, 96, 97, 17; their correct dates are June 8, June 22, June 25 and October 14, 1736 respectively.

were to be given to the Peshwā in *jāgir* on the explicit term that the various rulers of the various States within that area would not be harassed, if they submitted and paid their tribute.

(7) A sum of 15 lakhs to be paid immediately from the Bengal treasury to help the Peshwā to pay off some of his huge debts.

(8) The holy places of Prayāg, Benares, Gaya and Mathurā to be given in *jāgir* to the Peshwā.

(9) All the arrangements in the Deccan to be made through the Peshwā.

(10) Bāji Rāo agreed to go to Agra, whence he should be conducted by Jai Singh and Amir Khān and presented to the Emperor during a ride. Soon after he should be given leave to return home.

The Emperor naturally refused to accept these terms and all negotiations with the Imperial Court ended for the time being. They were, however, not renewed until after the death of Bāji Rāo, by his son, Bālāji Rāo, in 1740-1.[1]

The Peshwā found that his terms had been rejected, but at the same time he received a secret invitation from Jai Singh. He left Punā on November 12, 1736, to carry the war to the gates

---

[1] Sarkar, I, 274-6; S.P.D., XV, pp.95-6.

Bāji Rāo marches into Mālwa; his attack on Delhi and return, 1736-37.

of Delhi.[1] He crossed the Narmadā and was at Depālpur on November, 29. From there he marched to Bhopāl and besieged the place. Yār Muhammad Khān came out of Islāmnagar with his forces and attacked the besiegers, but could not raise the siege and had to return to Islāmnagar. Leaving Holkar in charge of the siege of Bhopāl, the Peshwā went and besieged Islāmnagar also. Yār Muhammad Khān had to yield and he promised to pay 5 lakhs in all. On his paying Rs. 3½ lakhs in cash and presenting 5 horses, robes, grain and many other things, peace was made (*c.* Dec. 20, 1736). The Nizām was then moving towards Burhānpur, but he did not go to the help of Yār Muhammad Khān as the latter did not summon him for aid.[2] From Bhopāl the Peshwā went to Bhilsā and took it on January 11, 1737 after a siege of a fortnight. After realizing the dues from Bhilsā, the Peshwā moved on to Bundelkhand.[3] The Imperial generals were also active moving near Agra and in the territories north of the Chambal. The Maratha generals went into the Bhadāwar State and a struggle

[1] *Vamsh*, 3240; S.P.D., XXII, 341; Sarkar, I, 270-1.

[2] S.P.D., XIV, 43; XV, 18; X, 27. Its correct date is January 19, 1737.

[3] S.P.D., XXX, 192; XV, 5, 93.

ensued. The Peshwā led his cavalry into the environs of Delhi, sacked Kalkādevi and returned. The few defeats of the Marathas in the campaign and the activities of the Imperialist generals did not affect the political situation in Mālwa.

The Nizām summoned to Delhi, 1737.

The Emperor, however, was now advised by the Vazir and some others of his counsellors to summon the Nizām to the Court. The Vazir and his associates had realized their own weakness and inability to grapple with the situation. The Nizām too had not yet got over the temptation to control the Imperial affairs. His interest in the affairs of Mālwa had so far been limited to the establishment of peace within and the realization of the dues from his *jāgir* lands.[1] But with the increased activity and the expansion of the Maratha power, the Nizām had grown anxious and had begun to correspond with Sādāt Ali Khān and other nobles for preventing the satisfaction of the Maratha demands.[2] Khān Daurān Khān too, the worse opponent of the Nizām, realized the need for summoning the Nizām. Saiyyad Jamāl Khān was sent from Delhi to bring the Nizām to the Court. The Nizām showed great

[1] S.P.D., XXX, 125; XV, 88.
[2] S.P.D., XIV, 43; XV, 89, 91.

respect and received the *farmān* near Burhānpur on February 3, 1737.[1] He had reached Burhānpur on December 20, 1736, and had been waiting there to hear from Delhi. His agent had informed him that he would be granted the governorship of Mālwa and would be asked to proceed to that province to drive the Marathas out.[2] On receipt of the *farmān*, summoning him to the Court, the Nizām decided to go to Delhi. Hearing that he was at last coming to his help, the Emperor too promised on oath not to meet the Peshwā. The Nizām could leave Burhānpur only on April 7, 1737, and crossed the Narmadā near Handiā some time early in May.[3] The news of the Nizām going to Hindustan had its effect on Mālwa. The *zamindārs* near Indore refused to pay the dues to the Maratha agents. Yār Muhammad Khān who had already

---

[1] S.P.D., XIV, 45; XV, 93; *Ahwal,* 241 in Irvine, II, pp.299-300.

[2] S.P.D., XXX, 194; X, 27; its correct date is January 19, 1737. In Sec. 2 of this letter (page 23 line 9) Chhatra Sāl should be read as Chhatra Singh. It refers to Chhatra Singh Kachhāwāh of Narwar and not Chhatra Sāl Bundelā. The latter would never have dreamed of making an alliance with the Nizām against his protectors, the Marathas.

[3] S.P.D., XV, 25, 26, 27, 37; *Ahwal,* 245a in Irvine, II, 300.

paid half of the dues, now declined to pay anything of the remainder.[1]

The Nizām reached Sironj on May 10, and the Maratha agents in the town left the place. The Nizām stopped at Sironj until May 29, and tried to sense the movements of Bāji Rāo, who was now on his way back to the Deccan. While returning from the North, Pilāji Jādhav met the Nizām on May 28, and the latter duly honoured him. At the request of the Nizām, Pilāji and his son escorted for some marches the army of the Nizām, which had stayed behind at Sironj. Stopping at Shāhdaurā on May 31, and at Budhā Dongar till June 2, the Nizām moved towards Gwalior. He passed through Agra and reached the neighbourhood of Delhi by July 2, 1737.[2]

No sooner did the forces of the Nizām leave Sironj than Yār Muhammad Khān once again made friends with the Marathas and promised to pay up his remaining dues, requesting, however, that his territories might not be devastated. On his way to the Deccan the Peshwā was at Dhāmuni on May 29, and thence he hastened towards the Deccan. Rānoji

---

[1] S.P.D., XV, 27, 40, 42.

[2] S.P.D., XV, 40, 42, 48, 44, 49, 60; *Ahwāl,* 245a in Irvine, II, 300. *Mirat-us-saffa,* 634.

Sindhiā and Holkar were back in Punā by July 24. After settling the affairs of Sironj and Bhopāl, Pilāji too followed them.

The affairs at Delhi were in a huge mess. Though the Nizām had been summoned in April, 1737, Sādāt Khān again asked for the grant of Mālwa and other *subahs* on the promise to drive the Marathas out of Mālwa. Khān Daurān again opposed with success this request of Sādāt Khān.[1] The attitude of Jai Singh, who was still the nominal governor of Mālwa, was one of busy mediation for peace. But when the Nizām came to Hindustan, these things came to a stand-still for it was expected that the Nizām would place his own policy before the Emperor.[2]

The Nizām gets Mālwa for his son, Ghāziuddin Khān : August 3, 1737.

The Nizām was very well received at Delhi, was granted the title of '*Asaf Jāh*' and presented with the customary grants and robes. The Nizām promised to stop the Marathas from advancing beyond the Narmadā, in lieu of which he was promised to be rewarded with five *subahs* and one crore of rupees. On August 3, 1737, his eldest son, Ghāziuddin Khān, was appointed governor of Mālwa and Agra, thereby removing Jai Singh from

---

[1] S.P.D., XV, 48, 44, 45, 59, 30, 52; XXII, 358.

[2] S.P.D., XV, 33.

the governorship of both the provinces and Bāji Rāo from the deputy-governorship of Mālwa.[1] This was, however, done on paper, but to assume the governorship of Mālwa in practice, the Nizām and his son had to measure their strength with the Marathas.

SECTION 4.—THE LAST STRUGGLE FOR MALWA AND ITS FAILURE: THE LOSS OF MALWA: (AUGUST 3, 1737—JULY 4, 1741).

The Nizām goes to Mālwa to drive the Marathas out.

After securing the governorship of Mālwa from the Emperor, the Nizām decided to drive the Marathas out of the province and to bring it under his control. Soon after the rains were over, he and his son, Ghāziuddin, started. The troops with them numbered about 30,000 (but, according to the estimate of the Maratha informant, 60,000), in addition to his trained artillery, which was then considered to be the best in India. Leaving the direct route for Gwalior, he crossed the Jamunā below Agra and marched through Bundelkhand. By the end of November, he reached Dhāmuni. On the way, Hirde Shāh and the other sons of Chhatra Sāl

[1] S.P.D., XV, 53; Ashob, 128a, 130b; Irvine, II, 300-2.

Bundelā met him (November 11, 1736). The Rājās of Datiyā, Orchhā and the son of Jai Singh of Jaipur were with his army. Various other Rājās including the Ahir landholders and Rohilā chieftains, joined him. The Nizām expected more forces from Sādāt Khān and Durjan Sāl Hada of Kotāh. Early in December, he passed Sironj and moved towards Bhopāl. He had already sent orders to his younger son, Nāsir Jang, then his deputy in the Deccan, to see that the Peshwā might not leave the Deccan.[1]

The Peshwā too goes to Mālwa. The attempt to stop the Peshwā in the Deccan failed. No sooner did he hear of the Nizām's march towards Mālwa than Bāji Rāo hurried to the province. He gathered together an army of 80,000 horsemen and moved by way of Khargon and Punāsā towards the Narmadā. On December 7, he was at Pohānālia. A week later, the distance between the two rival armies was of 40 *koses* only.[2] Soon after he was joined by Rānoji Sindhiā, Holkar and others, who had already defeated and killed Mir Mani Khān, the *faujdār* of Shāhjahānpur, and

---

[1] S.P.D., XV, 56, 57; *Brahm.*, 134; Khush-hāl, 1082; Ashob, 130b; *Siyar*, 477; Sujān, 5; Rustam Ali in Elliot, VIII, 57; Irvine, II, 302.

[2] *Bramh.*, 134; S.P.D., XXX, 207; XV, 59.

1500 of his men in a severe battle near Dārāi Sarāi. Having killed the Maratha agent in Shāhjahānpur, Mir Mani Khān had taken hold of the place and was coming to the aid of the Nizām.[1] Sayāji Gaikawād had to encounter opposition from the Nizām when he came to join the forces of the Peshwā by way of Bhilsā, but he joined the Peshwā near Bhopal on December 14.[2]

The battle of Bhopāl: December 14, 1737.

The stage for the final struggle was fully set. On his way to Bhopāl, the Nizām sent his own heavy baggage to Rāisin fort and made ready for fight. On December 13, he reached Bhopāl after a forced march of 12 *koses*. The forces sent by Sādāt Ali, which were 10,000 strong, joined those of the Nizam.[3] The Nizām had, however, been overawed by the Marathas. Instead of boldly advancing towards the charging Marathas forces, he

---

[1] S.P.D., XV, 58, XXII, 365; XXX, 207; *Bramh.*, 33.

[2] S.P.D., XXX, 206.

[3] On the authority of Duff (I, 397), Irvine asserts (II, 304) that "Safdar Jang, nephew of Sādāt Khan, governor of Oudh and the Hādā Raja of Kotah when marching to the relief of the beleagured army were intercepted and defeated by Malhār Holkar and Jaswant Pawar." But S.P.D., XXX, 207, definitely states that the forces sent by Sādāt Ali Khān joined those of the Nizām even before December 13. Hence the statement of Irvine, in so far as it concerns the forces of Sādāt Khān, cannot be accepted.

took up a strong position in the neighbourhood of the fort with a tank on his rear and a rivulet in his front, and prepared to defend himself against the Marathas.[1] On December 13, the Maratha forces were still 8 or 9 *koses* away. The next day, when they were near Bhopāl, they were emboldened by the over-caution of the Nizām and plundered upto the very lines of the Mughal army. The Nizām now sent ahead the Rajputs and the Jāt forces under Jai Singh's son, Sabhā Singh Bundelā and other Rajput generals. His own artillery was also ordered forward. The Maratha forces, led by Rānoji Sindhiā, Pilāji Jādhav and Sayāji, attacked them, while the Peshwā waited in the rear for an opportunity to attack the Nizām. The Nizām was too shrewd to give him such an opportunity. The battle was fought in the evening of the December 14, 1737.[2] The Rajputs lost 150 men while the losses

---

[1] S.P.D., XV, 5; XXX, 207; *Bramh.*, 33; Rājwāde, VI, 117; Irvine, II, p.303.

[2] Bāji Rāo says (S.P.D., XXII, 368; *Bramh.*, 33, 34, 36) that the battle was fought on Ramzān 3 (December 14). The letter in Rājwāde, VI, (No. 17) gives the date as Ramzan 4 The difference is caused by the fact that the battle was fought in the evening. The day according to the Muslim calendar changes at sunset and the writer of the letter in Rājwāde evidently dates the event a day later as the battle had not

of the Marathas numbered 50 or 60 men only. The number of the wounded on the Maratha side was 200 to 400 men and 500 to 700 horses. The artillery of the Nizām not merely caused havoc among the Maratha army, but it also saved the Nizām's forces from being badly routed. The Nizām soon recalled his forces and in the action neither party gained any decisive advantage.[1]

For three or four days the Nizām remained entrenched. The Rajputs and the Nizām became distrustful of each other and the former thought of deserting the Nizām, but could not do so as their baggage was kept in the city under his control. The Marathas besieged the Mughal forces and the horses of the Nizām's army began to starve. Lack of heavy artillery made it impossible for the Marathas to do much save to cause disorder in the Mughal army by throwing burning rockets in the midst of its ranks and camp.[2]

The Nizām had been waiting for help from Delhi and the Deccan. But soon after the battle

---

concluded before sunset. The battle was fought on December 14, in the evening.

[1] Rājwāde, VI, 117 gives different details but the statement of Bāji Rāo should be relied upon. *Bramh.*, 33.

[2] *Bramh.*, 33; Irvine, II, 303-4.

The Nizām gets no help.

of December 14, it was reported that no help would come from the capital. On receiving the request for additional forces from the Nizām, the Emperor told the Vazir and Khān Daurān that they should accompany him when he himself marched against the Marathas. The Emperor was not expected to move out in the near future.[1] A reinforcement from the Deccan assembled at Aurangābād only by the middle of December, 1737. The forces that were collected to march into Mālwa were 20,000 strong. The Peshwā had also written to Rājā Shāhu for help, and to Chimāji urging him to arrange for aid from Dābhāde, Bānde and other Maratha generals, who had so far abstained from helping him. Bāji Rāo wrote to Raghuji Bhonsle also. Nāsir Jang mobilized his forces at Aurangābād and on December 18, was preparing to march towards Burhānpur. He awaited the arrival of Shujāt Khān from Elichpur, who on his way to Aurangābād was completely defeated by Raghuji Bhonsle. Chimāji had already taken a strong position on the Tāpti and his forces were soon to be strengthened by the arrival of Dāmāji Gaikawād. Nāsir Jang found himself in a very bad position. He knew that he

[1] *Bramh.*, 33; Irvine, II, 304.

would be leaving Aurangābād at the mercy of Raghuji Bhonsle. After long discussions and consultations Nāsir Jang left Aurangābād and moved towards Burhānpur. Chimāji now attacked him in the rear. But soon after the news that peace had been made between the Peshwā and the Nizām was received (c. December 20-30, 1736),[1] and Nāsir Jang decided not to advance.

The failure of the first peace talks.

The Nizām was sending messenger after messenger summoning Nāsir Jang to Bhopāl. But, before any news from the Deccan could reach him, the army of the Nizām had actually begun to starve and he sent Anand Rāo Sumant to discuss terms of peace with the Peshwā (December 24, 1736). Bāji Rāo sent Bābuji Rāo Malhār to the Nizām. On the next day representatives of both the sides met and settled the terms, but the Nizām was yet thinking whether or not to accept them.[2] On

[1] S.P.D., XV, 58, 59, 63, 82; XXX, 207; XXII, 369; *Bramh.*, 33; Irvine, II, 304-5; Rājwāde, VI, 107, too refers to the events of this campaign. Its correct date is between December 20 to December 30, 1737.

[2] S.P.D., XXII, 369, refers to these peace terms. Nāsir Jang's decision not to advance further was probably taken on the news of the beginning of these peace talks. The terms were :—

(*i*) Handing over of the province of Mālwa and its full control.

December 26, under the guise of peace talks, he made an attempt to move, but failed. The Marathas were awaiting the final acceptance of the terms, but no reply was forthcoming. After moving for some distance, all of a sudden the Nizām turned back and marched towards Bhopāl. Now Awāji Kāwade and Yeshwant Rāo Pawār attacked him in the rear and an action began between the Marathas and the Jāt forces. The Nizām ordered forward his artillery, which was continuously in action for full six hours. Covering his retreat with his artillery the Nizām entered the fort of Bhopāl. Thereupon the Maratha forces besieged the fort and cut off all his supplies of food and fodder.[1]

The final retreat of the Nizām: January, 1738.

Very scantily informed about the situation in the Deccan, the Nizām still awaited help from there. Bāji Rāo could not cause a breach in the walls of the fort due to lack of artillery, but the burning rockets, which were being continuously thrown into the fort by the Marathas, conspired with the lack of provisions to force the Nizām to make

---

(*ii*) The Marathas not to cross the Chambal.

(*iii*) Some cash payments. (According to S.P.D., XV, 63, the Nizām promised 65 lakhs, while the Marathas were demanding 85 lakhs).

[1] *Bramh.*, 34; Irvine, II, 305.

another attempt to break through the Maratha besiegers. The baggages were deposited in Bhopāl and Islāmgarh. He began his peace talks afresh. The unwieldy Mughal army could not move faster than 1 or 1½ *kos* a day. The Marathas hovered round the Mughal army, cutting off all supplies, but without any great gain. The situation in the Mughal camp was, however, becoming desperate, rice was selling at one rupee a *seer* and even on payment of that price it could not always be had. Horses had to go hungry as no grass was available. On January 5, the Muslims ate up the artillery oxen, while the Rajputs were utterly starving. The Nizām now decided to make peace. He called Ayāmal of Jaipur and sent him with Said Lashkar Khān and Anwarullāh Khān to the Maratha camp. The peace terms were settled and on January 6, 1738, the Nizām wrote down with his own hand and signed the convention accepting the demands of the Marathas. The chief terms of the convention were as follows :—

The convention of Durāhā Sarāi : January 6, 1738.

(1) Grant of the whole of Mālwa to the Peshwā.

(2) The grant of the complete sovereignty of the territories between the Narmadā and the Chambal.

(3) A promise by the Nizām to obtain confirmation of this peace from the Emperor.

(4) A promise to use his best endeavour to obtain a sum of 50 lakhs from the Emperor to pay for Bāji Rāo's expenses. The Nizām would not part with money, but he promised to pay according to his own circumstances, if the Emperor did not pay anything.

The convention was signed at the Durāhā Sarāi. Soon after, the Nizām sent all the Rājās, landholders and other nobles of Mālwa to meet the Peshwā. By this convention the Nizām accepted the Maratha domination in Mālwa. The province was now practically lost to the Empire.[1]

After making peace with the Marathas the Nizām started for Delhi and reached the capital in April, 1738.[2] The Empire was being threatened by a new and at the same time, a greater danger, the impending invasion of Nādir Shāh of Persia.[3] At

---

[1] *Bramh.,* 35, 36, 116; S.P.D., XV, p.87; Irvine, II, 305-6; S.P.D., XV, No. 66 says that the peace was made on Paus, Vid 13 (January 7). He, however, states this on the basis of bazar gossip and cannot be fully relied upon.

[2] *Mirāt-us-Saffā,* 63b; Irvine, II, 306.

[3] According to *Siyar,* (p.477) the Nizām made peace with the Peshwā and hastened to Delhi to meet the new and yet

Delhi all were engrossed with this new problem and the convention of Durāhā Sarāi had to await its ratification from the Emperor for full three years.[1]

After the departure of the Nizām, the Peshwā stayed at Bhopāl for a fortnight. He sent Rānoji Sindhiā and Malhār Holkar to Kotāh to take their vengeance on Durjan Sāl Hādā, Mahārāo of Kotah, who had marched towards Bhopāl to help the Nizām but had had to retreat when intercepted and defeated by Malhar Holkār and Yeshwant Rāo Pawār. The Peshwā too followed Holkar to Kotāh and plundered and devastated the whole district. When Kotāh was besieged, the Mahārāo fled to the fort of Gāgron and made peace by promising to pay Rs. 10 lakhs by February 10. Only eight lakhs could be paid in cash and for the remaining two lakhs a bond was given which remained unredeemed for more than a year.[2] After

Bāji Rāo and the Kotāh affair: Feb.-Mar. 1738.

---

greater danger of Nādir Shāh's invasion. According to Rustam Ali, the Nizām courted his own failure and was secretly in league with the Marathas (Elliot, VIII, 57). Both these statements are wrong.

[1] According to Rustam Ali, the Emperor removed the Nizam and appointed Bāji Rāo instead as the governor of Mālwa, (Elliot, VIII, 57). But this again is wrong.

[2] S.P.D., XV, 65, 68; XXII, 129; XXX, 299; *Bramh.*, 134; Irvine, II, 304; Sarkar, I, 272; *Vamsh.*, 3249 states

settling the affairs of Kotāh, the Peshwā went to Datiyā and Orchhā by way of Ahirwādā (March, 1738).[1] But the Bassein affair demanded his personal attention and therefore he had to hasten to the Deccan.

Nādir Shāh's invasion and Mālwa: Feb.-May, 1739.

Northern India had to suffer from the threatened calamity of Nādir Shāh's invasion and the Peshwā decided to proceed to Hindustan (March, 1739), especially when it was remoured that Nādir Shāh would proceed from Delhi to Ajmer to visit the tomb of the saint. Bāji Rāo planned to meet Nādir Shāh's forces on the northern bank of the Chambal and to stop him from entering Mālwa. Nādir, however, did not move towards Mālwa but left Delhi to return to Persia (May 5, 1739). Before leaving Delhi he sent *farmāns* to Rājā Shāhu and Bāji Rāo (April 25, 1739) informing them that he had made friends with Muhammad Shah, that the latter was

---

that Kotāh was bombarded for 40 days at the end of which a contribution of 10 lakhs was paid. He dates the event a year earlier and says that the siege was laid by the Peshwā when on his way back from Delhi (1737).

Bālāji Yashwant Gulgule arranged the settlement with the Marathas and was rewarded by Mahārāo with the grant of a village which was confirmed by the Peshwā on February 24, 1738. Phālke, II, 1.

[1] S.P.D., XV, 68; *Bramh.*, 136.

once again the Emperor of India and that it was their duty to serve him.[1] The effect of the invasion, though indirect, was great. All the shops of the traders in all the cities and towns of Mālwa remained closed during the invasion. Disturbances broke out in various parts of the province and the Maratha generals were sent there to restore peace and order. The Peshwā was in southern Mālwa, watching the situation in northern India; he returned to the Deccan only in July.[2] The invasion of Nādir Shāh had one great effect on the affairs of Mālwa. It shattered the already tottering Empire, and the reputation of the Imperial government fell so low as to make the Maratha agent at Delhi ask the Peshwā whether he should go to the Emperor or only deal with the Nizām.[3] The loss of Mālwa to the Empire was accomplished in fact, if not yet in theory and the blow dealt by the invasion made it impossible for the Emperor to oppose the demands of the Peshwā any longer.

Bāji Rāo, however, strengthened his position in Mālwa by coming to an understanding with the

---

[1] S.P.D., XXX, 222; XV, 75, 80, 83; Rājwāde, VI, 130-133.

[2] S.P.D., XV, 81; XXX, 249.

[3] S.P.D., XV, 80.

other Maratha generals on a scheme of partitioning the Mughal provinces among the rival Maratha generals as their "spheres of influence." Dhār was guaranteed to Yeshwant Rāo Pawār and Mālwa was recognized as the preserve of the Peshwā. The partition took place some time after February, 1739, and the Maratha king set the seal of his approval on it.[1]

Death of Bāji Rāo: Azimullāh appointed governor of Mālwa: May, 1740.

In spite of all this, the settlement with the Marathas was postponed until after the death of Bāji Rāo. He died on May 10, 1740, and once again the Imperial authorities thought of making attempts to regain the already lost province of Mālwa. At the suggestion of the Nizām, his cousin, Azimullāh (who had already acted as the deputy of the Nizām there during the years 1723-24) was appointed governor of Mālwa. He collected an army of 15,000 men and took leave of the Emperor to proceed to Mālwa. He entered the camp, but did not move from Delhi. The rains set in. The Maratha armies were encamped in Mālwa and Azimullāh dared not to go there.[2]

---

[1] Sarkar, I, pp.68-9.

[2] Rājwāde VI, 145; Duff, I, 423.

In the Deccan, Bālāji Rāo received the robes of Peshwā-ship on June 25, 1740. He decided to settle the affairs of Mālwa once for all. "The new Peshwā's diplomacy and tact", says Sir Jadunath Sarkar, "seconded, it must be confessed, by the utter disintegration of the Imperial government through Nādir Shāh's invasion, succeeded where the blustering tactics of his father had failed." The Peshwā heard of the efforts that were being made in Delhi to raise trouble against him and in December, 1740, he ordered Sindhiā, Holkar, Vithal Shivdeo, Nāro Shankar, Antāji Mānkeshwar and other leading generals to proceed to northern India and to check all the efforts of the Nizām and his associates. On their way, the Marathas took the fort of Dhār. The Mughal Emperor grew furious on hearing of the success of the Marathas and ordered Samsam-ud-daulāh, Azam Khān and Jai Singh to proceed against the Marathas and not to allow them to cross the Chambal. Jai Singh was promised 7,000 a day, while the other two were to be paid 5,000 only. Samsam-ud-daulāh camped out of Delhi and Jai Singh hastened to join him.[1]

Bālāji Rāo and Mālwa: 1740-41.

[1] Sarkar, I, 276-7; Rājwāde, VI, 145, 149; S.P.D., XIII, 4.

Bālāji Rāo and Jai Singh: Final peace negotiations.

In March, 1741, the Peshwā too set out from Punā and reached Gwalior. Realizing that opposition was useless, Jai Singh reported to the Emperor that the captains under him were quite inexperienced in warfare against the Marathas. Jai Singh sent envoys to the Peshwā and opened peace negotiations. He urged the Peshwā that he should remain satisfied with the grant of the province of Mālwa and Gujrāt and should pledge that the other parts of the Empire would not be disturbed. The Peshwā claimed the *chauth* of the whole of Hindustan, but showed his willingness to accept the terms offered by Jai Singh, provided an Imperial *farmān* was issued and the two provinces were legally conferred on him.

Mālwa granted to Bālāji: the terms of the *farman* and the grant: July-Sept. 1741.

The Emperor had no other option but to accept the terms dictated by the Peshwā. To save the Emperor's face Bālāji was made to submit a petition to the Emperor professing his loyalty to the throne and submitting that he had come down to serve the Emperor. The last doubts of the Emperor were removed and his mind was fully reassured when, at his request, Rānoji Sindhiā and the other Maratha generals gave him an undertaking in writing that they would abandon the Peshwā in case he turned disloyal to the Emperor.[1] Now the Emperor sent a *farmān* informing the Peshwā that he had conveyed his orders to Mahādeo Bhatt Hingane, the Maratha agent at the Imperial Court, who would carry the same to the Peshwā. On July 4, 1741, another *farmān* followed, by which the Emperor granted the *Naib-Subāhdāri* (deputy-governorship) of Mālwa to the Peshwā and called upon the newly-appointed deputy-governor to see that the welfare of the subjects was well attended to. Two months later, on September 7, 1741, a grant of the whole of Mālwa, including criminal jurisdiction (*faujdāri*) within the province, was made to the Peshwā and he was called upon to maintain peace within the province, to guard its cities, to make the roads safe for travellers and above all, to see that the subjects were not oppressed. This grant bore the seal of the Vazir. The Vazir had further recommended to the Emperor that, according to one of the terms of the settlement, the Peshwā should be given Rs. 15 lakhs by way of reward; the payment, however, was to be made in three instalments.[2]

---

[1] Malcolm, I, pp.94-5; its correct date is May 12, 1741.

[2] *Chahar Gulzar,* 376a, 377a; Sarkar, I, 277-8; S.P.D., XV, 86, 88, 89, 86, 97.

Bālāji Rāo's undertaking to the Emperor, 1741.

Bālāji Rāo, on his part, gave a written undertaking to the Emperor and promised (1) to visit the Emperor, (2) to see that no Maratha crossed the Narmadā, holding himself responsible for the acts of one, if any ever did cross, (3) not to disturb any province except Mālwa, (4) not to ask even in future for any money in addition to what was already granted, (5) to depute one Maratha general with 500 horses to serve in the Imperial army, (6) to join the Imperial army with 4,000 men whenever the Imperialists started for any campaign,—any additional help was to be paid for especially.[1]

The Peshwā visited Jai Singh near Dholpur on May 12 and the latter returned the visit three days later. On May 20, Bālāji started for the Deccan. Early in July, when the *farmān* was received, the peace was confirmed.[2]

The true nature of the transfer of Mālwa.

The loss of Mālwa to the Empire was complete. The grant of the *Naib-subāhdāri* was merely meant to disguise the completeness of the surrender. Again, as it later proved to be, it was unconditional as well. Mālwa ceased to be a part of the Empire, which shrank to the Chambal on its southern

---

[1] Sarkar, I, 278; S.P.D., XV, 86, pp.97-8.

[2] S.P.D., XXI, 2; Purandare, I, 149; Sarkar, I, 278.

boundary. The breakdown of the Imperial administration in the province had occurred after the return of the Bangash. The struggle, which had been going on between the Mughal and the Maratha forces, practically ended after the convention of Durāha Sarāi, but its end was thoroughly accomplished in 1741, and the Maratha domination over Mālwa was not merely accepted, but was legalized. The year 1741 marks the beginning of a new epoch in the history of Mālwa.

Causes of the failure of the Mughals in Mālwa.

The causes of the failure of the Mughal forces to oppose the Marathas in Mālwa were many. The Emperor and his Vazir were incompetent and given to pleasure. Their disregard of the affairs of State was greater than usual when those of Mālwa were concerned. During the days of the struggle, it had been the custom at the Court that whenever there was the report of a Maratha invasion on Mālwa, the Emperor was sent either on long visits to the various gardens round the capital or on hunting expeditions in order to have his mind distracted. The Vazir too sought relaxation by a visit to his country house, 12 miles away from Delhi; and the affairs of the Empire were at a standstill.[1] The Imperial

[1] Wārid, 121-3; Irvine, II, 278-9; Sarkar, I, 12.

officers in the province could not do anything against the invaders as they got no help from Delhi. The turbulent and disturbed state of Mālwa greatly reduced the provincial revenues and the governor found it too insufficient even to maintain his own status, let alone for maintaining an efficient army to keep the invaders out of the province. The need for monetary help was great and the Emperor and his Vazir could not send any money from the Imperial treasury, which was already impoverished. The governor was being continually harassed by orders from Delhi and at times removed from his high office if he dared to meddle with the vested interests in the province. The whole of Mālwa was divided into *jāgirs* and grants, and the governor had literally no space in the province to place his foot on. The interest of the grantees was limited to the realization of their dues. Their agents and the various Rājās and *zamindārs* found it to their advantage to ally themselves with the Maratha invaders. It ensured peace within their lands and brought greater gains if they gave shelter to the invaders in cases of dire necessity. Jai Singh encouraged this tendency, hoping that his own ends would be attained by the weakening of the Imperial authority in the province. Those who were still loyal to the Mughal throne, found themselves too weak to stem the Maratha tide. There was thus practically no opposition within the province. The Imperial campaigns from 1732-33 right down to that of 1737-38 exhibited the utter incapacity of the Imperial generals and the immobility of the Imperial army, rendering swift and decisive action or earnest and vigorous effort impossible. The disunity among the Imperial statesmen and generals was quite obvious. The lack of a decided and definite policy and the ever-changing mind of the Emperor afforded sufficient opportunities for a scheming person to gain his own ends. The Maratha armies, on the other hand, were very swift in their movements, and their generals and statesmen could easily out-shine their Mughal rivals. Moreover, while the Imperial administration in the province was breaking down, the Maratha hold was strengthening. The various generals received grants in Mālwa and their interest in it was increased by the various settlements of the province, in which these generals were assigned certain portions of land or a certain percentage of the provincial revenues. These early grants proved to be the nucleus round which the modern Maratha States began to crystallize and consolidate.

SECTION 5. THE DEVELOPMENT OF MODERN MALWA. (1730-1741)

The new factor in the provincial politics of Mālwa.

This period forms an important stage in the development of modern Mālwa. Three factors helped the beginning of the new state of affairs. In the first place, it was during this period that the modern Maratha States of Mālwa made their humble beginning; secondly, the breakdown of the Mughal government within the province was complete, which helped the establishment and growth of some principalities and led to deterioration in the position of others; thirdly, the Maratha contact with the States of Mālwa was established and in some cases the States felt the heavy hand of the invaders. The position was yet to change considerably with the legalization of the Maratha domination.

The beginning of the Maratha States in Mālwa.

Since his first great victory over the Nāgar brothers at Amjherā the Peshwā had been following a policy of extending his hold over the province by assigning the dues of various places to some of his generals. In 1729, Bāji Rāo granted the dues of the districts in Mālwa to Udāji Pawār and Malhār Holkar, reserving a certain portion for himself and his brother, Chimāji. On the return of the Bangash to Agra the struggle between the Mughal and the Maratha forces continued only in the northern front from Rāmpurā to Bundelkhand, thus leaving southern and central Mālwa at the mercy of the invaders. The Maratha statesmen would not let such an opportunity go. The feudal institution was once again used to extend the Maratha confederacy and a beginning was made in the foundation of the Maratha States in Mālwa.

The settlement of 1731.

Udāji's withdrawal left Holkar supreme in Mālwa, and on October 3, 1730, Holkar was granted a *saranjam* of 74 *parganahs* in Mālwa, with all rights pertaining to the grant. Soon, however, Sindhiā was also associated with Holkar in the management of the province. Rānoji's rise was rapid, and in 1731, he attained a position in Mālwa equal to that of Holkar. In the settlement of December 20, 1731, the division of the dues was thus made by the Peshwā :—

		Percentage.
Peshwā	...	... 8·5
Holkar	...	... 35·0
Sindhiā	...	... 35·0
Pawār	...	... 21·5

Though a share in the dues of the province was reserved for the Pawārs, it was not assigned to them.

The settlement with Anand Rāo Pawār was to come into effect from 1732-3. The other scions of the Pawār family, Tukoji and Jiwāji Pawār, were also associated with the affairs of Mālwa and on October 22, they were granted 7% out of the 21·5% reserved for the Pawārs, but they were to be paid out of the common purse. The supreme control of the affairs in the province was vested in Holkar and Sindhiā and on November 2, 1731, the Peshwā handed over the seals to both of them jointly.[1] By the year 1731, all the leading Maratha families appeared in Mālwa and the rise of each may be traced separately.

Holkar in Mālwa. Even after 1731, when the Peshwā associated Sindhiā with Holkar, the latter continued to enjoy a preferential treatment at the hands of his chief. In 1731 he was given additional new grants, many of which were from districts outside Mālwa. The individual grants to Holkar in Mālwa were at first renewed year after year with slight modifications. On January 20, 1734, he was signally honoured by the Peshwā by a grant in perpetuity to his family. In addition to some lands in the Deccan he was

[1] S.P.D., XIII, 54-56; XIV, 58; XXII, 50, 55; XXX, pp.300-301, 304-306, 306-307.

given the district of Maheshwār in Mālwa and nine villages from Indore district (*viz.*, Harsol, Sāver, Bārloi, Depālpur, Hātod, Mahidpur, Jagoti, Karanj and Mākdon). These *khāsgi* lands in Mālwa, as they were termed, were expected to yield Rs. 2,63,000 a year, a sum which was not to be included in the *saranjām* of Holkar. This grant evidently marks the beginning of the modern Indore State. The other lands which were held by Holkar in lieu of his military services and duties of management, continued to be with him and were termed *daulatshāhi*. The management of the province, which was vested in him in 1731, continued to be with him till his death in 1766.[1]

Grant of the *khasgi* lands to the Holkar family: Jan. 20, 1734.

The rise of Sindhiā in Mālwa was very rapid. When Udāji Pawār withdrew from Mālwa, the Peshwā did not think it advisable to let the affairs of Mālwa remain in the hands of Holkar alone, and he nominated Rānoji Sindhiā also to work jointly with Malhār Rāo.[2] Though Rānoji was assigned

Rānoji Sindhiā in Mālwa.

---

[1] S.P.D., XXX, p.305; XXII, 82; Bhāgwat, *Purva*, I, 2-3. the *khasgi* lands in the Deccan were granted from the district of Chāndwad and yielded an income of Rs. 36,010-10-0 per year.

[2] According to *Holkaranchi Kaifiyat* Rānoji's rise was due to Holkar (pp.8-9). This appears to be a one-sided view. Rānoji was important even before his coming to Mālwa

a percentage of the dues from Mālwa, he does not appear to have received any individual grant in Mālwa. He, however, made Ujjain his head-quarters even as early as 1735.[1]

The Pawārs of Dhār. The position of the Pawārs in Mālwa declined with the withdrawal of Udāji. His brother, Anand Rāo retrieved the situation by consenting to accept the terms of the Peshwā, and he was granted a *saranjām* from the year 1732-3. He had, however, been closely associated with the affairs of Mālwa since the day of his brother's active co-operation. In 1733 the *saranjām* of Anand Rāo included the districts of Nālchhā, Badnāwar, Dharampuri, Bakāner, Sāver, Tāl, Khairābad and many others. He was granted a portion of the tributes from the Bānswādā and Dungarpur States also. The State of Dhār may be said to have been founded from the year 1733; the district and city of Dhār were, granted only in 1735, at the time of the annual renewal of grants. In June, 1736, Anand Rāo died and he was succeeded by his son Yeshwant Rāo

---

(S.P.D., XIII, 50; XXX, 28). His entry into Mālwa affairs must have been solely due to the Peshwā, who naturally did not like that Holkar should be allowed to become the sole manager of affairs in Mālwa.

[1] S.P.D., XIV, 29.

Pawār, and the *saranjam* of his father was confirmed on him (August, 1736).[1]

Pawārs of Dewās.

Tukoji and Jiwāji Pawār, cousins of Anand Rāo, were introduced into Mālwa only in 1731, when they were to be paid 7 per cent of the dues collected in the province. They received their individual *saranjām* in 1734, which was renewed on August 17, 1735. The two brothers thus jointly received the districts of Dewās, Sārangpur, Bāgod, Ingnod and a portion of the tributes from Bānswādā and Dungarpur. The grant of these districts marks the beginning of the modern State of Dewās. The joint grant led to the founding of two distinct princely branches in one place.[2]

The breakdown of the Mughal administration in Mālwa: its results.

The founding of these Maratha States was made possible by the breakdown of Mughal rule in the province after the withdrawal of the Bangash in 1732. The fact that all the States were founded in southern Mālwa shows that the Maratha hold on the province was strongest in the south. During the second stage of the Maratha-Mughal struggle, Mālwa was entirely without any system of adminis-

---

[1] S.P.D., XIII, 54-6; XIV, 48; XXII, 54, 331; XXX, 320; Athalye's Dhār, 28, 29, 31, 33, 34. The final partition between Anand Rāo and Udāji was effected in August, 1732.

[2] S.P.D., XIII, 55; XXII, 57, 87; XXX, 306-07, 319.

tration. The Marathas were busy in their own struggle with the Mughal armies, and therefore, their efforts to extend their hold on Mālwa were naturally very fitful, and were such as would cause the least resistance. The main interest of the Marathas lay in the realization of their own dues. Year after year, when on their way to the North, the Maratha armies came to Mālwa, their presence helped their agents in the province to realize their dues. These agents were appointed by the Peshwā and were ordered to work under the directions and on behalf of the generals in charge of the place. The Peshwā thus hoped to check the accounts and the activities of his generals. The Marathas saw to it that the agents and officers did not oppress the people and also asked the various *zamindārs* to see that more lands were put under cultivation.[1] During these years the Maratha armies encamped in Mālwa only once, during the rains of 1736, when the Emperor had accepted the Peshwā as a deputy of Jai Singh.

The breakdown of Imperial rule not only helped the Marathas to strengthen their position and to increase their hold on the province, but it also

[1] Rājwāde, VI, 620; A.M.D., 151, 153, 154, 161.

Strengthening of the various States: Increase of their powers and status.

strengthened the position of the various landlords and Rājāhs. The Marathas felt that it was to their benefit to continue all those who were in possession of lands and in control of districts, only if they were willing to accept them as their ally and to pay their dues. Hence, when Nandlāl Mandloi died, his son was confirmed in his father's place.[1] The Marathas also recognized those Rājāhs as masters of the land they held, if they agreed to meet their demands. Thus, this period of struggle gave the various princes of Mālwa sufficient time to strengthen their own position and to raise their status. The breakdown of Mughal rule naturally left these *zamindārs* and Rājās supreme masters of the lands which had been granted to them with various reservations, and of which now they assumed full sovereign powers. Thus, during the period the province was further divided into a great number of full-fledged States without any unity among them, which made the work of the Marathas at once easy and difficult. The lack of unity among them and lack of any strong individual State in Mālwa gave the Maratha power a commanding influence over the newly-created States, while their number made it necessary for the

[1] Rājwāde, VI, 613, 614, 607.

invaders to settle their affairs individually with each State.

States of Mālwa and the Maratha aggression: Southern Mālwa.

The relation of the Maratha power with the various States of Mālwa varied with their changing fortunes in the struggle. They changed from place to place. The internal affairs of the province were very few and more mainly intertwined with the Maratha aggression in the province, and as such cannot be dealt with separately. The Maratha hold on southern Mālwa was very firm. Since their early raids and their decisive victory at Amjherā, they dominated over the States of Jhābuā, Barwāni and Amjherā. Taking advantage of the minority, resulting from the succession of Shiv Singh, the posthumous son of Anup Singh of Jhābuā, the Marathas took over the control of the State. It was managed by officers appointed by Holkar. The danger from Jai Singh of Sailānā to the State of Jhābuā forced its well-wishers to rely on Maratha help.[1] The affairs of Amjherā were in confusion and the ruler of the State found it difficult to pay the dues of the Marathas regularly, which necessarily gave the invaders opportunity to interfere in its internal affairs and the State was practically managed by Maratha

[1] *Jhabua Gaz.*, p.4.

officers.[1] In Barwāni a civil war began among the sons of Mohan Singh. The last years of Mohan Singh were not happy and he felt the heavy hand of the invaders, who deprived him of the districts of Nāgulwandi and Brahmangāon. In March, 1731, the Nizām invaded the State and was about to take the fort of Rājaur, when he was called away to the Deccan. Mohan Singh now abdicated in favour of his second son, Anup Singh. Mādho Singh, the eldest son of Mohan Singh, secured the help of Maratha leaders like Udāji Pawār and Kanthāji Kadam Bānde, who were opposed to the Peshwā, and they ravaged the territories of the Barwāni State; but the Peshwā sided with Anup Singh and Pahād Singh and thus by helping them secured his hold over the State.[2]

The relations of the Marathas with other States varied from time to time. In his campaign against the Marathas, the Bangash got very little help from the rulers and that too was given very reluctantly. The other *zamindārs* of Mālwa sent their agents to the Marathas, as soon as the latter crossed the Narmadā, fixed the amount of the black-

---

[1] A.M.D., 173.

[2] *Barwani Gaz.*, pp.4-5. Vād, I, 202, 203; *Khajista*; *J.A.S.B.*, 315.

mail to be paid, exchanged their turbans with the Marathas and entered into alliance with them. Jai Singh, too, could rally very few rulers on the Imperial side. Later, the campaigns took place only on the northern border of the province. The princes were again summoned in 1737-8, when the Nizām led his campaign to Bhopāl, but his defeat only ruined the cause of the States which then sided with him, and soon afterwards the heavy hand of the invaders was on them. Kotāh was attacked by the Peshwā immediately after the Maratha victory at Bhopāl. The attitude of the Rohilā of Bhopāl also changed with time, but practically everytime he paid the Maratha dues. Jai Singh of Amber had also a personal interest in Mālwa even after he had ceased to be its governor. He was managing the affairs of Rāmpurā for his son, Mādho Singh. Jai Singh consented to pay the tribute for Rāmpurā to the Marathas and often allied himself with the Marathas, giving them shelter and promoting their cause in Mālwa.[1]

The affairs of Rājputānā also produced their own repercussions on Mālwa. The two efforts to bring about unity among the princes of Rajputānā

[1] *J.A.S.B.*, 319; Rājwāde, VI, 150-1.

and Mālwa had failed and the affairs of both the provinces drifted along. Bundi was yet in a state of trouble. The efforts made on behalf of Budh Singh have already been referred to. Even Maratha aid could not restore Budh Singh's rule in Bundi for long. He died on April 26, 1739, and it was only after 1741 that his son Ummed Singh began his efforts to recover Bundi. Yet the continuous struggle that went on for Bundi practically ravaged this part of the province.

Affairs in Rājputāna and their effect on Mālwa.

Again, in 1736, when Bāji Rāo visited Udaipur and when a treaty was signed between the Mahārānā and the Peshwā, the Māharana promised to pay Rs. 1,60,000 annually by way of tribute and to cover the tribute the Mahārānā assigned the district of Banhadā to the Marathas. Banhadā was then held by Sardār Singh, a descendant of Bhim Singh, brother of Mahārānā Jai Singh. Sardar Singh also ruled over the districts of Badnāwar and Nolāye, which comprised his independent possessions in Mālwa. He, however, grew anxious to save his estate of Banhadā and concentrated his forces there. Finding Badnāwar and Nolāye unprotected the Maratha took them over and the Peshwā granted

Disappearance of the Sisodiā State of Badnāwar, 1736.

them to Anand Rāo Pawār. The Sisodiā State of Badnāwar, in central Mālwa, finally disappeared from its political map after 1736.[1]

The political relations of the Maratha power with the States of Mālwa were completely revolutionized by the grant of the *farmān* of 1741. The Peshwā became the lawful deputy-governor of Mālwa and the relations of the ruler of Mālwa were now no longer with the Emperor at Delhi, but had to be kept up with the Peshwā at Punā.

The condition of the province and of its people.

The condition of the province during this decade was going from bad to worse. The anarchy that prevailed in it ruined the whole province. Its revenue declined and the breakdown made it impossible to realize any thing during the closing years of the period. Northern Mālwa was completely devastated and the invaders felt the possibility of encountering troubles and difficulties between Narwar and Agra. The Nizām too had to change his course, when leading his campaign to Bhopāl. The existence of local rulers in various places proved to be advantageous to the people, as they saved their

---

[1] Tod, I, 493-4; *Vamsh,* 3236-7; Ojhā, *Udaipur,* II, 630-1; Sarkar, I, 262.

lands from devastation at the hands of the invaders by agreeing to pay the dues to the Marathas. The disturbed state of the country made prosperity impossible and trade suffered from the same cause.[1]

[1] Rājwāde, VI, 606, 620; S.P.D., XIV, 5, 52, 54; XV, 89, 90. A.M.D., 104, 105, 153, 154; Irvine, II, 302; *J.A.S.B.*, pp.318, 323.

CHAPTER VI

THE CONSOLIDATION OF THE MARATHA HOLD ON MALWA AND THE END OF THE EPOCH. (1741—1765).

SECTION 1.—THE MAIN CURRENTS OF THE PERIOD: 1741—65.

With the formal cession of Mālwa to the Marathas by the Emperor, the struggle for the province ended and the Marathas became its master. During the early years of the first decade Holkar and Sindhiā were busy consolidating their hold on the province, but time and again they had to go to Bundelkhand and also to attend to the affairs of Jodhpur. After 1747 the Marathas became interested in the war of succession in the Jaipur State, and no sooner did it end than the Maratha generals were summoned to Delhi to oppose the Afghan invaders led by Ahmad Shāh Abdāli.

Soon, however, civil war broke out among the leading ministers of the Court of Delhi, and the Maratha generals became an important and powerful factor. Each of the two contending parties tried to win them over, and this struggle continued till 1755.

But next year, Ahmad Shāh Abdāli invaded the Punjab and reached Delhi in January, 1757. The Marathas had to send their armies and generals to fight the invaders. Raghunāth Rāo led the expedition and Malhār Holkar accompanied him. Ahmad Shāh retreated in April; Raghunāth Rāo led his expedition to the Punjab and on his way back went to Rājputānā.

In December 1758, Dattāji Sindhiā reached Delhi and a complete reversal of the Maratha policy in northern India took place. A political crisis occurred at Delhi, and on its heels came the news of a fresh invasion by Ahmad Shāh Abdāli. Once again the Maratha forces were entangled in the affairs of Delhi and the battle of Pānipat followed. Thus, for full twenty years after 1741 Maratha statesmen and their two leading generals, Holkar and Sindhiā, who were in charge of Mālwa, were kept busy with affairs outside Mālwa.

During the years that followed the disaster of Pānipat Malhār Holkar dominated the affairs of Mālwa till his death in 1766. In 1761, he had to restore order and once again to strengthen the Maratha hold on the province, which had been badly shaken by the disaster of Pānipat. But during this period Bālāji Rāo had died and with the succession of Mādhav Rāo there began troubles at Punā. Hostilities with the Nizām also kept the Marathas busy in the Deccan, and thus there was a lull in the affairs of Mālwa. The last three years of the period 1763-65 were marked by inactivity. Malhār Holkar was dying, the question of a successor to Jankoji Sindhiā was being finally decided and the affairs in Rājputānā were slowly taking shape.

Evidently, the first phase of this period of anarchy in the province was ending, and the long neglect of Mālwa affairs by the Maratha statesmen was coming to an end. With their scope restricted, the Marathas now applied themselves to making a home and creating a full-fledged dominion for themselves in Mālwa, and this policy in its result completely revolutionized the political order and social relations of the races of Mālwa in the course of the two generations that followed the death of Malhār Rāo Holkar. Yet the long period of drift followed by the Marathas in respect to Mālwa had its own effect on provincial politics. During these twenty-five years the various States and principalities which had arisen on the fall of the Mughal Empire took root and became crystallized into political entities. Thus, the political situation in Mālwa in the year

1765 was very different from what it had been in 1741.

It cannot, however, be denied that by the year 1765, the Maratha domination of Mālwa had become an established fact. The Maratha administration in the province was not yet organized, nor was the Maratha hold over the province very strong, but the Maratha power had come to stay in the province, and the various generals Holkar, Sindhiā and the Pawārs had become established in Mālwa. The Maratha power in Mālwa had become consolidated. The Maratha rule, however, crystallized only during the second phase, *i.e.*, after 1765.

SECTION 2.—THE CONSOLIDATION OF THE MARATHA POWER: 1741—59.

The grant of a *farmān* by the Emperor bestowing the deputy-governorship of Mālwa on the Peshwā, secured peace to the Empire on its southern boundary. The Marathas too gained their end: they virtually became the masters of the province. The position of the Maratha generals, working under the Peshwā was also strengthened; they were recognized as guarantors for the loyalty of the Peshwā to the Government of Delhi. Mālwa was also freed from all possibilities of interference by any other Maratha general, such as Raghuji Bhonsle.

The settlement of the affairs of Mālwa; 1741 and after.

Holkar and Sindhiā now set themselves to consolidating their holdings in Mālwa and also to settling their relations with the Princes of Mālwa. These early relations established by the Marathas were more or less in the nature of a contract to leave the territories of the Princes unmolested if the Maratha dues were regularly paid. The settlements with Yār Muhammad Khān of Bhopāl and the Mahārāo of Kotāh give us good examples of Maratha policy.[1] In many cases the dues could not be paid regularly, and force had to be brought to bear on a Prince to make him pay, but it could be done only when the Maratha generals found their hands free of any engagements elsewhere. Thus alone can the repeated reminders for the arrears due from the Mahārāo of Kotāh be explained.[2]

Sindhiā and Holkar were, however, busy during the year 1742 in settling the affairs of Jodhpur.

[1] The policy of the Marathas was to conciliate the Hindus and to exact money without resort to fighting if it could be so managed.

[2] The Vols. I & II of Shinde Shāhi I.S. (Phālke) abound in letters and reminders to Gulgule to make the Mahārāo of Kotāh pay his dues. Holkar and Sindhiā even threatened to invade Kotāh if the dues were not paid.

Rānoji returned to Ujjain in March by way of Sironj, while Holkar went to Kālābagh to meet the Vazir; but as the latter had gone back to Delhi, Holkar collected the Maratha dues from that province.[1] During the rains of 1742 the Maratha army encamped in Mālwa. This caused alarm in the hearts of the people of the province, but they were assured that if the dues were paid no additional levy would be imposed.[2]

When the year 1743 opened the two generals were still in Mālwa. Raghuji Bhonsle was trying his best to put obstacles in the way of Holkar and Sindhiā; Sawāi Jai Singh, though on his deathbed, was once again thinking of driving the Marathas out of Mālwa. One Gulāb Singh promised to undertake the campaign. Ramchandra Bābā was warned by the Maratha agent at Jaipur to strengthen the defences of the forts in Maratha hands in Mālwa. The situation was a bit menacing, and Purandare suggested to the Peshwā that for another year in continuation, Holkar and Sindhiā should encamp in Mālwa. The Maratha soldiers were tired of being

During the year 1743.

---

[1] S.P.D., XXVII, 2; XX, 4.

[2] Vād., III, 6; Rājwāde, VI, p.164; S.P.D., XXI, 6. The date of the letters appears to be about July, 1742.

away from their homes in the Deccan.[1] Bālāji dealt with the situation very tactfully, and on August 31, 1734, renewed the settlement regarding Mālwa with Raghuji Bhonsle, made by Bāji Rāo a few years before. According to this settlement, Mālwa with Ajmere, Agra and Allahabad were conceded by Raghuji to be the preserve of the Peshwā, while the Peshwā promised not to interfere with the provinces given to Raghuji Bhonsle.[2]

Destiny too helped the Peshwā, as Jai Singh died on September 23, 1743. Before his death he gave half the rights of the district of Māndugarh (26 *sarkārs*) to the Peshwā. Many of these had been already granted by the Peshwā to Holkar, Sindhiā and the Pawār. The Peshwā now sent instructions that half of the dues should be regularly paid to the agent of the Jaipur State.[3]

During the year 1744.

The period of the treaty made in 1740 by Bāji Rāo with Yār Muhammad Khān of Bhopāl for three years, having expired early in 1744, a new treaty was made with him and a satisfactory settlement of the dispute about lands was arrived at, as also of the dues in arrears. The affairs of Khichi-

---

[1] S.P.D., XXVII, 5; XXI, 8, 9.

[2] *Aiti. Patra,* I, 35, 36.

[3] Vād., III, 18.

wādā were also concluded. As the situation in Bundelkhand required personal attention, Holkar and Sindhiā went there leaving Mālwa in the charge of Laxman Pant, Govind Ballāl and Dādā Mahādeo, who moved from place to place and tried to bring the country under their control. All refractory *zamindars* were driven out and Maratha outposts were set up at important places. But soon after the rains, troubles began and one Durgā Singh of Kotāh, who was in charge of the Maratha lands there, fought a skirmish with the Maratha agents and was killed. Gopal Keshav reduced Ahirwādā and conquered the fort of Narsinhgarh and ten other minor fortresses.[1]

Early in 1745, the Maratha forces attacked and took the fort of Bhilsā, on March 11, 1745. These hostilities made it essential for the Peshwā to make another settlement with Yār Muhammad Khan.[2] The delay in the payment of the dues from the Kotāh State continued to be a perennial source of trouble between that State and the Marathas. Kotāh was, however, warned not to meddle with the territories of the "Pātan" district, which was

---

[1] Vād., III, 202,20, 21, 75; S.P.D., XXI, 10, 11; Phālke, I, 28 probably refers to this skirmish.

[2] S.P.D., XXI, 7, 12.

then under Maratha control, and the Marathas were desirous of making this place—a prosperous town.[1] Holkar and Sindhiā were busy in Bundelkhand. On July 19, 1745 Rānoji Sindhiā died at Shujālpur (in Mālwa) and was succeeded by Jayappā Sindhiā.[2]

The year 1746 was occupied in the Maratha conquest of the stronghold of Jaitpur in Bundelkhand. In the year following, while Antāji Mānkeshwar was busy subjugating the district of Gwalior, Malhār Holkar was requested by Sindhiā to punish the Rājā of Narwar, to exact their dues and to subjugate his territories.[3]

Yeshwant Rāo Pawār of Dhār and the Peshwā, 1748-1751.

In 1748, Yeshwant Rāo Pawār fell into disgrace due to his quarrels with his fellow officers and his excesses in the State of Bānswādā (May). Early in June, the Peshwā was at Dhār, and to please him Yeshwant Rāo gave up Dhār and Māndu to the former and moved to Badnāwar with his family. The Peshwā then gave him a *jagir* of 3½ *mahals* and took him into his service once again (June 14, 1748). Soon afterwards the Peshwā went back to the Deccan. Yeshwant Rāo, however, continued to request the Peshwā for the

[1] Phālke, I, 26, 29, 31, 33, 34, 38, 39.
[2] S.P.D., XXI, 13, 15; Phālke, I, 37.
[3] S.P.D., XXI, 16, 18, 3; XXVII, 29, 23.

restoration of the fort of Dhār to him, and at last on August 15, 1751 his request was granted. He was also granted his percentage in the dues of the province from the year 1751.[1] During the rains of 1748, the Maratha armies stayed on in Mālwa and Jayāji Sindhiā spent his days in camp.[2]

Rāmpurā affairs: 1727-1751.

During the years 1747-50, Holkar and Sindhiā were busy with the affairs at Jaipur. In 1727, the district of Rāmpurā, which was then under Mewād, had been granted to Mādho Singh, the infant younger son of Jai Singh, of the princess of Udaipur. The administration of Rāmpurā was carried on by Jai Singh's officials till September 7, 1743, when at the Mahārānā's desire Jai Singh withdrew his men. Mādho Singh had lived at Udaipur all these years. After the death of his father, his eldest surviving brother Ishwari Singh ascended to the throne of Jaipur and was recognized by the Mughal Emperor. Mādho Singh, however, claimed the *gadi* for himself on the basis of the

---

[1] Purandare, I, 172, 175; Vād., III, 38, 33, 183; Phālke, I, 74, 104; Rājwāde, VI, 141. Its correct date is June 25, 1748. The Peshwā, however, continued the grants made by Yeshwant Pawār in the district of Dhār. Māndu was given to Holkar and Sindhiā on June 7, 1755. Vād., III, 83.

[2] Phālke, I, 77, 78.

Triple Treaty of 1708. The Mahārānā of Udaipur helped his cousin and a civil war ensued. The two parties tried to secure Maratha help and the long civil war ended in 1750, when Ishwari Singh, hearing of the approach of a revengeful Maratha horde led by Malhār Holkar, committed suicide and Mādho Singh became the King of Jaipur (December 29, 1750). On January 6, 1751, the Marathas put up a new demand for at least one-fourth of Jaipur territory in addition to the cession of Ranthambhor etc., already agreed to before. Mādho Singh was alienated, and on January 10, the Maratha visitors to his capital were massacred. Mādho Singh explained away the massacre to Holkar and Sindhiā. Rāmpurā was thus once again held by Jaipur State and Mādho Singh became directly interested in the politics of Mālwa.[1]

---

[1] S.P.D., XXVII, 64, 65; II, 31; XXI, 40; Sarkar, I, pp.295-305; *Vamsh.*, IV, 3622; *Vir Vinod,* II, 1236, 1241; S.P.D., XXVII, 64 & 65 suggests that the Marathas practically got nothing. S.P.D., XXI, 40 asserts that Mādho Singh had promised to pay the levy and the arrears. But S.P.D., XXVII, 152a, says that Rāghobā demanded the province of Rāmpurā from Holkar which means that Rāmpurā was with Mādho Singh even in 1757. Hence it can be conclusively said that Rāmpurā was not transferred in 1751 as *Vir Vinod* (II, 1241) asserts. The change of ownership took place only in 1757.

The affairs of Delhi during the years 1748-53.

In the meanwhile, the Emperor Muhammad Shāh had died on April 18, 1748, and was succeeded by his son Prince Ahmad Shāh. On the occasion various new appointments were made, but the Imperial officials did not think of Mālwa and the Peshwā was left undisturbed there. He made Abul Mansur Khān Safdar Jang of Oudh his Vazir, which made Asaf Jāh's son, Ghāziuddin I, dissatisfied. In 1749, intrigues began at the Imperial Court and Nāsir Jang was summoned to Delhi. Safdar Jang entered into alliance with the Marathas, and hearing that Nāsir Jang had actually started for the North, he posted Holkar and Sindhiā in Kotāh to intercept his rival's march. On April 7, 1748, the Emperor made friends with Safdar Jang again and Nāsir Jang was written to to go back to the Deccan.[1]

In 1752, when Abdāli once again led his forces into the Punjab, Safdar Jang was away in Oudh; on hearing of the invasion from the Emperor, he summoned his Maratha allies to Oudh and there arranged a defensive subsidiary treaty with the

[1] S.P.D., II, 12, 12c; Sarkar, I, p.354-6; *Hadiqat-ul-Alam*, II, 191. Purandāre, I, 156, 157. These letters are of the year 1749. The "Rānabā" referred to is not Rānoji Sindhiā, but some one else.

Peshwā. To satisfy the Emperor, the two Maratha generals, Holkar and Sindhiā, were asked to give a written undertaking for the fidelity of the Peshwā. To stop treacherous Maratha encroachments he proposed to send Bakht Singh and other Rajput princes to hold the line of the Narmadā against them. But this treaty soon became a mere scrap of paper, as Emperor Ahmad Shāh made a cowardly submission to Abdāli and surrendered the Punjab and Sindh to him, just twelve days before Safdar Jang returned to Delhi.[1]

Safdar Jang was anxious to extend the power of the Empire, and during the last months of 1752 he wrote to Salābat Jang in the Deccan to keep the Marathas engaged there so that he could drive them out of Mālwa with the help of the Jāts and Mādho Singh. This as well as the later schemes of Mādho Singh and Bijay Singh to recover the provinces from the Marathas came to nothing.[2]

Raghunāth Rāo passes through Mālwa, 1753-55.

In 1753 Raghunāth Rāo marched into Hindustan and on his way passed through Mālwa. Crossing the Narmadā near Maheshwar on Sept. 22, 1753, he moved by way of Indore and Ujjain to

---

[1] Rājwade, I, 1; Sarkar, I, pp.360-4.

[2] S.P.D., XXI, 44; XXVII, 119; Sarkar, II, pp.182-3.

Mukund-durrāh and crossed the Chambal on November 3. On his way back two years later, he took the important fort of Gwalior on June 7, 1755, which was evacuated by the Jāts of Gohad. It was then put in charge of Gopāl Ganesh Barve. Thence he marched through Mālwa, traversed Khichiwādā and Umatwādā and re-crossed the Narmadā at the ferry of Barwāhd on July 11, 1755.[1]

By May, 1756 the Maratha forces had vacated Rājputānā and Hindustan, north of Chambal; Antāji Mānkeshwar and his small contingent alone remained in Delhi. On February 10, 1757, Antāji write to the Peshwā, "No general from the Deccan is coming; so (the Durrānis) think that if they can drive me out of Faridābād, they would conquer Mālwa also." In March, 1757, it was rumoured that Abdāli would make Agra his headquarters and attack Mālwa. Holkar and Raghunāth Rāo were ordered by the Peshwā to go to the border of Mālwa to oppose him.[2] Holkar and Raghunāth Rāo had reached Indore on February 14, 1757. Passing through the territory of Mewād and exacting a ransom of

Rāmpurā affairs : 1751-1759.

[1] S.P.D., XXI, 68, 87, 88; XXVII, 79, 110; Vād., III, 83.
[2] S.P.D., XXI, 99; XXVII, 166; Sarkar, II, p.136-7.

one lakh from Jāwad (near Neemuch), the Maratha forces reached Barwādā in Jaipur State and besieged it. Kani Rām the Jaipur minister came to satisfy Raghunāth Rāo by paying the tribute promised before. Raghunāth Rāo would not be satisfied with that and demanded the cession of Rāmpurā-Bhānpurā, Tonk and two other districts in addition to the monetary payments and transfer of the *jagir* of Ranthambhor (c. April 12, 1757). At first Mādho Singh made ready for fighting rather than grant these demands. Soon the Marathas lowered their terms. Mādho Singh transferred the districts of Rāmpurā-Bhānpurā, Tonk and two others to Holkar in order to win him over to the policy of peace. Thus again the districts of Rāmpurā-Bhānpurā reverted to the province of Mālwa.[1]

Cases of succession at Kotāh : 1756-58.

Raghunāth Rāo on his return march, after settling the affairs of Delhi, passed through Mālwa. At Kotāh the new Mahārāo, who had succeeded in 1756, had died, and the question of his succes-

[1] S.P.D., XXI, 107, 120, 121; XXVII, 152a; Rājwāde, I, 71; Sarkar, II, pp.137-8, 191-2. The Marathi authorities do not mention this fact. But S.P.D., XXI, 177 definitely mentions that in Dec., 1759, Rāmpurā was in Malhār's hands. The transfer, therefore, must have taken place between 1757 and 1759. No other probable opportunity occurred after 1757 when it could have been transferred.

sion had been settled by Sindhiā.[1] Here Holkar came, met Jankoji Sindhiā and removed the misunderstanding which had long existed between them. In northern India it was feared that Mādho Singh might open hostilities once again and invade Mālwa, and Raghunath Rāo was requested not to hurry back to the Deccan; but he continued his march to the Deccan and crossed the Narmadā early in September, 1758.[2]

Holkar now returned to Indore where he was taken ill. After his recovery, he went to Punā in January, 1759. There he used all his tact and diplomacy to remove an impression created in the mind of the Peshwā, that he had been opposing the interests of the latter. Soon after he returned to Mālwa carrying with him the full trust of his chief and all his former powers.[3]

At Bhopāl too there had come about a change. Yār Muhammad Khān died and was succeeded by Faiz Muhammad Khān. In 1753 the Peshwā renewed the settlement of lands made nine years before with that State. During these years the dues of the State were being paid regularly. The fort

Bhopāl affairs : 1753-1759.

[1] S.P.D., II, 66, 96; Phālke, I, 196.
[2] S.P.D., II, 88; XXVII, 229, 230; Phālke, II, 62.
[3] S.P.D., XXI, 167, 172; Sarkar, II, pp.195-6.

of Bhilsā was taken back by the Bhopāl State and continued to be in its hands.[1] There was, however, trouble brewing in Khichiwādā and Rājā Balbhadra Singh had not paid his dues. Constant fighting between him and the Mahārāo of Kotāh was going on.[2]

But the attention of the Maratha generals was once again centred at Delhi and they began to prepare for the final struggle with Ahmad Shāh Abdāli, and the settlement of many questions in Mālwa had to be postponed till their struggle with the Afghans was over.

The fluid condition of the province.

Thus the year 1759 marks the end of a period during which the Maratha hold on Mālwa continued to be strengthened and their authority in the province was never challenged. They continued to rule over the province, but the attention that they paid to its affairs and government was very scanty and fitful. Owing to the total disappearance of Imperial authority from the province and the delay in the establishment of full Maratha administration in its place, the unruly elements utilized the interval every time that the leading Maratha generals were

[1] Vād, III, 75; S.P.D., XVII, 145, 316, 217.
[2] Phālke, I, 213, 215, 217.

called away to Bundelkhand, Delhi or the Deccan—and the *zamindars* and *Grassiahs* (predatory classes and outlaws) of Mālwa displayed turbulence. In short, the province was in a fluid condition for ten years or more. The weakness of the Maratha administration becomes evident from the way in which all *zamindars* and petty rulers try to encroach on the lands belonging to the Marathas.[1] The Bhils living in the Vindhya range and near about were continually in a state of revolt and disturbed the peace of the country round, and the Marathas levied an additional tax on the States which comprised the area, in order to compensate them for the loss. But whenever the local rebels threatened to cut off communications with the Deccan, efforts were made to clear the path.[2] Much trouble in the province was caused by internal friction among the Maratha generals. For long Holkar and Sindhiā were not on good terms with each other, with the result that their assistants were also opposing one another. The friction among other minor officers also disturbed the peace of the country.[3]

---

[1] S.P.D., II, 22; Phālke, I, 29, 31, 38, 39, 139.
[2] S.P.D., XXI, 167; Vād, III, 226, 234.
[3] Phālke, I, 219, 29; Rājwāde, VI, p.303.

The vast Maratha armies which traversed Mālwa during the years 1751-1760 were destined for Rājputānā or Delhi and they did not touch Mālwa. The only effect they produced on the province was to cow down any intended rebellion, and the States on the way, *e.g.*, Kotāh, Khichiwādā etc., paid their dues.

During all these years the Marathas hoped to effect vast gains in Rājputānā and northern India, and hence they did not pay much attention to Mālwa. Mālwa, however, was yet to be really subdued and the Maratha administration there was still to be organized. It was not yet a paying concern. This fact accounts for the comparative neglect of Mālwa in their records during these early years. The province too did not go through any great convulsion, nor was there any event which would have revolutionized the politics of the province. Hence the references to its internal events are few and very brief.

SECTION 3.—THE DURRANI CLASH, THE BATTLE OF PANIPAT AND AFTER, 1759—1765.

Early in 1759, the skies on the north-western frontier were overcast by a fresh invasion of Ahmad

Shāh Abdāli. With his inroad into Hindustan, and defeat and death of Dattāji Sindhiā (Jan. 9, 1760), the eyes of the Maratha statesmen were fixed upon the affairs at Delhi and vast preparations were made to drive Abdāli out of India.

The Maratha army marches through Mālwa. April-May 1760.

The grand Maratha army led by Sadāshiv Bhāu started northwards in March, 1760. It crossed the Narmadā at Hāndia on April 12, and reached Sironj by way of Sihor and Bersiā on May 6. Here the Bhau stopped for some days in order to cash the *hundis* received from the Peshwā, payable at Ujjain and Indore. He tried to collect some dues from Balbhadra Singh Khichi, who had not paid anything for some years past. When the Bhāu marched beyond Sironj through the Ahirwādā country the Ahirs rose in his rear and made the roads unsafe for traffic and communications. The Bhāu, however, pushed on to Araun and Narwar. He reached Gwalior on May 30, 1760.[1]

During his march through Mālwa, the Bhāu was dependent on Holkar and Govind Bundelā for information as to the exact position of things in northern India. The Bhāu had sent letters to Jaipur,

[1] Rājwāde, I, 174, 176, 180, 186; S.P.D., II, 125; Khare, I, 18, 22; Phālke, I, 213, 215, 217; Sarkar, II, pp.241-3.

Jodhpur and Kotāh calling upon their rulers to join him in his campaign against Abdāli. Mādho Singh promised help, but the Kotāh Mahārāo kept quiet and his chastisement had to be postponed till after the defeat of Abdāli. The invasion of Abdāli had caused terror among the Maratha collectors (*Kamāvishdārs*) of Mālwa.[1]

The Marathas defeated at Pānipat: Holkar's escape: The Peshwā and Mādho Singh.

The Maratha army suffered a crushing defeat at the hands of Abdāli on January 14, 1761, and Malhār Holkar alone saved himself from the catastrophe. The Peshwā had marched into Mālwa early in January, and on the 24th of that month, when he was at Bhilsā, he intercepted a banker's letter from Delhi, giving the fatal news of the battle of Pānipat. He stayed at Bhilsā till Feb. 7, and then marched by way of Sihor and Sironj to Pachhār (32 miles north of Sironj), hoping against hope that the rumours of the escape of the Bhāu and other chiefs would prove true. At this time, the Peshwā received a letter from Mādho Singh summoning him to Bundi, and proposing to combine with him and march once again against the Afghans. Mādho Singh and other Rajput princes had been summoned to Delhi by Abdāli who asked

[1] Phālke, II, 10, 11; Rājwāde, I, 176; S.P.D., II, 118.

for a certain sum. But the reply of the Peshwā was a stern reprimand to the Jaipur Rājāh for his not having helped the Marathas in the campaign of Pānipat. He, however, added that if Abdāli advanced the Marathas would retreat south of the Narmadā. Soon after this, the survivors of Pānipat met the Peshwā and asked him to retreat to the Deccan. He left Pachhār on March 22, and soon afterwards crossed the Narmadā.[1]

The effect of the defeat in Mālwa.

The Maratha defeat at Pānipat rudely shook the Maratha power in Mālwa; a reaction against their domination began in the province. The disaster encouraged the original chieftains and land-holders who had submitted to Maratha rule or who had been ousted by them; they now rose in rebellion and talked of driving the southern intruders out of the province. For full three months or more the position of the Marathas in Mālwa was very critical. Their vast armies had been practically annihilated at Pānipat; the survivors were yet terror-stricken, leaderless and disorganized; the government had become bankrupt; the efforts of the Peshwā to make money by confiscating the grants to Yeshwant Pawār

[1] S.P.D., XXI, 204; XXVII, 260-72; Purandare, I, 402; Rājwāde, VI, 415, 416; Sarkar, II, pp.359-60, 502 *n*; Khare, I, 26, 28.

and the Sindhiā family had only caused dissatisfaction and weakened the Maratha power in Mālwa. It was really an excellent opportunity for the Rajputs, but no unity among them was possible; nor did there rise any great leader among them, who could take advantage of the situation. Mādho Singh of Jaipur was least fitted to undertake any such expedition.[1]

Holkar saves the situation in Mālwa.

Malhār Rāo Holkar, who was now put in supreme control, not only of Mālwa but of the whole of Hindustan, rose to the occasion, and the veteran leader by his indefatigable energy turned the table against all the enemies of Maratha rule. On his return from Pānipat he recouped himself at Gwalior for some time, gathered together the remnants of the Bhāu's army, and then went to Indore. He found that not merely had the Rajputs risen in revolt, but that the administration had also broken down and various minor officials were becoming disobedient.[2]

He, however, decided to restore his authority first by putting down the revolts of the Rajputs and other tribes. Rāmpurā, now in the *jagir* of Holkar,

---

[1] S.P.D., II, 142, 143; XXIX, 18; Sarkar, II, 502-4.
[2] S.P.D., XXVII, 268; XXIX, 10.

had been captured by the Chandrāwat family, which formerly ruled there. Holkar marched against the usurper, but before his arrival Krishnāji Tāndev (an officer of Santāji Wāgh and revenue collector of Mahantpur) had defeated the Chandrāwats and recovered Rāmpurā. The Chandrāwats lost about 400 men, and their *Diwan* was captured.[1]

The third day after this success, Holkar went to the country of the Hādās, and by way of Gahukhedi advanced to Gāgurni, where Abhay Singh Rāthor, one of the officers of the Mahārāo of Kotāh, had ousted the Maratha officers. Malhār Rāo besieged the Gāgurni for fifteen to twenty days, but he could not do anything until the heavy guns ordered from Indore were received. Soon after, the fort was taken (early in June, 1761). The immediate result of this success was to restore the awe and prestige of the Marathas in north-west Mālwa. Holkar moved on to Mewād.[2]

Vithal Shivdev was busy restoring order in Gohād and other neighbouring countries on the

---

[1] S.P.D., XXVII, 271; Phālke, II, 64.

[2] S.P.D., XXVII, 269, 271. Holkar had asked for forces from Raghunāth Rāo while at Gāgurni. S.P.D., XXVII, 267.

Efforts in eastern Mālwa, 1761-62.

northern frontier of Mālwa.[1] The situation in Ahirwādā and the country near it also needed urgent attention, and the Peshwā had sent Gopāl Rāo and Jānoji Bhonsle to put down the troubles there. Gopāl Rāo had restored order by the beginning of May, 1761, and went on to Sāgor by way of Sironj, but no sooner had he left Mālwa than there was another rising of the Ahirs and they began to build new forts. The rains had set in and as the Ahirs were joined by Izzat Khān and the Khichis, the Marathas thought of waiting till the end of the rains. They, however, strengthened their control over Narsinghgarh and maintained good relations with Visāji Pant, who though a Mughal officer, had great influence in the province. In November, 1761, the chief Maratha official in Ahirwādā sent pressing calls to Holkar, then near Kotāh, and Holkar went as far as Sāngāner but had to return as his wound received at Māngrol was festering. Hence in December, 1761, Nāro Shankar asked his son Vishwās Rāo to go to Sironj, to meet Izzat Khān and Govind Kalyān, to make friends with them and to capture Jhānsi with their help. Govind Kalyān was ordered by the Peshwā to take up the

[1] S.P.D., XXVII, 270, 272.

affair of Sironj and Ahirwādā, to conciliate the *zamindars*, to bring under his control all the out-posts of the place and manage the district. He was further ordered to recover the fort of Bhilsā, recently taken by the Nawāb of Bhopāl.[1]

In the meanwhile, Mādho Singh had been intriguing against the Marathas and planning to over-throw their predominance. He went down to Ratlām (on May 14) and probably secretly intrigued to gain help from the States of central Mālwa. Khichi, Bundi, Kotāh and many other chiefs joined him or promised to do so. The rains prevented Holkar from doing anything. Late in October, 1761, Mādho Singh began his offensive. Holkar had been summoned to Punā, but he could not go there; on the other hand, he marched from Indore towards Kotāh to meet the invading Jaipur forces. On November 29, the battle of Māngrol was fought and the forces of Mādho Singh were decisively beaten. The Mahārāo of Kotāh sided with the Marathas. The effect of this victory was decisive; all possibilities of the formation of any anti-Maratha

Mādho Singh defeated by Holkar: Oct.-Nov., 1761.

[1] *Aiti.*, II, 188; I, 101; S.P.D., XXIX, 12, 22, 37, 43; XXXIX, 3; Rājwāde, I, 296.

coalition were lost, and the prestige of the Maratha arms once again soared high.[1]

During the rains of 1761 and afterwards the Peshwā made a series of new appointments; Holkar was awarded new lands, Vithaldeo Rāo was appointed a *Saranjamdar*, and Bahiro Anant also received *saranjams*, while Kedārji and Mānāji Sindhiā got grants of lands when they were accepted as heirs to Jankoji.[2]

But age had begun to tell on Holkar. The wound that he had received at Māngrol kept him in bed for more than three months. No vigorous policy was possible in Mālwa. During the years 1762 and 1763 the Maratha forces were kept busy in the Deccan by the invasion of the Nizām on Punā and the civil war between the Peshwā and Raghunāth Rāo. In the years 1764 and 1765, Malhār Rāo was induced to march to Hindustan in order to join Jawāhir Singh Jāt in his attack on Najib Khān in Delhi. In May, 1765, he was bribed by Shujā-ud-daulāh the Vazir to fight against the English in the Doab. Mādho Singh had realized the hopeless-

---

[1] S.P.D., XXVII, 276; XXIX, 20, 22; II, 57; XXI, 91, 92, 93, 94; Phālke, I, 266, 267; II, 65: Sarkar, II, 506, 509.

[2] Vād, IX, 158, 189, 190, 193, 338, 105, 159, 160, 161, 162, 194.

ness of his own situation by now, and he made friends with the Marathas and the more so on realizing the new danger that had arisen from the European-drilled forces of Jawāhir Singh Jāt.

In Mālwa itself, there was now a lack of great leaders. Malhār Rāo Holkar was dying, and he left no great successor to continue his work. The Peshwā had on the other hand not yet realized the fact that Mahādji Sindhiā was the man of the future. He did not appoint any successor to Jankoji till March 17, 1763, when Kedārji Sindhiā was awarded the robes of honour; but that did not settle the question. On September 16, 1764, Mānāji Sindhiā was also recognized, and the two were ordered to work jointly. This estranged Mahādji, who left Punā without orders and went to Mālwa. He eluded those, who had been ordered to intercept his march, reached Ujjain, and thence went on to Kotāh to exact tribute.[1] The situation in Mālwa at this time, though apparently calm and peaceful, was really full of ominous signs and there was a great danger that if no efforts were made Mālwa would also be lost to the Marathas.[2] Inactivity and lack

The situation in 1765.

[1] S.P.D., XXIX, 130, 48, 70, 67, 62, 64, 92, 96; XXXIX, 32, 33; Vād, IX, 159, 160, 161, 163.

[2] S.P.D., XXIX, 103.

of a vigorous policy weakened the Maratha power in Mālwa. Holkar was dying, and there was yet none to take up the supreme command and the lead in the affairs of Mālwa, that he would relinquish at his death.

SECTION 4—THE END OF THE EPOCH.

With the year 1765 the first stage of the age of anarchy in Mālwa ends. The Maratha hold on the province was well-established by now, and it had survived the great shock of the battle of Pānipat. Mughal rule in Mālwa had broken down early, and the falling Empire had neither the energy nor the will left to re-assert its authority here. With its formal cession in 1741, the Mughal Emperor, and his ministers and officers had abandoned Mālwa for good.

The Maratha disregard of the affairs of Mālwa.

The long struggle between the Mughal and Maratha forces thus ended with the withdrawal of the former and the Peshwā became the *de facto* master of Mālwa, and Maratha generals controlled the province and attended to its affairs. But neither their army nor its generals had much time to consolidate and organize a regular administration there. The Maratha statesmen expected much greater gain from other provinces like Allahabad, Oudh and the

Punjab, and tried hard to establish their hold there, and consequently they neglected Mālwa, taking care, however, to see that the province was not lost to them. Thus, even though the administration was not yet organized, the Maratha power came to stay and the various Maratha generals who were granted *saranjams* and lands in Mālwa, first to help the conquest of the province and later to keep it under Maratha dominion, made these grants the basis of their power and in time carved out new States in the province.

The strengthened position and increased status of local States in Mālwa.

This fluid condition of Mālwa afforded excellent opportunity to local adventurers and powerful *zamindars* as well as to the former Mughal grantees. They seized the chance, and seeing that the Marathas were too strong for them to oppose, they agreed to pay money tributes and went on strengthening their own hold over their possessions. Slowly these States crystallized into political entities, and taking advantage of the situation their rulers formed full-fledged States. Thus, the Marathas inadvertently helped the rise and strengthening of a new factor in Mālwa, which was later to prove a source of real danger to their domination over the province, and this process went on unchecked even after 1765.

The coming phase of the period of transition: Main points of difference.

Soon after 1765, however, a series of events began which definitely marked the beginning of a new stage in the life of the province. Once again the Maratha forces march northwards, and their generals were engaged in reducing Bundelkhand and fighting against the Jāts of Gohād and Bharatpur. Raghobā led the expedition of 1766 against the latter. But one great star had set. Malhār Holkar died on May 26, 1766. His life's work of establishing the Maratha hold on Mālwa was completed, when he restored the Maratha prestige and ruthlessly put down the newly-formed opposition to Maratha domination in the province after the battle of Pānipat. And with Malhār Rāo ended the predominance of the Holkar family in Mālwa. The man of the future, the arbiter of the coming age, was Mahādji Sindhiā, who was still struggling to rise above his compeers. The question of the headship of the Sindhiā family was raised in 1761, but was finally decided only after 1765, and with Mahādji's rise the House of Sindhiā overshadowed that of Holkar. A number of new personalities dominate the coming age; Mahādji Sindhiā, Ahilyābāi Holkar, Tukoji Holkar, Zālim Singh Jhālā, and lastly Amir Khān Pindhāri, all rose after 1765 and shaped the course of events during the second stage of the age of anarchy.

After 1765 the Maratha policy in Mālwa also radically changes. The immediate effect of the battle of Pānipat in Mālwa was wiped out by the vigorous action of Malhār Holkar and other generals who re-imposed peace on the whole province. But its far-reaching results became apparent only after 1765. "The ambition and aims of the revived Maratha Power in the north", says Sir Jadunath Sarkar, "were hence-forward cooped up within the barren sands of the Rājputānā and the broken, infinitely chequered wilderness of Bundelkhand—all Hindu territory—and their activities there for forty years, 1765-1805, have left a legacy of hatred for the Maratha name in Rajput hearts, which has not yet died out."[1] Thus, it was only when all hope of Maratha domination in the politics of Delhi was lost (January, 1765) that the Maratha generals in the North turned earnestly to Mālwa. But that was after 1765. Mahādji's organization of full-fledged Maratha rule in Mālwa was a later affair, and it was only after 1775 that the Maratha administration of Mālwa (as distinct from legal

---

[1] Sarkar, II, 357-8.

possession) was established. This organization of Maratha rule in the province and these efforts of the Maratha generals to make the province a paying concern, brought them into a clash with the Rajput States, principalities and chieftains. By the year 1765, all hope of any outside help, such as the Imperial forces, the Rajput confederacy in Rājputānā or a Rajput-Jāt combination, had died out, and the Rajput princes of Mālwa felt their own helplessness, when they were hit hard by the new Maratha policy.

By the close of the year 1765, another new factor was being added to the politics of Mālwa. The Pindhāris had begun to enter Mālwa as an appendage to the Maratha forces. Though restricted at first (when a pass for their movements was necessary to take them north of the Narmadā),[1] they were soon to become a constant menace to the peace and prosperity of the province and an additional cause for alienating the local princes and *zamindars* from the Maratha patrons of these predatory bands.

These alienated Rajputs and the bitterly estranged Muslims knew that against any other Indian power the Maratha forces would prove

---

[1] Vād, IX, 351.

stronger, but when pitted against a foreign power they would not be able to hold their own, and thus when the English entered into the political arena of Mālwa they appeared as the redeemers of the harassed princes and the impoverished peasantry.

But all these events have no direct bearing on the subject of this work, save as pointing out the main respects in which the second stage differed from the first. They would, naturally be treated at length in any history of the second stage.

CHAPTER VII

CONDITION OF MALWA DURING THE PERIOD (1698—1765).

The political situation summed up.

Politically, the province of Mālwa ceased to be a part of the Mughal Empire in 1741, and thenceforth it became one of the various preserves of the Peshwā. Under the Mughals Mālwa had been one of the most important provinces. But, when the invasions of the Marathas grew frequent, it became a most difficult and dangerous business to rule over it.

With its cession to the Marathas, Mālwa was completely cut off from the Empire. The cession was nominally formal, but final. For all practical purposes no effort was ever officially made by the Empire to recover the province. The officers of the Empire too abandoned it. But Mālwa did not get that unity of administration which it had enjoyed under the Mughal Empire. The expansion of the Maratha power was achieved by the feudal system, and as the Marathas came to dominate over it the province was parcelled out into a number of fiefs.

The Maratha statesmen did not limit the application of the feudal principle to men of their own race. Their need for money was greatly responsible for its extension to the landholders and princes of Mālwa. The provincial unity was lost, and Mālwa became a jumble of principalities ruled over by Maratha generals and officers, Rajput princes and Afghan adventurers.

Administrative.

Guided by feudal ideas and with their attention diverted to affairs outside Mālwa, the Marathas did not introduce any regular administration in the province to take the place of the Mughal system which had already broken down. The early Maratha rule took the form of establishing various centres in the province and appointing officers to them to collect their dues. Many of these officers, though appointed by the Peshwā, worked under or on behalf of some Maratha general to whom the dues of the place or the right to levy a certain contribution had been granted by the Peshwā. The main work of these minor official was only to collect money and to render accounts of the same. The Peshwā thus hoped to obtain his share in the revenue of the place. In some instances, however, these officers acted as agents or *Vakils* of the Maratha Government, specially when they were posted in a State.[1]

Leaving aside the principalities and States, which had been recognized by the Maratha power as independent and liable to pay a fixed tribute only, much of the remaining land of the province was directly held by the Maratha power. Stray portions from these were granted as *Saranjāms* to the various officers, like Holkar, Sindhiā, the Pawār, Pilāji Jādhav and others. These *Saranjām* lands formed the basis round which the Maratha States of Mālwa crystallized and took definite shape. The lands which were not granted as fiefs were, however, placed in charge of the generals for management. Pilāji Jādhav, his son, Satvoji Jādhav and later Nāro Shankar were put in charge of eastern Mālwa, which included the tract from Narwar down to Sironj. The dues from Bhopal were also to be realized by this officer, who generally resided at Sironj.[2]

---

[1] The Gulgules (a family of Sāraswat Brāhman *Kamavishdars*) of Kotāh are an example of it. They collected the dues from the Mahārāo of Kotāh and the neighbouring States, and from the lands which had been assigned to the Marathas. At the same time they had to watch lest the Mahārāo should oppose the Maratha forces or their cause.

[2] Tieffenthaler, I, p.348. Pilāji Jādhav was also referred

The rest of Mālwa was put under the joint control of Sindhiā and Holkar. All the revenues were collected in a common purse and then divided between the Peshwā, Holkar, Sindhiā and the Pawārs according to the settled percentage of each. The joint control of Holkar and Sindhiā often led to trouble. It was specially the case during the years 1745-59, when there existed a misunderstanding between the heads of these two families, and their assistants carried the bad relations of their masters to the bitter end.

The administration was essentially a military occupation of the province; and this system of government continued for twenty years or more. Hence, when the organization of a regular administration was taken up, it could merely be an amplification of the system which had hitherto continued. The systematic organization of the administration on modern lines in the Maratha States of Mālwa took place only during the latter half of the 19th century, when the British Government called upon them to consolidate their territories and organize their administration.

---

to as *Subahdar;* he enjoyed a status equal to that of Holkar and Sindhiā. S.P.D., XIV, p.21; Rājwāde, VI, 406.

Their army in the province was also of a very rudimentary standard. Forces had to be kept by the various *Saranjāmdārs* and these were necessarily of the militia type and not of the high standard of the Household cavalry of Punā. Mālwa was considered more or less a foreign province, and whenever the Maratha armies encamped there they subsisted by plunder or on dues exacted from the farmers, Rājās or other rich people. The camping of the Maratha army in the province was, hence, considered a calamity. The situation changed a little for the better after the seventies of that century.[1]

Justice and public peace.

During the period of the Mughal administration in Mālwa, it was the duty of the Imperial authorities to administer justice, which was rough and ready in most cases. They were also responsible for maintaining peace in the land, the only exception being that of the States, which enjoyed full criminal powers. In the case of these States, the burden fell on the shoulders of the ruler of the State.

With the advent of Maratha rule many of the criminal powers so far reserved by the Imperial authorities, were usurped even by States which did not enjoy them before. Still, as the Marathas

[1] Vād., III, 6; Phālke, I, p.77, 78.

claimed to be officers of the Mughal Empire, they did, meddle with cases of murder committed in these States.[1] The Maratha, however, accepted the usurpation of criminal powers by many of these States of Mālwa as an established fact; these States were made responsible for maintaining peace and keeping the roads open and safe throughout their territories. In cases of continuous neglect of this duty, they were forced to make good the loss caused to wayfarers by their neglect.[2]

The justice administered by the Maratha officers was also very rough and ready. In civil cases attempts were made to effect a compromise, and when they happened the State realized a certain sum as fee for its efforts to bring about a settlement.[3] In many cases a *Panchāyat* was appointed to settle the dispute. The work of the *Panchāyat* was generally done orally, but the result of the inquiry was most

---

[1] Vād., II, p.70 mentions such a case, when Lāl Singh of Panched (in Ratlām State) murdered a Brahman in Panched. When appealed to by the relatives of the murdered Brahman the Peshwā ordered the confiscation of twelve villages held by Lāl Singh in *jagir* and granted some land in Panched in *inam* as compensation to these relatives. Jankoji Sindhiā was ordered to execute the orders of the Peshwā in this matter.

[2] Vād., III, p.226, 234.

[3] Vād., II, 40; III, 229.

often committed to writing (*Mahazarnāmāh*), when required to do so by the higher authorities.[1]

New routes in Mālwa.

The trade and other routes which passed through Mālwa also changed to some extent with the establishment of the Maratha power in the province. In the seventeen-thirties when the struggle was going on, the Maratha forces generally moved up to Garha and Saugor and entered Mālwa near Kurwāi. Their footing in Mālwa had not yet been established. But with the strengthening of their position in south-western Mālwa, the Akbarpur ferry and the fords near Barwāh gained importance. The route to Burhānpur by way of Handiā was practically abandoned as it passed through the territories of the principalities of Bhopāl, Khichiwādā and Ahirwādā, where anti-Maratha feeling prevailed more often than not. The new route followed by the Maratha armies in the fifties was this :—they crossed the Narmadā generally at Barwāh and went to Ujjain, thence to Rāmpurā,, crossed the Chambal at Kotāh, and entered Rājputānā,. As this route passed through lands inhabited by the Sondhiās, a class of early Rajput settlers in Mālwa, the Marathas had to put

[1] Phālke, I, 107, prints the papers relating to a case settled by a *Panchayat*. It throws much light on the procedure of the *Panchayat* courts.

them down to make the roads safe.[1] The armies going to Delhi moved from Kotāh to Shivpuri, Narwar and Gwalior. This change in route greatly reduced the political importance of Sironj, which, however, continued as a stronghold of the Marathas, because from this point they controlled Ahirwādā, Khichiwādā and Bhopāl.

Economic condition of the province.

The long-drawn struggle between the Mughal-Maratha forces and the continuous neglect of the affairs of the province, made the economic condition of Mālwa pass from bad to worse. Since 1700, the revenues of the province had begun to decline. In 1704 Bidār Bakht informed his father that southern Mālwa was practically ruined by the Maratha invasions.[2] The condition of the peasants and the landholders was equally bad.[3] Hence the revenue, which stood at Rs. 1,02,08, 667 in 1700 was reduced to Rs. 1,00,97,97,541 (or Rs. 1,00,99,516 according to Jag Jivan Dās) in 1707. The affairs of the province did not receive much attention during the thirteen years that followed the death of Aurangzib and the revenue fell further to

[1] Tieffenthaler, I, 350.
[2] Ināyetullāh, fol. 15a, 60a, 61a.
[3] Nawāzish, 7b, 8a, 8b-9a; Ināyetullah, 132b.

Rs. 90,04,593 in 1720.[1] The Nizām could, however, realize about Rs. 40 lakhs in 1724-5, but even these could not be collected later and the governor of the province in 1730 found it difficult with his resources to maintain a strong contingent and to carry on the administration of the province.[2] When the Marathas ruled over Mālwa the revenue was divided, and Tieffenthaler found it impossible to give any estimate of the total revenue returns of the province in his time (*circa*, 1750-60).

During the years 1741-65, the province was not a paying concern. The dues and the subsidies were not paid regularly by the States. The management by the Maratha collectors was also not very efficient, which resulted in a fall of the revenue of the province. The Maratha forces were mainly busy invading northern India, and these expeditions left the generals bankrupt. They were quite unable to devote any money to the province or its people.

In addition to Sironj and Ujjain, Indore was now becoming a flourishing centre of trade and commerce. The traders, who were mainly Bohrās, imported goods from foreign lands. Indore had its

---

[1] *India of Aurangzib*, lix, lx, 56, 141; Manucci, II, 413.
[2] S.P.D., X, 66; *J.A.S.B.*, 323-4.

bankers too, who used to cash *hundis* from the Deccan.[1]

The internal trade in grain was carried on by the Banjārās, and the Marathas had to seek their help.[2]

All the principalities enjoyed the right to levy custom duties on the transit of goods through their limits, but many times they could be exempted if the government of the place was pleased to do it.[3] Wherever it was the monopoly of the Maratha government the collection of the tax used to be farmed out.[4] There existed internal barriers even in lands held by one officer or general. All the custom dues which were being collected from the Mughal times continued to be levied under the Maratha rule.[5]

In addition to the usual levies and dues,[6] new exactions were also made by the Marathas to solve

---

[1] Vād., II, 229; S.P.D., II, 128.

[2] Vād., II, 195.

[3] Manucci, I, Introduction, lvii-lviii; Ch. XVIII; Tavernier, I, 37; *J.P.H.S.*, 90; Phālke, I, 16, 27.

[4] Vād., III, 71.

[5] Vād., III, 454.

[6] Vād, III, 410, mentions the dues which were to be regularly collected and paid to the government in addition to the land-revenue. They were :—

(*a*) Octroi; (*b*) *Sarkari Batta* (discount) at the rate of

their eternal problem of debt or to finance new expeditions.[1] They levied special occasional contributions to build public works like temples.[2]

As regards the lands held by the Maratha generals it was naturally their concern to make them prosperous.[3]

Agricultural and industrial products of Mālwa.

The fertility of the province, however, could not be affected by anarchy, and Mālwa continued to produce plenty of wheat, opium, linseed and oil-seeds. Mustard seeds, chick peas and common peas (besides linseed) were also grown in eastern Mālwa near about Bhadaurā. Rice could also be grown there. Near Sārangpur for fourteen miles at a stretch the traveller came across nothing but fields of growing wheat (*circa* 1750). The oxen of Mālwa were admirable, of great height, and robust frame and used to be exported to other countries as a valuable breed.[4]

3·125%; (*c*) *Sadil* or contingent allowances of 3%; (*d*) *Bhets* from villages (*i.e.* presents to officers on tour); (e) *Masala* fees levied from persons summoned to *huzur* to answer a charge (bailiff's costs); (*f*) *Havaldari* dues; (*g*) Fines and *Kamavis-bab*.

[1] Vād, III, 489, 495.

[2] Vād, III, 511.

[3] A.M.D., 104; Vād, III, 329, 362; Phālke, I, 38, 39, 41.

[4] Tieffenthaler, I, 342, 349, 350, 351.

The industries of Mālwa also continued to exist, though they suffered a set-back due to the anarchy and the disturbed state of the roads, which interfered with export. Cotton cloth of extreme fineness was made and exported from Chanderi. The people of Sārangpur lived by weaving, embroidery or commerce. At Sironj, cloth of various colours, ornamented with flowers, were made. They served as bed-covers and were exported abroad. Tents too were a speciality of Sironj and were ordered for the Maratha armies.[1]

Social changes in Mālwa.

Socially, the province was greatly changed during this period (1698-1765). A new factor was introduced in the provincial life by the Marathas, who came not merely as a passing blast of raiders but as settlers and overlords. They brought with them new ways of life and dress, and above all different ideas. The rough manners and defiant attitude of these men from the hills of the Deccan did not appeal to the people of Mālwa at large. Still they added another source of variety into the already cosmopolitan society of the province. The Rajputs, however, looked upon them as mere up-starts.

[1] Tieffenthaler, I, 349, 351, 354; Vād, II, 243.

The coming of the Marathas to the province resulted in completely cutting off the connection with Delhi and the Mughal Empire. Evidently the influence of Muslim culture began to wane. The Maratha influence penetrated the existing society and a mixed culture began to grow up. The effect becomes most evident in the gradual but definite change in the dress of the men-folk.[1] The Hindu culture in the province received an added impetus from the Marathas,[2] and the Maratha domination in Mālwa led to the adoption even by the Rajput States of

---

[1] The archives of Sitāmau State contain a complete set of the portraits of the rulers of the State from its foundation in 1702 to present times. A study of the dress (especially the head-dress) of the various rulers shows the slow but steady change. The modern form of the turban in Mālwa (which also is now being replaced by the more cosmopolitan form Sāfā) has evolved from the Mughal court turban with changes caused by the influence of the Maratha turban.

[2] The Marathas tried to infuse more of the religious spirit into the Brahmans of Mālwa. Rules were laid down which regulated their conduct in all walks of life. Even matters mainly conventional, such as those of dress, were given a religious colouring and efforts were made to inculcate a particular ideal. The Peshwā called upon his generals in Mālwa to do all they could to enforce such edicts. Special attention was paid to the character and learning of the Brahmans who conducted public worship in the temples. *B.I.S.M.Q.*, VI, pp.148-151, 153-6.

certain ways and thoughts of these invaders. Many of the Maratha customs, *e.g.*, the worship of Ganesh in the month of Bhadrapad and the distribution of *Til* and sweets on the Makar Sakrānti day, became the practice of the Rajput courts also.

Again, the various Rajput princes, who based their claims on Imperial Mughal favours and grants, now rose in social estimation. The difference, which once marked the grades and their status at the Mughal court was wiped out, and against the Maratha invaders all the States, small or great, became independent States of equal status and position. With their rise in political position from mere landlords to sole masters of the States, they became dictators in social affairs also. They no longer remained mere puppets in the hands of the princes of Rājputāna but became the heads of Rajput society in their State, and their opinion in social matters received due recognition in other Rajput States also.

Society as a whole was still mediaeval. Belief in witch-craft prevailed everywhere as it does even now in rude villages. Dancing girls plied their trade for the pleasure of those who could afford to engage them.

The Maratha settlement in Mālwa marks a new epoch in the linguistic history of the province.

Linguistic and literary movements. The local dialect of Hindi, generally termed *Mālwi*, which had already been a queer mixture of various languages like Vrij-bhāshā, Gujrāti, Dingal or Rajasthāni, Urdu and Persian, was further influenced by the Marāthi language. Vast hordes of Maratha soldiers passed through Mālwa, at times camped and stayed for months together, while many of them settled in Mālwa itself : and they all influenced the *Mālwi* dialect. This dialect continued to be the chief medium of expression and was used in the Rajput courts in their letters and in other documents. To the common man of the villages also this dialect was the only medium of conversation.

Vrij-bhāshā, however, continued to be the language most used in poetry. It received patronage at the hands of the Rajput princes, who were pleased to hear the poets extolling them in high terms. Lāl Kavi was the court poet of Chhatra Sāl Bundelā and wrote *Chhatra-Prakāsh*, giving a poetical account of the valiant deeds of his patron. Jadunāth Kavi composed the *Khānde Rāi Rāso* in 1749, in which he has given an account of the events in eastern Mālwa during the years 1704-1744 A.D. It mainly describes the exploits of Khānde Rāi, a brave fighter and a minister of the Narwar State. The sons of Khānde Rāi also took prominent part in the affairs of the States near about. The poet quotes the verses of some other poets, and merely mentions the names of many more. During this period, western and central Mālwa continued to be barren in literary production, while eastern Mālwa and Bundelkhand produced many poets, though very few of them were of a high order.

In the courts of the Maratha generals and officers, Marāthi was used. This language was also being slowly influenced by its long contact with the Hindi-speaking people. The court of the Rohilā chief of Bhopāl patronized Persian, which was the court language there. It was at that court that Rustam Ali wrote his history, *Tārikh-i-Hindi* (in 1741 A.D.). This work was the only one of its kind, and no other Persian work, worthy of note in this field, was produced there.

The fine arts and architecture.

On account of the long period of anarchy and continuous upheavals, the cultural life of the province received a great set-back, and the period is barren so far as the fine arts and architecture are concerned. No patronage from the central government was forthcoming. The Maratha generals were men of war with no taste for the fine arts and things of the mind. They were too busy with conquest and the establishment of their rule to turn to the intellectual and cultural side of provincial life. After the establishment of the observatory in Ujjain by Jai Singh, nothing more was done to develop the science. Education too did not receive any help from the State. To the Marathas Mālwa was yet a foreign province; it had not yet become their home. The Rajput princes also were busy consolidating their hold on the States, which had not long been under their domination. The economic pressure on these States by the Maratha generals impoverished them and the States could not find enough revenue even to maintain their own rulers much less to devote to the fine arts and architecture.

The period is transitional and hence devoid of any great creative effort.

The whole period (1698-1765) was naturally one of transition and the province saw great changes which revolutionized its society, culture and ideals, introduced new factors, and above all gave an entirely new colour to its political map. It took a long time to adjust the opposing forces, clashing interests and divergent ideals. Only after the new order had completely taken shape was it possible for Mālwa to show the final result of the changes in a striking form. During the period of upheaval and disorder any great creative effort was naturally wanting. A general degradation of the intellectual life of the province was inevitable during the period.

Whether the impact of the Marathas would help Mālwa to rise once again to its former greatness, could only be answered by a study of the second phase.

BIBLIOGRAPHY

THE NATURE OF THE HISTORICAL MATERIAL RELATING TO THE HISTORY OF MALWA DURING THE PERIOD: 1698-1765.

Except for a few chapters in Sir John Malcolm's *A Memoir of Central India*, which are very scrappy and need complete revision in the light of later researches no attempt has so far been made to write a continuous history of Mālwa during this period. The student has, therefore, to reconstruct the history of the period entirely from the original sources. In this effort he is greatly helped by the works on the decline and fall of the Mughal Empire by William Irvine and Sir Jadunath Sarkar, who tried to use all the available authorities. But since Irvine wrote his work, much new Marāthi material has become known and the history of the period need to be reconstructed in the light of the fresh evidence. Sir Jadunath Sarkar wrote with his eye fixed on the centre of the Imperial Government, and hence he has omitted all details of purely provincial interest.

The whole period can, however, be divided into three main sections according to the nature of the extant authorities on each. The first section (1698-1719) is pre-eminently Mughal and the authorities are Persian, save for the few references

Authorities for the first phase: 1698-1719.

by Marāthi historians or news-writers, which relate mainly to the early Maratha invasions on Mālwa. *Māasir-i-Alamgiri* supplies the dates of Imperial appointments, while Khāfi Khān gives details of certain incidents in the province. Bhimsen's *Nuskhā-i-Dilkasha* also gives a few additional facts. The Court bulletins (*Akhbārāts*), however, supply the main series of incidents of the period. Ināyet-ullah's précis of Aurangzib's orders, *Ahkām-i-Alamgiri*, adds much to our knowledge of the viceroyalty of Bidār Bakht in Mālwa. The few letters published in *Vir Vinod* throw much light on the incident of Gopāl Singh Chandrāwat's rebellion. Nawāzish Khān, who was the *faujdār* of Māndu from 1700 to 1704, gives us the details of the early Maratha invasions of Māndu and depicts the condition of southern Mālwa during these years.

As the *Akhbārāt-i-Durbār-i-Muallā* for the eighteen years immediately after the death of Aurangzib (1707-24) are lying idle in the archives of Jaipur State and have not been permitted to be copied or examined by scholars as yet, the historian has got to fall back upon the Persian works of

Kāmwar, Mirzā Muhammad and other contemporary historians for the details of the affairs in the province during that period. William Irvine almost exhausted all the Persian authorities on the period, but he omitted to note events of provincial interest, *e.g.*, the battle of Sunerā between Ratan Singh of Rāmpurā and Amānat Khān in 1712, and the facts relating to such events had to be culled out of these works, which are mostly in manuscript. The Marāthi sources here just begin to throw a little light on the scene, and the volumes of *Selections from the Peshwā's Daftar* give a few details of the early efforts of the Marathas in Mālwa soon after the rise of the Peshwā to power in 1713. The sixth volume of Rājwāde also publishes many important letters on the period, but the dates of many of them need correction.

There is yet another source of information about this period. The various travellers who came to India and visited the Imperial Court have given descriptions and noted incidents in Mālwa during the period. Manucci and the Dutch travellers are noteworthy in this respect. Dr. J. Ph. Vogel of the Kern Institute has translated the journal of Ketelaar and hopes to edit those of other travellers from Holland.

Authorities for the second phase: 1719-41.

Soon after the year 1719 the importance of the Persian sources diminishes. The interest of the Persian historians at Delhi in the affairs of Mālwa is definitely on the wane. Their attention is concentrated on the centre of the Empire and hence after 1723 they cannot devote more than a couple of lines to Mālwa affairs, and these too only to record some new appointment. Thus, no account is found in the Persian histories of Chimāji's campaign in Mālwa and the defeat and death of Girdhar Bahādur in 1728, and the historian has to depend on the private (Persian) letter-book of Girdhar Bahādur's family and the Marāthi records to settle the long-drawn out controversy on the point. The details of the governorship of the Bangash in Mālwa are also given on the basis of his private letter-book, *Khajistā Kalām*.

Later, the Court historians deal with the struggle raging on the northern border of Mālwa between the Maratha and the Mughal forces, but the details of the movements of the Mughal generals alone are mentioned. The intricate currents and cross-currents of the policy of peace and war confound the narrator of these events stationed in Delhi, and thus we have to supplement and correct the Persian authorities with the very valuable original

Marāthi records. The expedition of the Nizām to Bhopāl and its failure is the only thing dealt with by the Persian historians in detail.

During this period the importance of the Marāthi records vastly increases, and as years pass they slowly begin to take the first place. The authentic records recently published in the volumes of *Selections from the Peshwā's Daftar* make it easy for the historian to compare and correct the dates of many other documents published before by scholars like Pārasnis, Vād and Sāne.

The local material is also important and it can throw a good deal of light on the condition of the province and give many details of provincial interest, but this field is yet unexplored. Leaving out the Mandloi *Daftar* of the *zamindār* of Indore and the small collection of similar letters published by Rājwāde in his Vol. VI, much material of this class remains undiscovered. The archives of the State of Bhopāl may possibly contain records, but they await examination. The Hindi poets, too, do not appear to have written much. The history of the Bundelās was written by Lāl Kavi, while Jadunāth and other poets went recording the exploits of Khānde Rāi of Narwar, which are put together in *Khānde Rāi*

Rāso. But they do not give us any information about central Mālwa.

Authorities for the third phase: 1741-65.

With the formal cession of Mālwa to the Marathas in 1741, the Persian historian of Delhi had no longer any interest in the province. The Mughal officers totally abandoned Mālwa, and, therefore, it was nobody's interest to write a Persian history of the occurrences there during the period (1741-65), or to collect any Persian letter-book, because no chief had any occasion to write Persian letters. Thus, the material available to the historian is one-sided. The Maratha material is the sole basis for the history of Mālwa from that year (1741) onwards. Even in this language very little material has survived. Mālwa had no doubt come under Maratha control, but the interest of the Maratha generals and statesmen was centred further north, with the result that only political disturbances or a few movements of their marching armies are noted by them in the extant Marāthi dispatches. The other material in Marāthi has been lost by reason of the fact that as the Maratha grantees had not yet consolidated their administration and as the provincial affairs were under the control of Holkar and Sindhiā, the records remained with the descendants of the hereditary *diwans* and accountants of these two chiefs and not in the State archives of the *Peshwās*. Thus, the only Marāthi material available is that published from the *Daftar* and the diaries of the Peshwās and other private collections like that of the Mandloi of Indore, which have somehow or other become available to the public.

The unexplored local material is our only hope for the history of internal affairs during the period 1741-65. The first two volumes of Phālke's *Shindeshāhi Itihāsānchi Sādhanen* publish letters from the Gulgule *Daftar* of Kotāh, but these chiefly relate to the payment of their dues by Kotāh and other neighbouring States, and as such do not add much to our knowledge of the affairs of Mālwa. The scarcity of local material makes it difficult for the historian to write with certainty or fulness on the economic condition and the cultural movements of the province in the middle of the century.

THE SOURCES

A. Persian.

1. *Maasir-i-Alamgiri* by Sāqi Musta'd Khān. Bib. Indica. Calcutta.
2. *Nuskha-i-Dilkasha* by Bhimsen. Sarkar MSS.

   It is a work which has been most used by Sir Jadunath Sarkar in his *History of Aurangzib.* The brief references to the events in Mālwa during the first nine years of period dealt with by me are useful as throwing light on some important events in the province, *e.g.*, Gopāl Singh Chandrāwat's rebellion.
3. *Akhbarat-i-Durbar-i-Mualla*

   Tod's gift (originally belonging to Jaipur archives) to the Royal Asiatic Society, London, copied for Sir Jadunath Sarkar, supplemented by transcripts secured by Sir Jadunath of the remaining *Akhbarat* from Jaipur.
4. *Chahar Gulshan* by Chatarman Saksenā. O.P.L. MS. Translated in Sir Jadunath Sarkar's *India of Aurangzib* (1901).
5. *Ahkam-i-Alamgiri* compiled by Ināyetullah. Vol. I. Sarkar MS. containing the text as given in the Rāmpurā State Library MS., with the variants in O.P.L. MS. noted.

   It is deficient in dates, and the letters too are not chronologically arranged. The dates of many letters have been settled by me.
6. *Khulasat-ut-Tawarikh* by Sujan Rai. O.P.L., Patna MS.

   Useful for the description and other details of the province.

7. Nawāzish Khān's Letter-book. The Sarkar MS. is the only MS. as yet known.

    A small collection of letters. It throws much light on the state of affairs in southern Mālwa during the years 1700-04. It gives us a few details of the Maratha invasion of Māndu in 1704.

8. *Kalimat-i-Tayyibat.* A.S.B. MS.

    It gives us a few important letters of Aurangzib which throw light on the affairs of Mālwa.

9. *Azam-ul-Harb.* Br. Museum, Or. 1899.

    Rotographed for me. It gives an account of the march of Azam to the battle-field of Jājau. It contains a few details of Mālwa affairs during Feb.-May, 1707.

10. *Mirat-i-Ahmadi.* G.O. Series, 3 Vols.

11. *Ajaib-ul-Afaq.* Br. Museum, Or. 1776.

    Rotographed for me. It is the letter-book of Girdhar Bahādur and his son Bhawāni Rām, containing the letters addressed to them by the Emperor and his chief officers, and their replies thereto. The letters relating to Girdhar Bahādur are very few and do not add much to our knowledge of his governorship. They are, however, the primary Persian source for the events during the short but eventful governorship of Bhawāni Rām.

12. *Tarikh-i-Hindi* by Rustam Ali. Br. Museum, Or. 1628.

    Written in Bhopāl in 1741-42. Rotographed for me.

13. *Muntakhab-ul-Lubab* by Khāfi Khān. Vol. II. Bib. Indica, Calcutta.

14. *Masir-ul-Umra.* Vols. I—III. Bib. Indica. Calcutta.

    A compilation from other sources, but very useful.

15. *Khajista-Kalam.* India Office MS. 1815. The letter-book of Muhammad Khān Bangash, compiled by Sāhib Rāi.

Rotographed for me. It was fully used by W. Irvine in his "Bangash Nawābs of Farrukhābad". *J.A.S.B.*, 1878, part IV.

16. *Roznamcha* by Mirzā Muhammad. Sarkar MS.
It contains a few references to the affairs of Mālwa during the reign of Farukhsiyār.

17. *Tarikh-i-Chaghtai* by Kāmwar Khān.
It is very useful so far as the details and dates of appointments and other incidents are concerned.

18. *Munawar-i-Kalam* by Shiv Das. Br. Museum, Or. 26.
Rotographed for me. It gives very few details regarding Mālwa, but is a primary source for the period it covers.

19. *Tarikh-i-Shahadat-i-Farukhsiyar wa Julus-i-Muhammad Shah* by Ashob. 2 Vols. I.O.L. MS. Transcript made for Sir J. N. Sarkar.

20. *Mirat-i-Waridat* by Wārid Tihrāni. Udaipur MS.

21. *Hadiqat-ul-Alam* by Mir Alam (Litho. Hyderabad).
Only the portion referring to Asaf Jāh in Mālwa. A derivative authority.

22. *Siyar-ul-Mutakherin* by Ghulām Ali. N. K. Press, Litho.
A purely derivative and late work of no independent value.

NOTE :—All the Persian authorities have been almost exhausted by W. Irvine in his *Later Mughals.*

B. MARATHI.

23. *Selections from the Peshwa's Daftar.* Edited by G. S. Sardesai. Vols. 2, 7, 8, 9, 10, 12, 13, 14, 15, 20, 21, 22, 23, 25, 27, 29, 30, 31, 39.

24. *Marathyanche Itihasanchi Sadhanen* by Rājwāde. Vols. 1, 2, 6, 8.

25. *Aitihasik Lekh Sangrah* by Khare. Vol. I.

26. *Selections from the Peshwa's Diaries* edited by Vād and Pārasnis. Vols. I, II, III, IV, VII and IX.

27. *Bramhendra Swami Charitra* by Pārasnis.

28. *Peshwe Daftarantil Sanad-patrantil Mahiti* (*Itihas-Sangrah*) by Pārasnis.

29. *Aitihasik Patravyavahar Lekh* by Sardesāi. Vols. I-II.

30. *Holkarshahi Itihasanchi Sadhanen* by Bhāgwat. *Purvardha*. I.

31. *Shindeshahi Itihasanchi Sadhanen* by Phālke, I-II.

These volumes contain letters from the Gulgule *Daftar*. They, however, mainly contain details of payment of dues etc.

32. *Dharchya Pawaranche Mahatva* by Oak and Lele.

It is a long-winded essay showing the early importance of the Dhār family. It is useful for the few unpublished documents given in it.

33. *Dhar Sansthan cha Itihas* by Oak and Lele. Vol. I.

Very brief.

34. Dhar *Daftar*. (Unpublished).

Transcripts taken from the collection of Mr. S. V. Athalye of Shiposhi.

35. Mandloi *Daftar*: (Unpublished).

The collection contains letters from the *Daftar* of Nandlāl Mandloi and his descendants. I have got two collections. One was made by Mr. B. R. Bhalerao, which contains copies of the seven vernacular letters which were published in Sardesāi's *Marathi Riyasat* and aroused a storm of controversy. The other letters in this collection are all given in Rājwāde's Vol. VI. The second collection, made by Mr. S. V. Athalye of Shiposhi, is larger and more authentic. It does not contain those seven letters, but gives hundreds of others not included in Rājwāde, VI. It gives many important letters, which have hitherto remained unpublished.

36. Purandare *Daftar*. Vol. I and III. B. I. S. Mandal, Poona.

Many letters give new facts, but their dates had to be corrected.

37. *Marathi Riyasat* by Sardesāi. *Purvardha, Madhyabhag,* Vol. I-IV.

38. Chandrachud *Daftar*. Vol. I. B. I. S. Mandal, Poona.

The letters of Holkar's *Diwan*, from the time of Malhār Rāo Holkar I onwards.

39. *Holkaranchi Kaifiyat*. 2nd Ed. by Bhāgwat.

Mainly traditional and hence, not reliable.

C. Hindi and Rajasthani.

40. *Khande Rai Raso* by Jadunāth Kavi. (Unpublished).

Written in 1744 A.D. The references are given to the pages of the MS. of the transcript copy of Sardar Phālke. It gives a few incidents of provincial importance only and throws much light on the condition of the country near about Narwar during the period 1704-44 A.D.

41. *Vir Vinod*. Vols. I., II.

The printed but unpublished history of Udaipur and the neighbouring States written by Kavirāja M. M. Shyāmaldāsji. It is useful for the various *farmans*, letters and other documents printed in its text.

42. *Rajputane ka Itihas* by Ojha. Vols. I-III.

It gives the history of Udaipur and Dungarpur as based on *Vir Vinod* and other works.

43. *Vamsh Bhaskar* by Suraj Mal. Vol. IV.

Written in 1841, it gives the history of the Bundi-Kotāh States. Other incidents are also given when they relate to the main theme. It forms the only authority on the Rajput side. It does not, however, throw any light on the later history of Mālwa.

44. *Chatra Prakash* by Lāl. Or A Poetical History of the Family of Chhatra Sāl Bundelā. (Kashi Nagri Pracharini Sabhā Edition.

45. *Sujan Charit* by Sudan. K. N. P. Sabhā Ed.

There are only a few incidents relating to the history of Mālwa.

46. Bule's *Bakhar*. Hindi MS. from Mr. S. V. Athalye's collection.

It appears to have been written in the early years of the 19th century, and as such the events relating to the early Maratha invasions are merely traditional. Of no higher degree of credibility than Gazetteer history.

D. English and other European Languages.

47. *Aurangzib* by J. N. Sarkar. Vol. III.

Ends with 1681. Vol. V., gives the main incidents during the last eight years of Aurangzib's rule in outline, but not in detail.

48. *The Fall of the Mughal Empire* by J. N. Sarkar. Vol. I & II.

They summarize much of the new Marāthi material. They, however, deal solely with the incidents that bear on Imperial affairs.

49. *India of Aurangzib* by J. N. Sarkar.

Useful for topographical details and statistics relating to the province of Mālwa in the 17th and 18th centuries. Based on Persian sources and Tieffenthaler.

50. *Later Mughals* by W. Irvine. Vols. I-II. Ed. by J. N. Sarkar.

Based exclusively on Persian authorities. The incidents relating to Maratha history are taken from

Grant Duff. The published Marāthi records were unknown to Irvine and have been utilized in Sarkar's notes only so far as they were available in 1920.

51. *A Memoir of Central India* by Sir John Malcolm. Vols. I-II. (1823 Ed.).

The work was written from what little information could then be had. Its chapters relating to history are very brief and the incidents are confused. There are many mistakes of dates also. It is now entirely antiquated.

52. *Report on Malwa and Adjoining Districts* by Sir John Malcolm.

The text of the report is practically the same as that of the *Memoir*. 1927 reprint cited.

53. *Storia de Mogor* by Manucci. Vols. I-IV. Ed. by W. Irvine.

It gives a few details of the early Maratha invasions of Mālwa. Some light is also thrown on the condition of the province on the eve of the 18th century.

54. *Travels in India by Tavernier,* Vols. I, II. Ed. by Ball. (MacMillan).

It gives the trade routes and some details of the economic aspect of provincial life.

55. *Administrative System of the Marathas* by S. N. Sen.

56. *Military System of the Marathas* by S. N. Sen.

57. *Journal of the Travels of John Ketelaar.* Translated by Dr. J. Ph. Vogel. Published in the *Journal of the Punjab Historical Society.* Vol. X, Part I.

It gives a good account of the condition of Mālwa in 1712.

58. Gazetteers of the States of Sitāmau, Ratlām, Sailānā, Rājgarh, Narsinghgarh, Dewās, Jhābuā, Barwāni and Alirājpur.

The historical account given by these gazetteers has to be taken with reserve and the dates have to be verified.

59. *History of the Deccan* by Scott. Vol. II.
Contains the useful memoirs of Irādat Khan in translation.

60. *History of India as told by its own historians* by Elliot & Dowsan. Vols. VII & VIII.
The translation has been verified by comparison with the original, whenever the latter has been accessible to me.

61. *History of the Marathas* by Grant Duff. Vol. I. (Oxford Edition).

62. *Annals and Antiquities of Rajasthan* by Tod. Vols. I-III. Oxford Edition.

63. *The First Two Nawabs of Oudh* by A. L. Srivāstava.
Sādāt Khān and Safdar Jang in connection with Mālwa affairs.

64. *Description de L'Inde.* par le père Joseph Tieffenthaler, S. J.—publié en François par M. Jean Bernoulli; Tome 1. Berlin, 1786.

12. La Province de Mālwa, pp. 342-358, gives an account of the condition of Mālwa and an account of its chief towns and cities as in 1760 A.D. He, however, does not give an estimate of the revenue returns in 1760.

Tieffenthaler stayed at Narwar for twenty-one years (1740-1761 A.D.) and moved about in the neighbouring country as a poor priest. Hence he got very good chances of meeting the people and knowing their condition. He could also note the condition of the province, its agriculture, villages and cities. Other details of State income and divisions etc. in the province are taken by him verbatim from Persian works like *A'in-i-Akbari* and *Khulasat.*

INDEX

Abbas Afghan, 69.

Abdali (Ahmad Shah Durrani), 288 *ff.*, 299 *ff.*, 304, 307 *ff.*

Abdulla Khan,
—Deputy-Governor of Malwa, 38 *f.n.*, 40, 91.
—replaced by Nijabat Khan, 93.

Abhaya Singh (Marwad), 173, 209, 231, 236.

Abhaya Singh (Rathor of Kotah), 311.

Abdul Mansur Khan, *see under* Safdar Jang.

Abu Nasar Khan (Shayista Khan II),
—and Gopal Singh affair, 50.
—and the Marathas, 33-34, 62.
—as Governor of Malwa, 33-34.
—his dismissal, 34.

Adaru, 237.

Afghans (the) in Malwa, 13, 14, 23, 67, 288, 304, 308, 323.

Agaunch, 229.

Agra, 35, 75, 105, 125, 132, 139, 150, 212, 221, 225, 247, 252, 294, 301.

Ahilya Bai, *see under* Holkar.

Ahirwada, 75, 168, 227, 242, 264, 307, 312, 328.

Ahkam-i-Alamgiri, 35.

Ahmadabad, 98, 146.

Ahmad Khan, 214.

Ahmadnagar, 39, 91.

Ahmad Shah Abdali (Durrani), *see under* Abdali.

Ahmad Shah (Emperor), 300.

Ahu, 166.

Ahwal-ul-Khawaqin, 140 *f.n.*

A'in-i-Akbari, 8.

INDEX

Ajaib-ul-Afaq, 167 *f.n.,* 177 *f.n.,* 200.

Ajit Singh (Marwad), 136.

—and Bahadur Shah, 96, 116 *f.n.*

—and Durgadas, 119.

—and the Princes of Malwa, 119 *ff.*

Ajmere, 96, 264, 294.

Akbar (Emperor), 48, 73, 75, 76, 119.

Akbar (Prince), 24.

Akbarpur ferry, 92, 140, 146, 151, 157, 216, 328.

Akhabarat-i-Durbar-i-Mualla, 342.

Alam Ali Khan, *see under* Saiyyad.

Ali, 147.

Ali Mardan Khan, 38 *f.n.*

Ali-Rajpur, 147.

Allahabad, 65, 132, 139, 176, 233, 294, 316.

Alot, 80.

Amanat Khan (Shahmat Khan, Mubariz Khan), 143.

—created Mubariz Khan, 98.

—created Shahmat Khan, 98, 118.

—fights with Ratan Singh, 98, 118, 121.

—Governor of Malwa, 98, 118 *f.n.*

—Struggle with the Nizam, his defeat and death, 152 *ff.,* 155.

Amanullah Khan, 38 *f.n.,* 40.

Ambaji Pant Trimbak Purandare, 154, 156, 157, 158 *f.n.,* 159, 184, 191.

Amber, 115, 128, 135, 136, 284.

Amin Khan, 103 *ff.*

Amir Khan, 133, 247.

Amir Khan (Pindhari), 318.

Amjhera, 146, 155, 158 *f.n.,* 166, 169, 201 *ff.*

—affairs of the State of, 78-79, 134, 184, 274, 282.

—battle of, 163 *ff.,* 193, 201 *ff.*

Anand Rao Sumant, 259.

Antaji (Anthu) Mankeshwar, 216, 218, 267, 296, 301.

INDEX

Anup Singh (Jhabua), 147, 155 *ff.*, 185, 282, 283.
—his son, 185.
Anup Singh (Narwar), 74, 94, 95, 121-22.
Anwarullah Khan, 261.
Arabic Era, 87.
Araun, 307.
Architecture, *see* Fine Arts.
Art, *see* Fine Arts.
Asaf Jah, *see under* Nizam.
Athalye (S. V.), 197.
Aurangabad, 35, 37, 152, 191, 258, 259.
Aurangzib, 15, 24 *ff.*, 121.
—and Jai Singh, 36, 86.
—and the Marathas, *see under* Marathas.
—his death, 40, 107, 111 *f.n.*, 112, 329.
—his fanatical policy, 47, 187.
—his wars in the Deccan, 10, 24 *ff.*
see chapter II *also.*
Awaji Kawade, 260.
Awasgarh, 35, 69, 78, 215.
—zamindar of, *see* Mohan Singh.
Ayamal, 240, 261.
Azam (Prince),
—defeat and death at Jajau, 94, 115.
—in Gujrat, 37, 39, 59, 61, 76, 81.
—made Governor of Malwa, 39 *ff.*
—marched through Malwa to Jajau, 92 *ff.*
—proclaimed himself the Emperor, 91.
—sent to Malwa in 1700, 49, 49 *f.n.*
—starts for Malwa (1707) but returns, 40, 40 *f.n.*, 91.
Azam Khan, 267.
Azimullah, 149, 153.
—his deputy-governorship, 149 *ff.*
—made Governor of Malwa, 266.
Azim-ush-shan (Prince), 97.

Babu Rao Malhar, 242, 259.
Badaksha (Bolasa), 145 *f.n.*, 146.
Badnagar, *see* Nolai.
Badnawar, 278, 285, 296.
—Granted to Bhim Singh, 74, 82.
—The State and the Marathas, 82-83, 167.
Badshah Quli Khan, 93.
Bagad (State of), 3, 3 *f.n.*, 279.
Baghmal, 50.
Bahadur Shah (Muazzam), 9 *f.n.*, 75, 108, 115.
—and Jai Singh, 94, 95, 113, 116 *f.n.*
—death, 97.
—Rajput Policy, 112, 116.
—victory at Jajau, 94.
—march through Malwa, 96 *ff.*
—march to Jajau, 94.
Bahiro Anant, 314.
Baji Bhimrao Jadhav, 237.
Baji Rao Peshwa, *see under* Peshwa,
Bajranggarh (Raghogarh), 73, 75, 83.
Bakaner, 161, 201, 278.
Bakht Buland, 26, 49, 54 *f.n.*, 66-67.
Bakht Singh (Jodhpur), 300.
Balaji Rao, *see under* Peshwa.
Balaji Vishwanath, *see* under Peshwa.
Balaji Yeshwant Gulgule, 263 *f.n.*
Balbhadra Singh (Bajranggarh), 304, 307.
Bangash, Muhammad, 208, 211 *ff.*
—and Jai Singh, 221, 238, 271.
—and the Marathas, 127, 214, 216, 219 *ff.*
—and the Nizam, 213 *ff.*, 215.
—causes of his failure, 221.
—Governor of Malwa, 211 *ff.*
Banhada, 285.
Banhauli, 43.

Banjaras, 20-21, 331.
Baniyas, 21.
Banswada, 3 *f.n.*, 77, 170, 185, 223, 278, 279, 296.
Baran, 45 *f.n.*, 114.
Barloi, 277.
Barna, 45 *f.n.*
Barod, 113, 178.
Barwada, 302.
Barwaha, 151, 152, 174, 227, 301, 328.
Barwani, 36, 66, 78, 185, 282, 283; *see also* Awasgarh.
Bassein, 263.
Beausse, 7.
Bidar Bakht, 33, 48, 49, 51, 70, 84.
—and Chhatra Sal, 46.
—and Gopal Singh, 48-49.
—condition of his forces, 38, 42, 59.
—Governor of Malwa, 34-35.
—Governor of Gujrat, 37-38, 91.
—in Malwa on his way to Jajau, 91 *ff*.
—on Malwa, 329.
—ordered to go to Malwa, 59, 64, 65.
Begham, 227, 242.
Benares, 233, 247.
Bengal, 247.
Berar, 10, 14, 57.
Beri Sal, 124.
Bernier, 9.
Bersiah, 123, 307.
Betwa (The), 3, 231.
Bhadaura, 332.
Bhadawar, 248.
Bhakra, 123.
Bhalerao, B. R., 197.
Bhambholao, 241.
Bhamgarh, 61.

Bhanpura, 169, 302.
Bharatput, 36, 318.
Bhats, 20.
Bhawani Ram, Raja Chimna Bahadur, 200.
—and Jai Singh, 165, 174, 175, 176 *f.n.*
—and the Emperor, 165, 167, 170, 172, 173, 175.
—and the Marathas, 166, 167, 173 *ff.*
—and Saiyyad Najmuddin Ali, 165 *ff.* 171, 172.
—his dismissal and reinstatement, 174 *ff.*
—his final supersession, 175.
—his financial difficulties, 172 *ff.*
—his governorship, 165 *ff.*
Bhilalas, 12, 20.
Bhils, 11, 305.
—rebellion of, 35, 65, 69, 126, 305.
Bhilsa, 26, 43, 109 *f.n.*, 134, 220, 248, 255, 295, 304, 308, 313.
Bhim Sen, 49, 54.
—on Shahu's escape, 92 *f.n.*
—on the battle of Sironj, 92 *f.n.*
Bhim Singh (Badnawar), 74, 82, 285.
Bhim Singh (Kotah), 49.
—and the Saiyyads, 100 *ff.*, 105, 126, 135, 136.
—battle of Khandwa and death of, 140.
Bhonsle,
—Janoji, 156, 312.
—Kanhoji, 109 *ff.*
—Raghuji, 258 *ff.*, 292, 294.
—Santoji, 157, 162.
Bhopal, 135.
—and the Marathas, 148, 214, 227, 248, 251, 284.
—state of, 102, 121, 148, 292, 304, 313, 324, 328, 337.
—struggle at, 209, 214, 253 *ff.*, 284.
Bihari Das, 132.
Bijagarh, 2, 8, 62, 70, 79.
—Shahu's *jagir* in, 111 *f.n.*

Bijai Singh (Jodhpur), 300.
Bijapur, 24.
Bijay Singh (Amber), 94, 115 *ff*.
Bohras (the), 330.
Bolasa, *see* Badaksha.
Bordi, 155.
Boregaum, 148.
Bori, 185.
Brahmangaon, 283.
Brahmans, 18.
Brahm Dev Sisodia, 69.
British Government (the), 70, 74, 325.
Budha Dongar, 225.
Budh Singh (Bundi), 76, 94 *ff*., 101, 113 *ff*., 134, 136, 227, 241, 285.
—and Farukhsiyar, 101, 105, 113.
Bule's *Bakhar*, 155, 185.
Bundelkhand, 3, 14, 44, 60, 65, 164, 220, 223, 231, 238, 248, 253, 275, 288, 295, 296, 305, 318, 319, 337.
Bundi, 76, 135, 136, 158, 168, 226, 227, 232, 241, 285, 308, 313.
—and Jai Singh, 100 *ff*., 114, 135, 136, 179, 181.
—and the Saiyyads, 100, 114 *ff*.
—its extension, 76.
—tussle with Kotah, 94, 100, 105, 113 *ff*., 121.
Burhanpur, 2, 6 *f.n.*, 37, 39, 49, 57, 59, 60, 66, 103, 139, 141, 248, 250, 258, 259, 328.

Calabag, *see* Kalabag.
Chahar Gulshan, 3 *f.n.*, 4 *f.n.*, 348.
Chambal (The), 3, 93, 138, 238, 246, 259 *f.n.*, 261, 264, 267, 270, 300, 328.
Champaner, 223.
Chanderi, 3, 4, 168, 174, 175, 227.
—cotton cloth made at, 333.
Chandwad, 277 *f.n.*

Charans, 20.
Chechat, 113.
Chhabada, 113.
Chhabileram Nagar, 132, 144.
Chhatra Mukut Bundela, 44.
Chhatra Prakash, 43 *f.n.*, 336, 353.
Chhatra Sal Bundela, 26, 33, 75, 134, 250 *f.n.*, 253 *ff.*, 336.
—and Malwa, 42-47, 58, 65.
—makes peace with Aurangzib, 38-39, 39 *f.n.*, 47.
Chhatra Sal Rathor, 80-81, 81 *f.n.*, 123.
—and the modern State of Ratlam, 81, 81 *f.n.*, 123.
Chhatra Singh (Narwar), 218 *ff.*, 222, 250 *f.n.*
Chikalda, 173, 179, 216.
Chimaji Ballal, 156, 180, 205, 211, 274.
—and Daya Bahadur, 203 *ff.*
—and Girdhar Bahadur, 163 *ff.*, 201 *ff.*
—and Nasir Jang, 258.
—and the Emperor Muhammad Shah, 242 *ff.*, 245.
—his campaign in Malwa (1728-9), 163 *ff.*, 169, 189 *ff.*, 199 *ff.*
—his debts, 190.
—his later expeditions, 220, 223 *ff.*
Churaman Jat, 101.

Dabhade, 215 *ff.*, 258.
—Khande Rao, 110.
Dabhoi, 216.
Dadaji Mahadeo, 295.
Dadaji Pant, 240.
Dado Bhimsen, 162.
Dag, 113 *f.n.*
Dalel Singh Hada (Bundi), 179, 228.
Dalpat Rao, *see* Rao Dalpat.
Dancing girls in Malwa, 22.
Dastur-ul-Amal, 7 *f.n.*
Datiya, 176, 227, 236, 254, 264.

Daud Khan Pani, 108.
Dawalji Somvanshi, 109.
Daya Bahadur,
—and Jaziya, 194.
—and the Maratha invaders, 157 *ff*, 189, 202 *ff*., 205 *ff*.
—at the battle of Amjhera, 163 *ff*., 204 *ff*.
—controversy over the date and place of his death, 200, 202 *ff*.
—defeat and death of Daya Bahadur, 164, 206.
—in Malwa, 153.
Delhi, 104, 110, 119, 124, 135, 136 *f.n.*, 149, 153, 212, 218, 224 *ff*., 228, 231 *ff*., 239 *f.n.*, 240, 242, 245, 248, 249, 250, 251, 252, 257, 262 *f.n.*, 263 *f.n.*, 265, 266, 272 *ff*., 286, 288, 291, 293, 299, 301, 302, 304, 306, 307, 308, 314, 319, 329, 334.
Deogarh, 20, 54 *f.n.*, 68.
Deolia (Partabgarh), 3 *f.n.*, 48, 128 *f.n.*
—crated an independent State, 76.
Depalpur, 97, 166, 213, 237 *f.n.*, 248, 277.
Desoji Bagh, 178.
Devi Singh Dhamdhera, 46.
Devi Singh (Sisodia), 69.
Dewas, 279.
Dhamuni, 26, 43, 44, 54, 61, 68, 171, 251, 253.
Dhamdhera—Basis of, 74-75.
Dhanna, 58.
Dhar, 4, 8, 37, 49 *f.n.*, 51, 63, 86, 156, 163, 167, 169, 175, 214 *ff*., 237, 246, 266, 267, 278, 296*f*.
Dharampuri, 54 *f. n.*, 85, 162, 170, 175, 202, 278.
Dharmat,
—battle of, 79.
Dhiraj Singh (Bajrangarh), 75.
Dholpur, 238, 270.
Dhondho Pant, 244.
Dingal (Rajasthani), 336.
Dip Singh, 180, 208, 212.
Doab (The), 314.

Dost Muhammad Khan, 102, 118, 214, 240.
—and the Matharas, 140.
—and the Nizam, 135, 140 *f.*, 147, 148, 149, 152.
—and the Saiyyads, 135.
—founds the state of Bhopal, 121.
Duff, 93 *f.n.*
Dungarpur, 3 *f.n.*, 77, 223, 237, 278, 279.
Durjan Sal (Kotah), 163 *f.n.*, 165, 171, 175, 183, 231, 254, 263.
Durjan Singh (Chanderi), 168, 174, 175.
Durgadas, 96, 115, 118.
Durraha Serai, 92, 98 *f.n.*
—convention of, 261 *ff.*, 271.

Education in Malwa, 21.
Elichpur, 258.
Elliot, 131 *f.n.*
English (the) 314, 321 ; *see under* British *also.*

Faiz Muhammad Khan (Bhopal), 303.
Faridabad, 225, 301.
Farukhsiyar (Emperor), 80, 99.
—and Jai Singh, 100 *ff.*, 105, 114.
—and Muhammad Amin Khan, 102 *ff.*
—and the Marathas, 109 *f.n.*, 110.
—and the Saiyyads, 100 *ff.*, 114.
—his deposition, 105, 135.
Farukkhabad, 212 *f.n.*
Fasli Era, 87.
Fateh Singh, 219.
Fine Arts and Architecture in Malwa, 21, 337, 338.
Firuz Jang, 34, 38, 46, 49, 59.
—Wins the battle of Sironj, 60.

Gadha (Mandal), 4, 61, 68, 231, 328.
Gagron, 3, 36, 45 *f.n.*, 70, 263.

Gagurni, 311.
Gahukhedi, 311.
Gaikwad, 215.
—Damaji, 258.
—Pilaji, 146.
—Siyaji, 255, 256.

Gaj Singh (Narwar), 94, 95, 101, 121 *ff.*, 136.
Ganges (the), 150, 235.
Garh, 3, 8.
Gaya, 233, 247.
Gharibdas Bundela, 44.
Ghaziuddin, 252, 253, 299.
Ghuraura, 43.
Ghyas Khan, 134.

Girdhar Bahadur (Rajah), 135.
—and the Marathas, 144 *ff.*, 157, 159, 189.
—controversy over the date and place of his death, 199 *ff.*
—first governorship of Malwa, 142, 144 *ff.*
—his defeat and death, 163 *ff.*, 165, 199 *ff.*
—his exactions in Malwa, 186, 194 *f.*
—his *jagir*, 167, 170, 172, 191.
—letter-book of, 200; *see* Ajaib-ul-Afaq *also*.
—second governorship of Malwa, 153 *ff.*

Gohad, 301, 311, 318.
Gojaji Devkate, 156.
Gokul, 136.
Golkonda, 24.
Gonds (the), 11, 14.
Gondwana, 3, 10, 14.
Gopal (Chaudhari of Sironj), 60, 62, 68, 93.
Gopal Ganesh Barve, 301.
Gopal Keshav, 295.
Gopal Rao, 312.

Gopal Singh Chandrawat, 182.
—and Azam, 117.
—and Maharana, 117, 118 *ff*.
—and Triumvirate, 117.
—his first revolt, 33, 34, 37, 48, 49, 50, 52, 76.
—his second revolt, 51, 67.
—in Delhi, 119.
—in Rampura, 100, 117.
Govind Ballal, 295.
Govind Bundela, 307.
Govind Kalyan, 312.
Grassiahs, 92, 305.
Gugair, 113.
Gujrat, 3, 5, 10, 37, 39, 49, 51, 59, 77, 91, 98, 108, 110, 120, 145, 147, 150, 151, 158, 160, 185, 219, 223, 224, 236, 237.
Gujrati Language, 336.
Gulab Singh, 293.
Gulgules (the), 292 *f.n.*, 325.
Gwalior, 46, 92, 93, 212, 213, 217, 236, 238, 251, 253, 296, 307, 310, 329.
—falls into Maratha hands, 301.
Gyan Chand Bundela, 134.

Hadawati (Hadoti), 3, 97.
Hafiz Khidmatgar, 222.
Haidar Quli Khan, 145, 147.
Haiderabad (Deccan), 50.
Hamid Khan ("Jangli Shahzada"), 54 *f.n.*, 68, 147, 160.
Handia, 3, 8, 58, 66, 109 *f.n.*, 145, 148, 250, 307, 328.
Harda, 229.
Harris *Voyages*, 9.
Harsol, 277.
Hasilpur, 7.
Hate Singh, 81, 81 *f.n.*
Hidayatullah, 42 *f.n.*

Hindi Language, 336, 337.
Hirde Shah, 253.
Holkar,
—Ahilya Bai, 318.
—Malhar Rao, 293, 294, 300.
—and Rampura, 284, 298 *f.n.*, 302 *f.n.*
—gets family grants, 276.
—given the seals for Malwa, 218, 276.
—grants in Malwa, 161, 173, 213, 275 *f.*, 297, 314.
—his death and its effect, 315, 318.
—in Malwa, 162, 174, 178, 181, 208, 213, 214, 218, 220, 223 *ff.*, 226 *ff.*, 232, 239, 245 248, 254, 256, 263, 267, 275, 277, 289, 292, 293, 301, 303, 307.
—saves the Maratha power in Malwa after 1761, 289, 309 *ff.*, 314.
—Tukoji Holkar, 318.
Hushangabad, 57, 58, 148.
Hussain Ali Saiyyad, *see under* the Saiyyads.

Iftikhar Khan, 49.
Ikhlas Khan, 104.
Inayet Khan, 152.
Inayetullah, 120.
Inayetullah (author of *Ahkam*), 35 *f.n.*, 342, 348.
Indore, 2, 156, 196, 250, 277, 301, 303, 307, 310, 313, 330.
Ingnod, 279.
Irvine, W., 93 *f.n.*, 131 *f.n.*, 158 *f.n.*
Ishwari Singh (Jaipur), 182, 298.
Islamgarh (Islamnagar), 148, 149, 248.
Izzat Khan, 146, 312.

Jadhav,
—Pilaji, 169, 235, 237, 242.
—grants in Malwa, 235, 324.
—his position in Malwa, 324.

—in Malwa, 226, 230, 245, 251, 256.
—Satvoji, 324.

Jadunath Kavi, 336.
Jafar Ali, 45.
Jagjivan Das Gujrati, 9, 329.
Jagoti, 277.
Jagrup Rathor (Amjhera), 78, 134, 184.
Jahandar Shah (Emperor), 98 *ff.*, 118.
Jahangir (Emperor), 75.
Jahangirpur (Jahangirabad), 63, 152.
Jahan Shah (Prince) Khajista Akhtar,

—absentee Governor of Malwa, 95 *ff.*
—his death, 98.

Jahazpur, 241.
Jaichand Bundela, 134.
Jains, 21.

Jaipur, 112, 120, 178 *f.n.*, 225, 228, 232, 233, 235, 236, 240, 242, 254, 261, 288, 293, 294, 297, 302, 307, 309, 310, 313.

Jairup Rathor (Amjhera), 78, 134, 184.
Jai Singh (Maharana), *see under* Mewad.
Jai Singh Kachhawah (Sawai) of Amber (Jaipur), 17, 37, 97, 99, 105.

—and Aurangzib, 36, 86.
—and Bahadur Shah, 94, 96, 115.
—and Bhawani Ram, 165, 174, 175, 176 *f.n.*
—and Bundi, 100 *f.n.*, 179, 181, 229.
—and Farukhsiyar, 99 *ff.*, 101, 119.
—and Malwa, 28, 36-37, 86-87, 89, 99, 112, 119, 129, 177 *ff.*, 194, 210, 222, 251, 293 *f.*, 298.

—and Muhammad Shah, 162 *ff.*, 235 *f.*
—and Nekusiyar's revolt, 132.
—and Rajputana, 112 *ff.*, 210, 230-31.
—and Rampura, 117, 119, 182 *ff.*, 297.
—and the Jats, 101, 114, 121.

—and the Marathas, 36-37, 86-87, 89, 129, 177 *ff.*, 192, 209, 212, 223-24, 226, 231 *ff.*, 235, 240 *ff.*, 243, 247, 252 *f.*, 268, 293, 298.
—and the triple treaty, 115, 182 *ff.*, 297.
—his effects to bring about unity in Rajputana, 230.
—his first Governorship of Malwa, 90, 95 *f.n.*, 99 *ff.*
—his second Governorship of Malwa, 181 *ff.*, 221.
—his third Governorship of Malwa, 222 *ff.*
—observatory at Ujjain, 338.
—reasons for his pro-Maratha policy, 177 *ff.*, 194.

Jai Singh (Sailana),
—founds the State of Sailana, 125.
—Jhabua affairs and, 155, 184 *ff.*, 282.
Jajau, 76, 94, 113, 115, 121.
Jalan Khan, 121.
Jalalpur, 43.
Jalgaon, 144.
Jamal Khan, Saiyyad, 249.
Jamuna, (The), 129, 225, 253.
Janjira, 226.
Jats, 101, 121, 300, 314, 315, 318, 320.
—and Malwa, 11, 14.
Jawahir Singh (Jat), 314, 315.
Jaziya, 194.
—and Aurangzib, 17, 47, 79, 84.
—later reimposition and abolition, 120, 194.
Jhabua, 78, 83, 126, 145, 146, 154 *ff.*, 158 *f.n.*, 161, 282.
—affairs of, 146 *ff.*, 154 *ff.*, 184*ff.*
Jhalod, 154.
Jhalrapatan, 113.
Jhalrapatan Chhaoni (now Brijnagar), 44 *f.n.*
Jhansi, 43 *f.n.*, 312.
Jhuna, 44.
Jinji, 25, 26.
Jodhpur, 97, 173, 209, 231, 288, 292, 308; *also see* Marwad.

Jodh Singh (Barwani), 78.
Jujhar Rao, 68.

Kabul, 75, 131.
Kachirah (Kachir Kakar Wai), 43, 43 *f.n.*
Kakali, 216.
Kalabagh (Calabagh), 61, 233, 293.
Kalinjar, 26, 43, 46.
Kali Sindh (the), 178.
Kaliyadah, 97, 167, 168, 171, 173.
Kalkadevi, 249.
Kambakhsh (Prince), 96.
Kampel, 109, 156, 196.
Kamwar, 136 *f.n.*
Kanauj (*sarkar* of), 3 *f.n.*
Kaniram, 302.
Kanthaji Kadam Bande, 146, 147 *f.n.*, 150 *f.n.*, 158 *f.n.*, 184, 258, 283.
Kanthal (district of), 3 *f.n.*
Kara-Manikpur, 98.
Karanj, 277.
Karan (son of Rajaram), 55.
Kaulas, 50.
Kayasthas (in Malwa), 21.
Kayath (Kanth), 140, 217.
Kesari Singh (Ratlam), 124.
Keshodas, 109.
—founds the State of Sitamau, 80, 80 *f.n.*
Kesho Mahadeo, 156, 157.
—and Daya Bahadur, 157 *ff.*
Kesho Vishvanath, 156.
Ketare, 111.
Ketelaar, 98 *f.n.*, 118 *f.n.*, 125.
Khafi Khan, 49 *f.n.*, 55, 92 *f.n.*, 104 *f.n.*, 118 *f.n.*, 123 *f.n.*, 131 *f.n.*, 134 *f.n.*, 136 *f.n.*

Khadautu, 43.
Khairabad, 277.
Khairandesh Khan, 44, 46.
Khan Alam, 36, 38, 93.
—as Governor of Malwa, 40.
Khan Dauran, 213, 221, 226, 249, 252, 258.
—and the Marathas, 208, 228, 231, 233 *f.n.*, 233 *ff.*, 236, 239, 240, 243.
Khande Rai, 74, 94, 122, 227, 336.
Khande Rai Raso, 336.
Khande Rao Dabhade, *see under* Dabhade.
Khandesh, 35, 37, 39, 40, 56, 59, 65, 146, 148, 151.
Khandwa,
—battle of, 140, 147.
Khan Jahan Kokaltas, 99.
Khanjar Khan, 61.
Khargon, 57, 63, 65, 111, 174, 254.
Khatoli, 68.
Khelna, 86.
Khichiwada, 294, 301, 304, 306, 312, 313, 328.
see also Bajranggarh *and* Khilchipur.
Khimlasa, 219.
Khujista Akhtar (Prince), *see* Jahan Shah.
Khulasat, 2 *f.n.*, 348.
Khuman Singh (Dungarpur), 77.
Khwaji Quli Khan, 134.
Kirparam, 243.
Kirti Singh, 50.
Kishangarh, *see* Rupnagar.
Koki Jiu, 212.
Kolaras, 231.
Kolhapur, 90.
Kondana (Sinhgarh), 57.
Kotah (Kotrah in Bundelkhand), 43 *f.n.*, 45 *f.n.*
Kotah (Rajputana), 4, 15, 49, 101, 113 *f.n.*, 126, 163.

—and the Marathas, 158, 168, 217, 226, 228, 231, 254, 255, 263, 284, 292, 295, 299, 302, 304, 306, 308, 311, 312, 313, 315, 324, 328.
—creation of the State, 72, 75-76.
—Tussle with Bundi, 94 *ff.*, 100, 113 *ff.*, 121, 135 *ff.*
Kotri Paraya, 3, 67.
Krishnaji Hari, 156.
Krishnaji Sawant (invasion of Malwa), 33, 41 *f.n.*, 54, 54 *f.n.*, 86.
Kukshi, 150 *f.n.*, 237.
Kurukshetra, 233.
Kurwai, 230, 328.
Kusaji Ganesh, 213.
Kushal Singh (Banswada), 77.
Kushal Singh (Jhabua), 78, 147, 155, 184.

Lahore, 98.
Lakshman Pant, 295.
Lalgarh, 124.
Lal (Kavi), 43 *f.n.*, 336, 353.
Lal Singh (Panched), 327 *f.n.*
Lal Singh Rathor (Amjhera), 134.
Lashkar Khan (Saiyyad), *see under* Saiyyad.
Later Mughals (the), 197.
Lunawada, 237.

Maasir-i-Alamgiri, 86, 342, 348.
Madhav Rao, *see under* Peshwa.
Madho Bhil, 69-70.
Madho Singh (Jaipur),
—and Rampura, 182, 183 *f.n.*, 284, 298, 301 *ff.*
—and the Marathas, 298 *f.n.*, 308, 310, 313 *ff.*
—his birth, 182, 183 *f.n.*
Mahadji Sindhia, *see under* Sindhia.
Mahadeo Bhatt Hingane, 240, 244, 269.
Maheshwar, 152, 170, 277, 300.

Mahi (the), 145 *f.n.*, 158 *f.n.*, 223.
Mahidpur, 277.
Makdai, 145, 148, 277.
Malcolm (Sir J.), 19, 54 *f.n.*
—his memoirs, 186, 196, 199, 207.
—his mistake, 85 *ff.*, 95 *f.n.*, 108 *f.n.*

Malhar Rao Holkar, *see under* Holkar.
Malvi (dialect), 336.
Malvi Era, 87.

Malwa,
—and Jai Singh, *see under* Jai Singh.
—and Rajputana, *see under* Rajputana.
—and the Marathas, *see under* Marathas.
—and the Mughal Empire, *see under* Mughal Empire.
—and the Nizam, *see under* Nizam.
—and the Rajput princes, *see under* Rajputs.
—Cession of Malwa, 210, 268 *ff.*, 289, 291.
—It's true nature, 270.
—Condition of its people, 18 *ff.*, 84 *ff.*, 125 *ff.*, 156, 186, 193, 194, 286.

—Growth of modern Malwa, 70-82, 120 *ff.*, 277 *ff.*, 316 *ff.* *and* Ch. VII.
see also under Rajputs.

—Its administration, 16 *ff.*, 27 *ff.*, 41 *ff.*, 106, 169, 127 *ff.*, 274 *ff.*, 279 *ff.*, 304 *ff.*, 316, 322 *ff.*

—Its disappearance as a political entity, 1.
—Its governors, *see the contents of* Chs. II, III, IV & V.
—Mughal Malwa of 1698, 1-23.
—Muslim kings of Malwa, 11.
—Nature of Mughal grants in Malwa, 71-73, 83.
—Rajput colonization of, 15, 73 *ff.*
—Situation in Malwa in 1765, 315, 316 *ff.*
—Struggle for Malwa, 127 *ff.*, 208 *ff.*, 270 *ff.*
—The fluid condition of the province in 1759, 304.

—The year 1698 marks a change in the history of, 2, 26.
—the beginning of anarchy, 27, 32.

Manawar, 201.
Mandleshwar, 96 *f.n.*
Mandloi, *see under* Nandlal.
Mandloi *Daftar,* 196 *ff.*
Mandsaur (Mandeshwar), 3, 4, 55, 96 *f.n.*, 139, 172, 174, 213, 216, 225.

Mandu, 3, 4, 34, 51, 54 *f.n.*, 97, 103, 112, 161, 169, 175, 201, 203, 216, 246, 296.

—Raid on, 58, 58 *f.n.*, 62, 79, 85 *ff.*
—taken by the Marathas, 178, 192.

Mangrole, 313.
Man Singh (Ratlam), 119, 125.
Manucci, 1, 58, 58 *f.n.*, 60 *f.n.*

Marathas,
—administration in Malwa, 29-30, 315 *ff.*, 322 *ff.*
—and Aurangzib, 24-25.
See the contents of Ch. II; 111, 129, 187.
—and the Hussain Ali Saiyyads, *see under* Saiyyads.
—and Jai Singh, *see under* Jai Singh.
—and Rajputana, *see under* Rajputana.
—and the Bangash, *see under* Bangash.
—and the Deccan, 107 *ff.*, 187.
—and the Nizam, 108 *ff.*, 128, 141, 143, 249 *ff.*, 266.

—the final struggle with the Nizam, 253 *ff.*, *see also under* the Nizam.

—and the Peshwa, 108 *ff.*, *see under* Peshwa *also.*
—and the States of Malwa, 16, 72, 74, 83, 161, 184 *ff.*, 211, 274, 279 *ff.*, 316 *ff.*, 322, 324, 328, 331.
see also under Rajputs.
Rajputs.

—Cession of Malwa to, 192 *ff.*

—Consolidation of Maratha power in Malwa, 292 *ff.*, 304 *ff.*, 315.
—establishment of the Maratha hold in Southern Malwa, 127, 172, 184 *ff.*
—in Malwa, 23, 27, 29, 31-32, 109, 110, 144, 146 *ff.*, 150 *f.n.*, 151, 166 *ff.*; *also* Ch. V, VI & VII.
—invasion on Malwa by Chimaji Ballal, 162 *ff.*, 199 *ff.*
—peace talks with the Marathas, 179 *ff.*, 240 *ff.*, 259 *ff.*
—their failure, 243.
—Real cause of the Maratha invasion, 186 *ff.*
—Renewal of the Maratha invasions in 1715, 90, 100, 102, 109.
—Their early invasions on Malwa, 33 *ff.*, 52 *ff.*, 85 *ff.*, 128, 187.
—Their influence on society of Malwa, 334 *ff.*
—Their states in Malwa, 274 *ff.*, 326.
—Their struggle for Malwa, first phase, 127 *ff.*
see the contents of Ch. IV; second phase, 208 *ff.*
also see the contents of Ch. V.

Marathi Language, 336.
—and Hindi, 337.
Marahmat Khan, 103, 133, 135, 137.
Marwad, 187.
—and Bahadur Shah, 96, 115 *ff.*
Mataundha, 43.
Mathura, 136, 233, 247.
Mau, 44 *f.n.*
Mewad (Udaipur State), 48, 169, 187, 237, 297, 301, 311.
—and Bagad, 77.
—and Bahadur Shah, 96, 116 *f.n.*
—and Bhawani Ram, 165.
—and Deolia, 76.
—and Rampura, 48 *ff.*, 117, 118, 182 *ff.*, 296.
—Maharana of, 50, 51 *f.n.*, 74, 82.

Mewat, 228.
Mir Ahmad Khan, 35 *f.n.*
Mirat-i-Ahmadi, 158 *f.n.*
Mir Mani Khan, 255.

Mitra Sen, 132.
Mohan Singh (Awasgarh), 62, 65, 69, 78, 185, 215, 283.
Muazzam (Prince), *see* Bahadur Shah.
Mubariz Khan, *see* Amanat Khan.
Mughal Empire,
—and Malwa, 8, 16, 26 *ff*., 41-42, 210, 322, 326, 329, 334.
also see under Malwa.
—and the Marathas, 161 *ff*., 181, 186 *ff*., 208 *ff*., 240 *ff*., 267 *ff*.
also see under the Marathas.
—Its failure against the Marathas, 271.
—Its failure in Malwa, 18, 28 *ff*.
Muhammad Amin Khan, 138.
—as Governor of Malwa, 102 *ff*., 123, 131.
—as the Vazir, 142 *ff*.
Muhammad Bangash, *see under* Bangash.
Muhammad Shah, Roshan Akhtar (Emperor), 133, 144, 148 *f.n.*
—and Bhawani Ram, 165.
—and Jai Singh, 235 *ff*.
see also under Jai Singh.
—and Nadir Shah, 264 *ff*.
—and the Marathas, 151, 222 *ff*., 233 *ff*., 236, 240, 245, 247 *ff*., 267 *ff*.
—and the Nizam, 138, 141, 145 *ff*., 149 *ff*., 249 *ff*.
—and the Saiyyads, 132, 137.
Muhammad Umar Khan, 171.
Mukhtiyar Khan,
—and Rampura affair, 33, 48.
—Governor of Malwa, 33, 48.
Mukund-durrah, 97, 140, 231, 301.
Mukundji Mahant, 155.
Multan, 139.
Munawwar Khan, 39.
Murad, 102.

Muslims (the),
—in Malwa, 13, 22, 334.
—relations with the Hindus, 21.
Muzaffar Khan, 228.

Nadir Shah, 209, 262 *f.n.*, 264 *ff*.
Nagulwandi, 283.
Nahargarh, 80 *f.n.*
Najamuddin Ali Khan, *see under* Saiyyad.
Najib Khan, 314.
Nalam, 137.
Nalchha, 97, 163, 202, 278.
—Treaty of, 152, 154.
Nalgunda, 80 *f.n.*
Nandlal Mandloi (of Kampel), 197.
—and the Marathas, 109, 156, 163 *f.n.*, 167, 173, 191, 193, 169 *ff*., 213, 281.
—his descendants, 196 *ff*.
Nand Maharaj, 45.
Nandurbar, 3, 7, 70, 79.
Narmada (the), 3, 25, 54, 58, 62, 89, 115, 140, 150 *f.n.*, 213, 214, 219, 232, 234, 244, 248, 252, 270, 283, 320, 328.
Naro Shankar, 267, 312, 324.
Narsinhgarh, 75, 126, 219 *f.n.*, 295, 312.
Narwar, 4, 61, 136, 140, 150, 212, 225, 230, 236, 238, 286, 296, 307, 324, 329, 336.
—State of Narwar, 74, 95, 122, 219, 250 *f.n.*
Narwar (near Ujjain), 124.
Nasir Jang, 254, 258, 259 *f.n.*, 299.
Nasiruddin Khan Irani, 103.
Nathdwara, 233.
Nauhara pass, 97.
Nawazish Khan, 34, 41, 78.
—and the raid of Mandu, 62 *ff*.
—letter-book of, 70.

Neemuch, 300.
Nejabat Khan, 40.
—governor of Malwa, 40, 93.
Nekusiyar—his rising, 132, 138.
Nemad, 2 *f.n.*, 35, 109 *f.n.*, 152, 226.
Nijabat Ali Khan, 240, 243.
Nima Sindhia, 36, 46, 64, 66.
—Raid on Malwa, 57 *ff.*, 68.
Nisar Afghan, 68.
Nizam, the Asaf Jah (Nizam-ul-mulk), 283, 284.
—and Dost Md. Khan, 135, 148.
—and Malwa, 128, 249 *ff.*
—and Nekusiyar, 132, 138.
—and the Bangash, 215, 221.
—and the Emperor, 138, 141, 145, 149, 151, 222, 234, 249, 252 *ff.*, 266.
—and the Marathas, 108, 127, 141, 143, 150, 188, 216 *ff.*, 250 *f.n.*, 251, 265, 290.
—and the Peshwa, 128, 145 *ff.*, 148 *f.n.*, 151, 154, 160, 253 *ff.*, 286.
—and the Saiyyads, 106 *ff.*, 131, 132, 133, 137 *ff.*, 139 *ff.*
—as the Vazir, 127, 141, 145, 150.
—in the Deccan, 127, 139, 141, 152.
—in Gujrat, 145 *ff.*
—in Malwa, 145, 147, 149 *ff.*, 186.
—Governor of Malwa, 106, 127, 131 *ff.*, 149, 286.
—Struggle at Bhopal, 253 *ff.*, 286.
—Struggle with Mubariz Khan, 151 *ff.*
Nolai (Badnagar), 37, 51, 67, 167, 285.
Nurabad, 238.

Ojha, G. H., 96 *f.n.*, 119 *f.n.*
Orchha, 227, 236, 238, 254.
Oudh, 150, 209, 255, 299, 316.

Pachhar, 309.
Pachpad, 113 *f.n.*
Padap, 113 *f.n.*
Pahad Singh (Barwani), 283.
Pahori, 231.
Palkhed,
—battle of, 160.
Panchayat system (the), 327.
Panched, 327 *f.n.*
Pandher, 92.
Panhala, 81, 123.
Panipat, 289, 306 *ff.*, 318.
Parbat Singh (Barwani), 79.
Parnalia, 154, 184.
Parsu (Maratha), 37, 51, 66.
Partabgarh,
—State, *see* Deolia.
—town (founded), 77.
Partab Singh (Raoti), 124.
Patan (now known as Keshoray Patan), 76, 233, 295.
Patna, 131, 176.
Pawagarh, 223.
Pawar (the), 291, 324.
—Anand Rao,
—and the Peshwa, 208, 212 *ff.* 218.
—his death, 245, 278.
—in Malwa, 223, 224, 226, 237, 276, 278.
—Jiwaji, 218, 226, 245, 276, 279 *ff.*
—Krishnaji, 223.
—Tukoji, 218, 226, 245, 276, 279 *ff.*
—Udaji,
—and the Peshwa, 161, 208, 212, 215.
—grants in Malwa, 144, 154, 156, 159, 161 *ff.*, 174, 178.
—in Malwa, 86, 110, 146, 162, 166, 179 *f.n.*, 223.
—withdrawal from Malwa, 275, 278.

—Yeshwant Rao,
—and the Peshwa, 266, 296, 297 *f.n.*, 309.
—confiscation of his *jagir* after his death, 309 *ff.*
—grants in Malwa, 266, 278, 294, 297 *f.n.*
—in Malwa, 245, 255 *f.n.*, 260, 278, 291, 294, 296.
Payaghat (the), 146.
Penukonda, 81.
Peshwa (the),
—Baji Rao Ballal I,
—and Chimaji, 167, 169 *f.n.*, 189 *ff.*, 202.
—and Kotah, 263, 284.
—and the Nizam, 128 *ff.*, 143, 145, 148, 150 *f.n.*, 151 *ff.*,
—and Nadir Shah, 264, 265, 267.
—and the battle of Amjhera, 164 *f.n.*, 201, 205.
—and the Dabhade, 208, 216.
—and the Nizam, 128 *ff.*, 143, 145, 148, 150 *f.n.*, 151 *ff.*, 154, 160, 216, 249, 251, 252.
—the final struggle at Bhopal, 253 *ff.*
—attacks Delhi, 249.
—becomes the Peshwa, 109, 128, 143.
—expeditions in Malwa, 144 *ff.*, 147 *ff.*, 248 *ff.*, 255 *ff.*
—gets Imperial honours, 245.
—goes to Delhi, 110.
—goes to Rajputana, 237 *ff.*, 239 *ff.*
—hands over seals of Malwa to Sindhia and Holkar, 218, 275.
—his death, 247, 266.
—his demands from the Emperor, 209, 233 *ff.*, 240 *ff.*
—accepted by the Emperor, 243.
—they rise higher 243, 246 *ff.*
—his debts, 188 *ff.*
—his mother's pilgrimage, 233.
—his Naib-subahdari of Malwa, 243, 253.
—his purpose in invading Malwa, 186 *ff.*
—his schemes of conquest, 54, 109, 143, 186 *ff.*
—makes convention of Serai Duraha, 261 *ff.*

—Balaji Rao, 294.
—and cession of Malwa, 247, 267 *ff.*, 291.
—and Jai Singh, 268.
—and Malwa, 230, 300, 301, 303, 304.
—and Muhammad Shah, 247, 267 *ff.*
—and the battle of Panipat, 289, 308.
—and Yeshwant Rao Pawar, 297.
—Balaji Vishwanath, 188.
—goes to Delhi, 110 *ff.*
—his rise and the Maratha power, 54, 90, 108 *ff.*, 188.
—Madhav Rao, 290, 309, 314, 315, 316.

Peshwa's Daftar, Selections from, 200 *et seq.*
Pilaji Jadhav, *see under* Jadhav.
Pindharis (the), 318, 320.
Pirthi Singh (Deolia), 126 *f.n.*
Pohanalia, 254.
Pratap (Maharana), 52.
Pratap Singh (Deolia), 50, 77.
Pratap Singh Hada, 227, 239, 241.
Prayag, 247.
Puna (Poona), 237, 247, 252, 290, 303, 313, 315, 326.
Punasa, 254.
Punjab (the), 97, 289, 299, 317.
Puraghat, 44.
Purandare, 293.

Qamruddin Khan, the Vazir, 209, 249, 258, 269, 271.
—leads the Imperial expenditions against the Marathas, 225 *ff.* 231, 236, 244.

Qasim Hussain Khan, 38 *f.n.*

Raeyat Khan, 149.
Rafi-ud-darajat (Emperor), 105, 111, 120, 131, 133.
Rafi-ud-daulah (Emperor), 133.

Rafi-ush-shan (Prince), 98, 105.
Raghogarh, *see* Bajranggarh.
Raghuji Bhonsle, *see under* Bhonsle.
Raghunath Rao Ballal (Raghoba), 289, 300, 301, 302, 314, 318.
Rahim Beg, 117.
Raichand Bundela, 134 *f.n.*
Raipuria, 144 *f.n.*, 146.
Raisin, 3, 246, 255.
Rajaram, 25, 26, 31, 53, 55.
—effect of his death, 31, 55.
—introduces Feudalism, 53.
Rajaur, 283.
Raj Bahadur (Kishangarh), 99 *f.n.*
Rajgarh, 75, 126, 169, 217, 219 *f.n.*, 233.
Rajasthani, *see under* "Dingal".
Rajputana, 3, 10, 12, 13, 15, 19, 28, 73, 89.
—and Malwa, 112 *ff.*, 121, 210, 284, 328, 335.
—and the Marathas, 228, 229, 230, 232, 237, 239, 241, 289, 290, 301, 306, 319.
Rajputs in Malwa,
—their status in Malwa, 28, 29, 73.
—and Rajputana, 19, 28, 112, 335.
—and the Empire, 15 *ff.*, 28, 89.
—colonization in Malwa, 11, 73.
—rise in their political status, 272, 274, 281, 317 *ff.*, 326, 335.
—their weakness, 15 *ff.*, 28, 73.
—the Society, 11 *ff.*, 18 *ff.*, 28, 73, 74, 333 *ff.*
Rajwade, V. K., 198.
Ramchandra Bawa, 228, 232, 240, 293.
Ramchandra Pandit, 55.
Ramchandra Singh (Datiya), 176.
Ramgarh, 134.
Rampura, 229, 231.
—affairs of, 48 *ff.*, 76, 96, 99, 117*ff.*, 121.
—and Girdhar Bahadur, 160, 182.

—and Jai Singh, 100, 119, 182, 183, 284, 298 *f.n.*, 303.
—and Madho Singh, 182, 183, 298 *f.n.*, 303.
—and Maharana, 119, 121, 182, 183, 298 *f.n.*
—and the Marathas, 216, 231, 298 *f.n.*, 303, 311.
—the Chandrawats of, 311.
Ram Singh (Dungarpur), 77.
Ram Singh Hada, 17, 49, 75, 94, 113.
Ramuccio, 9.
Ranod, 43.
Ranoji Sindhia, *see under* Sindhia.
Ranthambhor, 302.
Rao Chand, 149.
Rao Dalpat Bundela, 17, 92 *f.n.*, 94.
Ratan Singh (Bori), 185.
Ratan Singh (Islam Khan), 48 *ff.*, 99, 117, 118.
—and the Maharana, 50 *ff.*
—fight against Amanat Khan, 117, 122.
—his conversion, 33, 48.
—in Rampura, 48 *ff.*
Ratan Singh Rathor, 74, 81.
Ratlam, 17, 167, 313, 327.
—first State of, 73-74, 81.
—modern State of, 81.
—troubles in, 81, 215.
Roshan-ud-dowlah, 212.
Rupnagar, 99 *f.n.*
Rustam Ali, 263 *f.n.*, 337.
Rustam Khan, 57, 60, 62.

Sabal Singh, 151.
Sabha Singh Bundela, 256.
Sadashiv Ballal (Bhau), 307 *ff.*
Sadat Ali Khan (of Oudh), 144, 233, 234, 236, 237, 249, 252, 254, 255.
Safdar Jang (Abdul Mansur Khan), 255 *f.n.*

Said Latif Khan, 45 *f.n.*
Sakho Mahadeo, 159.
Sailana, 124, 155, 184, 185.
Saiyyad (the),
—Alam Ali Khan, 138, 141.
—Brothers, 131, 132, 133, 135.
—and Bhim Singh, 99, 136, 139.
—and Dost Muhammad Khan, 122 *ff.*, 135.
—and Emperor Farukhsiyar, 99, 101, 105.
—and Rafi-ud-darajat, 105.
—and the Nizam, 137, 139.
—their fall, 142.
—Dilawar Ali Kham, 136, 138, 139, 140.
—Hussain Ali, 131.
—and Jai Singh, 100 *ff.*
—and the Marathas, 106 *ff.*
—and the Nizam, 137 *ff.*, 141, 142.
—in the Deccan, 100, 101, 103, 108.
—marches to Delhi, 103 *ff.*
—Najmuddin Ali Khan, 165, 168, 169 *f.n.*, 171, 172, 174.
—Qutub-ul-Mulk (the Vazir), 131.
—and the Emperor, 102, 105.
—his surrender, 142.
Salabat Jang, 300.
Salim Singh Hada, 136.
Sambhar, 232.
Sanganer, 312.
Sangram Singh Chandrawat, 119, 182, 183 *f.n.*
Sangram Singh Hada, 228.
Sansani, 36.
Sarbuland Khan, 98, 158, 159, 234.
Sarangpur, 3, 117, 137, 146, 159, 168, 213, 214, 217, 279, 332, 333.
Sardar Singh (Badnawar), 285.
Sardesai G. S., 92 *f.n.*, 108 *f.n.*
—and Mandloi Daftar, 196 *ff.*

Sarkar, Sir J. N. 14, 17, 26, 39, 41, 55, 58 *f.n.*, 67, 92 *f.n.*, 177 *f.n.*, 197, 199, 319.
Satara, 54, 82 *f.n.*, 144, 190, 206.
Saugor, 219, 312, 328.
Saver, 277, 278.
Sawai Jai Singh, *see* Jai Singh.
Sehore, 150, 152, 307, 308.
Serai Alahwardi Khan, 101.
Shahabad, 46, 95, 113 *f.n.*, 219.
Shahdaura, 213, 251.
Shah Jahan (Emperor), 73, 75, 78.
Shahjahanpur, 92, 117 *f.n.*, 155, 214, 217, 254.
Shahman Dhamdhera, 46.
Shahu (Raja), 157, 159, 164, 177, 178 *f.n.*, 220, 241, 258, 264.
—and Baji Rao, 143, 169, 189, 242, 246.
—and Hussain Ali, 108, 110.
—and the Emperor, 151, 152, 192.
—his escape, 92.
—his rule, 90, 107.
—in captivity, 31.
—obtains *farman*, 111 *ff*.
also see under the Marathas and Peshwa.
Shivpuri, 121, 231, 329.
see also under Narwar.
Shambaji (Raja), 25.
Shah Quli, 43, 45.
Shamsh-ud-daulah, 267.
Shankarji Malhar, 110.
Shayista Khan (I), 33.
Shayista Khan (II), *see* Abu Nasar Khan.
Sheogarh, 147, 155.
Sheolal, 85.
Sher Afkan, 43, 44.
Shergadh, 113 *f.n.*
Shiposhi, 197.

Shivaji (Raja), 45.
Shivaji II, 55.
Shiv Singh (Jaipur), 182.
Shiv Singh (Jhabua), 282.
Sholapur, 67.
Shujalpur, 296.
Shujat Khan, 258.
Shuja-ud-daulah, 314.
Siddis (the), 226.
Singhs (the),
—Revolt of, 97.
Sindh, province of, 300.
Sindhia (the), 291, 305, 324.
—Dattaji, 289, 307.
—Jankoji, 290, 303, 305, 310, 314, 327 *f.n.*
—Jayappa (Jayaji), 297, 300.
—Kedarji, 314, 315.
—Mahadji, 315, 318, 319.
—Manoji, 314, 315.
—Ranoji,
—and the Emperor, 268.
—entry into Malwa affairs, 208, 211, 275, 277.
—in Malwa, 256, 267, 275, 277 *ff.*, 288, 292 *f.n.*, 293, 295, 296.
Sinhgarh, *see* Kondana.
Sironj, 4, 46, 55, 58, 60, 62, 64, 75, 93, 125, 149, 150, 168, 213, 217, 236, 243, 252, 254, 293, 307, 308, 312, 324, 329, 333.
—Battle of, 46, 60 *ff.*
—cloth made at, 6.
—exchange house at, 5.
Sitamau, 334 *f.n.*
—grant of Sitamau by Aurangzib, 74, 80.
Siyaji Gurjar, 169.
Siyar-ul-Mutakherin, 199.
Slavery in Malwa, 22.

Sondhias, 12, 20, 328.
Soron, 150.
Sujan Rai, 7, 18.
Sultanpur, 62.
Sultan Singh (Badnawar), 82.
Sunera,
—battle of, 117.
Surajmal (Badnawar), 82.
Surajmau,
—battle and siege of, 43.
Surat, 5, 216.
Surati Ram, 227.
Suttee,
—practice of, 22.

Tal, 278.
Talam, 137.
Tapti (the), 258.
Tarabai, 31, 55-56.
—her counteroffensive, 53-54.
Tarikh-i-Hindi, 337.
Tavenier, 5, 7.
Tejkaran, 218.
Thandla, 155, 185.
Thurhat, 43.
Tieffenthaler, 330.
Tirla, 201, 206.
Titrod, 80.
Tod, 51 *f.n.*, 132 *f.n.*
Toda (?), 172, 174.
Toda tank, 239.
Tonk, 76, 302.
Torna, 61.
Trimbak Gangadhar, 156.

Triple Treaty (of Udaipur), 1708, 115, 120.
—and Amber, 115.
—and Rampura affair, 115, 182.
—its effect, 89 *ff*., 116, 181 *ff*., 297.
Tukoji Holkar, *see under* Holkar.
Tumari Pass, 92.
Turebaz Khan, 200 *f.n.*, 209.
Turkey, 7.

Udaibhan Saktawat, 50.
Udaipur, 96, 115, 119, 132 *f.n.*, 182, 229 *f.n.*, 233, 239, 241, 285, 298.
see also under Mewad.
Udaji Pawar, *see under* Pawar.
Udawat Singh (Raja), 176.
Ujjain, 4, 17 *f.n.*, 18-19, 34, 51, 57, 62, 64, 65, 69, 109 *f.n.*, 117, 133, 166, 180, 190, 214, 221, 278, 307, 328, 329.
—observatory at, 338.
—siege of, 166, 167.
Umar Khan, *see under* Muhammad Umar Khan.
Umar Pathan, 67.
Umatwada, 75, 219 *f.n.*, 225, 301.
Ummed Singh (Bundi), 285.
Urdu language, 336.

Vad, 158 *f.n.*
Valentyn, 98.
Vamsh Bhaskar, 76 *f.n.*, 86, 96 *f.n.*, 113 *f.n.*, 120 *f.n.*, 136 *f.n.*, 163 *f.n.*, 178 *f.n.*
Vazir (the), *see under* Qamruddin Khan.
Vir Vinod, 96 *f.n.*, 120 *f.n.*
Visaji Pant, 312.
Vishwas Rao, 312.
Vithal Deo Rao, 314.

Vithal Shivdev, 267, 311.
Vithoji Rao Bule (Bolia), 155 *f.n.*, 223.
Vrij Bhasha, 336, 338.

Witchcraft (beief in), 22, 335.

Yadgar Khan Kashmiri, 243.
Yar Muhammad Khan (Bhopal),
—and the Marathas, 214, 227, 246, 248, 250, 292, 294.
—and the Nizam, 148, 152, 248.
Yeshwant Rao Pawar, *see under* Pawar.

Zahir-ud-daulah, 142 *ff*.
Zalim Singh Jhala, 318.
Zorawar Singh, 174.
Zulfiqar Khan, Nasir Jang, 41, 60 *f.n.*, 64, 66, 99, 118 *f.n.*
—and Shahu, 93 *f.n.*, 108.

ADDENDA ET CORRIGENDA

PAGE	LINE		
xv	1	*Read*	*Peshwa Daftar* for *Peshwa's Daftar*
xv	11	„	Peshwas' Diaries *for* Peshwa's Diaries
1	5	„	structure of the Indian Empire *for* structure
2	25	„	*Chahār* also (1720) does not mention it, *for* Chahār does not mention it also (1720)
4	21	„	the Malwa routes *for* Malwa routes
18	23	„	*Memoir* for *Memoirs*
19	14	„	Rajput *for* Rajputs
19	21	„	this *for* these
23	6	„	a new factor *for* a few factors
23	7	„	was *for* were
25	15	„	up to *for* upto
33	4	„	some time *for* sometime
34	15	„	peremptorily *for* peremptorilly
35	22	„	diwān of *for* diwān sarkār of
35	23	„	*Naib-Subahdār* for *Naib-Subedar*
35	24	„	contain instructions *for* contain the instructions
36	8	„	1704 *for* 1703
39	4	„	filling up this *for* filling this
45	2	„	has a little *for* has little
45	27	„	Baran *for* Baron
48	11	„	Emperors *for* Emperor
50	5	„	Saktāwat *for* Sakatāwat
65	2	„	than *for* then
68	10	„	rose in *for* broke into
70	5-6	„	then that *for* then, that
76	8	„	Budh Singh *for* Budh
77	19 and on subsequent pages	„	Kushal Singh *for* Khush-hal Singh
78	21	„	Mohan Singh managed *for* Mohan Singh, however, managed
79	3	„	dispersed, by *for* dispersed by
80	20	„	*qiladār* for *quledār*
81	7	„	*qiladāri* for *qiledāri*
84	7	„	those who *for* those, who
85	5	„	*Memoir* for *Memoirs*
86	3	„	*Memoir* for *Memoirs*
86	11	„	*Masir-i-Alamgiri* for *Massir-i-Alamgiri*

PAGE	LINE		
87	6	*Read*	or *for* on
91	1-2	,,	denying the fact *for* denying fact
92	18	,,	Khush-hal Chand *for* Kushal Chand
93	21	,,	wrong, as Jai Singh *for* wrong, Jai Singh
95	14	,,	makes *for* make
95	22	,,	*Memoir* for *Memoirs*
110	15	,,	Khānde Rao *for* Phānde Rao
111	5	,,	lands held by Shivāji in 1680 *for* lands by Sivāji in 1681
111	17	,,	Duff's *for* His
114	9	,,	refugee *for* refuge
121	8	,,	benefited more by *for* benefited by
125	19	,,	the facts *for* he facts
128	26	,,	decadence *for* decadance
135	5	,,	*news* for *new*
136	2	,,	join *for* joini
142	14	,,	1720 *for* 1721
147	23	,,	1722 *for* 1772
158	18	,,	1726 *for* 1727
163	29	,,	horse *for* horses
174	20	,,	Khargon *for* Khargaon
176	22	,,	of Jai Singh, he *for* of Jai Singh. He
177	23-24	,,	In October, 1730 the Nizām told Dip Singh (the ambassador of Jai Singh), "Mālwa is taken out of your charge. The Bangash has become [the governor of Mālwa]." *for* The Nizām told Dip Singh not to interfere with the affairs of Bhawāni Rām.
185	23	,,	pp. 3-4 *for* pp. 314
192	marginal note 1.3	,,	keen *for* keep
194	marginal note 1.4	,,	Marathas. *for* Marathas?
197	8	,,	startling statements *for* startling facts
197	12	,,	Irvine's Later *for* Irvines Later
198	12	,,	fabrications *for* fabrication
198	14-15	,,	its claim *for* its a claim
198	17	,,	*Daftar* ceases *for Daftar*, ceases
199	13	,,	*Peshwā Daftar* for *Peshwā's Daftar*
200	7 & 18	,,	*Peshwā Daftar* for *Peshwā's Daftar*
200	20	,,	Turābāz Khān *for* Turebaz Khān
204	13	,,	rout *for* route
205	18	,,	was the decisive fact *for* was sufficient
208	3 (heading)	,,	1741 *for* 1749
209	4	,,	Turābāz Khān *for* Turebāz Khān
212	7 & 10	,,	The Bangash *for* Bangash
212	22	,,	1878 *for* 1678
213	16	,,	The Bangash *for* Bangash
218	18	,,	of *for* on
225	24-5	,,	Khush-hāl *for* Kush-hāl.

Page	Line		
226	9	*Read*	1732 *for* 1722
229	12	,,	after the rains *for* after rains
231	1	,,	Pāhori, Shivpuri *for* Pāhori Shivpuri
231	2	,,	to him by *for* to him, by
231	23	,,	Khush-hāl *for* Kush-hāl
238	5	,,	places *for* place
243	9	,,	waiting *for* awaiting
245	11	,,	went on *for* went over
246	7-8	,,	it, be given *for* it, to be given
256	17	,,	of December *for* of the December
261	17	,,	The horses *for* Horses
262	25	,,	*Mirāt-us-safā* for *Mirāt-us-saffā*
267	21	,,	promised Rs. 7,000 *for* promised 7,000
282	7	,,	and were *for* and more
290	20	,,	respect of *for* respect to
291	22	,,	Peshwā, was *for* Peshwā was
294	3	,,	1743 *for* 1734
297	11	,,	by the princess *for* of the princess
299	6	,,	The new Emperor *for* He
299	15	,,	1749 *for* 1748
301	8	,,	Barwāh *for* Barwāhd
301	13	,,	wrote *for* write
307	21	,,	Govind Bundelé *for* Govind Bundelā
315	17	,,	eluded those who *for* eluded those, who
318	4	,,	marched *for* march
323	21	,,	minor officials *for* minor official
327	3	,,	Marathas *for* Maratha
327	13	,,	compromises *for* a compromise
341	4	,,	researches, no *for* reseaiches no
341	13	,,	needs to be *for* need to be
343	12	,,	*Peshwā Daftar* for *Peshwā's Daftar*
344	13	,,	long-drawn controversy *for* long-drawn out controversy
345	8	,,	*Peshwā Daftar* for *Peshwā's Daftar*
345	24	,,	went on recording *for* went recording
346	12	,,	Marathi *for* Maratha
348	5	,,	MS. *for* MSS.
350	26	,,	*Peshwā Daftar* for *Peshwā's Daftar*
351	2	,,	*Peshwās' Diaries* for *Peshwā's Diaries*
353	4	,,	*Chhatra Prakash* for *Chatra Prakash*
353	6	,,	Edition.) *for* Edition.
353	17	,,	Vol. III., ends with 1681. *for* Vol. III.
353	18	,,	Vol. V., *for* Ends with 1681. Vol. V.
353	22	,,	Vols. I & II *for* Vol. I & II.
354	12	,,	Malcolm. (1820) *for* Malcolm.
355	8	,,	Dowson *for* Dowsan
355	19	,,	*L'Inde,* for *L'Inde.*
355	20	,,	Français *for* François
355	35	,,	*Ain-i-Akbari* for *A'in-i-Akbari*

PAGE	LINE		
355	36	*Add*	65. "The Bangash Nawabs of Farukhabad" by W. Irvine. Published in the *Journal of the Asiatic Society of Bengal*, Part IV., 1878. Irvine exhaustively used all the available Persian authorities, and as such fully gives the details of the history of the Bangash's governorship in Mālwa as mentioned in Persian works. It has to be supplemented by the additional information from the Marāthi sources.